THE WARSHIP ANNE

THE WARSHIP ANNE

Richard Endsor

C
CONWAY
BLOOMSBURY
LONDON · OXFORD · NEW YORK · NEW DELHI · SYDNEY

Conway
An imprint of Bloomsbury Publishing Plc

50 Bedford Square   1385 Broadway
London   New York
WC1B 3DP   NY 10018
UK   USA

www.bloomsbury.com

www.conway.com

CONWAY and the Conway logo are trademarks of Bloomsbury Publishing Plc

First published 2017

© Richard Endsor, 2017

Richard Endsor has asserted his right under the Copyright, Designs and Patents Act, 1988, to be identified as Author of this work.

All rights reserved. No part of this publication may be reproduced or transmitted in any form or by any means, electronic or mechanical, including photocopying, recording, or any information storage or retrieval system, without prior permission in writing from the publishers.

No responsibility for loss caused to any individual or organisation acting on or refraining from action as a result of the material in this publication can be accepted by Bloomsbury or the author.

British Library Cataloguing-in-Publication Data

A catalogue record for this book is available from the British Library.

Library of Congress Cataloguing-in-Publication data has been applied for.

ISBN: PB: 978-1-8448-6439-3

2 4 6 8 10 9 7 5 3 1

Design by CE Marketing

Printed in China by RR Donnelley Asia Printing Solutions Limited

Bloomsbury Publishing Plc makes every effort to ensure that the papers used in the manufacture of our books are natural, recyclable products made from wood grown in well-managed forests. Our manufacturing processes conform to the environmental regulations of the country of origin.

To find out more about our authors and books visit www.bloomsbury.com. Here you will find extracts, author interviews, details of forthcoming events and the option to sign up for our newsletters.

Contents

Preface		6
Introduction		7
Chapter 1:	The thirty new ships	8
Chapter 2:	Building the *Anne*	20
Chapter 3:	Laid up in Chatham	40
Chapter 4:	The Mediterranean	50
Chapter 5:	The Battle of Beachy Head	82
Chapter 6:	The guns of the *Anne*	102
Chapter 7:	The *Anne* today	118
Appendices		132
Appendix 1:	The approved principal dimensions for the third-rate ships of 1677	134
Appendix 2:	Scantling lists	135
Appendix 3:	Building contract for the Yarmouth	138
Appendix 4:	Contract for the carvings of the third-rate ships of 1677 built at Deptford and Woolwich	144
Appendix 5:	Duke of Grafton's instructions	145
References		148
Index		156

Preface

Not so many years ago, methods of seventeenth-century ship construction were little understood. Recent study of the subject has revealed the extraordinarily complete archive left to us by the bureaucracy of Samuel Pepys, Secretary to King Charles II's Admiralty Commission that sat between 1673 and 1679. In addition, many ship models survive from the period, as do drawings by the Dutch artists, the Van de Veldes, a couple of contemporary books and, finally, archaeological remains. The most useful of these are those of the *Anne*, one of the thirty ships constructed by Charles II as part of the 1677 building programme. My study of that programme eventually resulted in a book, *Restoration Warship*, published in 2009.

The enthusiasm of those who also have an interest in the *Anne* has resulted in this work about her building and career. Among them, and to whom I am deeply indebted, is Dr Peter Marsden, the archaeologist responsible for having the *Anne* legally protected. He has supported me over a period of many years and allowed me to help with some of the archaeological work he has carried out. Another archaeologist with whom I have spent time on the wreck and in the mud is Robert Peacock. Also essential to my work was Jacqueline Stanford, the appointed licensee of the wreck by Historic England and director of the Shipwreck Museum, Hastings, where artefacts from the *Anne* are held. I was a trustee at the museum but am now a volunteer as well as the long-standing Technical Historian to the Warship Anne Trust. My gratitude extends to Dr Peter LeFevre, who for many years has been the *Anne* historian and without whom this work would not have been possible. Another group of friends I could not have done without are the noted seventeenth-century naval historians Dr Ann Coates, Dr David Davis and Frank Fox, both for their expert advice and for attending events in support of the ship. Charles Trollope was also generous with his invaluable advice and opinion concerning the guns of the *Anne*. I would also like to thank Simon Stephens, the Ship Model Curator at the National Maritime Museum, for his help and for providing access to the models. Finally, I would like to thank my ever-supportive wife, Ilona, for putting up with my dubious reputation among family and friends for an unusual interest in seventeenth-century futtocks, buttocks and related ships' parts.

Above: The Stuart arms of King Charles II. *Author*
Left: The author appearing as Phineas Pett, the builder of the *Anne* at the Anne Conference in July 2015 at St Clements Church, Hastings.
Background image: The beach at Pett Level showing the remains of the *Anne*.

Introduction

The *Anne* is one of the most important shipwrecks along the southern coast of England. Laying on the beach at Pett Level near Hastings, her remains are sometimes visible at very low tides. She was lost in 1690 after the Battle of Beachy Head, defending the country from invasion. Sadly the *Anne* and the men who died aboard her are now largely forgotten. The battle prevented a French invasion which, had it been successful, would have dramatically and permanently changed English and European history. The exiled Catholic King James II would have been restored to the throne, his Catholic faith almost certainly imposed and the country dominated by the French.

Although the importance of Beachy Head ranks alongside the Armada Campaign and the Battle of Trafalgar it was not a glorious victory to celebrate and be remembered. In fact the outnumbered English and Dutch allies were forced into ignominious retreat during which the dismasted *Anne* was run ashore between Rye and Hastings and burned to prevent capture. She was the only English loss although many Dutch ships were abandoned, burned and sunk.

Anne was built midway between the *Mary Rose* and *Victory* and is the outstanding example of a warship from that era. The whole of the lower hull survives intact and is the most substantial known remaining shipwreck from the Navy of Charles II and his Secretary to the Admiralty Commission, Samuel Pepys. It is all the more important as she had not been rebuilt or altered.

The *Anne* was one of a fleet of 30 new ships begun in 1677 by Charles II that would transform his Navy into the world's supreme maritime power. He led the extraordinary military and political strategies that resulted in the huge investment in ship building. These started ten years before when the Dutch attacked his fleet in the River Medway for which Charles engineered the end of the Dutch Golden Age. The brilliant administration of Samuel Pepys ensured the building programme was a success but his devious talent for changing facts to suit his ends and preserve his reputation are exposed in his dealings with the *Anne*. Before the Battle of Beachy Head she was the flagship of a squadron sent to the Mediterranean to enforce peace treaties with the Barbary States. Today, she is owned by a charitable trust that runs the Shipwreck Museum in Hastings Old Town.

Chapter: 1 The Thirty New Ships

The Second Dutch War

The events that led up to the building of the *Anne* in 1678 started many years before during the Second Anglo-Dutch War. England and the Netherlands were the world's leading maritime trading nations and their rivalries spilled over into war in March 1665. Both sides were equally proud, confident and prepared to fight resolutely for their cause. It would be a bloody affair. It started well enough for the English with victory at the Battle of Lowestoft on 3 June 1665. The Dutch lost 19 ships and 5,000 men, including their flagship, *Eendracht*, blown up by the guns of James, Duke of York's flagship *Royal Charles*. Their losses were balanced when the French and Danes entered the war on the Dutch side in January 1666, an event that had a marked influence on the conflict. Not because of their fighting prowess but simply a result of their possible appearance at the next major battle.

The medal struck to commemorate the Peace of Breda with Britannia on one side and King Charles the other. *Author's collection*

This occurred on 1 June when Prince Rupert's squadron was detached from the English fleet to cover a French fleet that failed to appear. The remaining and outnumbered English met the Dutch and fought a tenacious battle over the next three days with the advantage veering one way then the other. Just as it seemed that defeat for the English was inevitable, Prince Rupert's squadron returned to save the day. This, the Four Days' Battle, was probably the hardest sea battle ever fought. Under normal battle conditions fleets are exhausted after one day's fighting and rarely do they extend into two days. Four days of hard fighting is a tribute to the quality and courage of both participants. By the end of it, England had lost 10 ships and the Dutch four. Both sides displayed extraordinary resilience and managed to set out fleets of equal size less than two months later.

On St James's Day, 25 July, they met off the North Foreland and again exchanged heavy fire until the Dutch were eventually forced to give way. The English Navy followed up the victory with an audacious attack by small warships on the Dutch merchant fleet in the Vlie. The action became known as Holmes's Bonfire. The number of merchantmen destroyed was put at 150 to 170, while the best, and most conservative estimate, is that the cargoes of those ships was worth at the time twelve million guilders, or a little over a million pounds.[1] The burning of the town of Westerschelling caused further damage.

King Charles II. *Author's collection*

The Dutch raid on the Medway

With honour satisfied, Charles II was happy to enter into peace negotiations. He was especially keen to do this as the national debt had soared, as a result of lower tax revenues following events including the Great Fire of London and the plague. The negotiations dragged on for months and assuming that the war was over, Charles laid up his fleet and paid off the crews.

Seizing the opportunity, Johan de Witt, the Grand Pensionary for Holland, authorised a long-standing secret plan for an attack on the Thames. In June 1667, ten months after the last hostile action, a Dutch fleet under de Ruyter attacked the unmanned and unarmed English fleet at Chatham. There was considerable damage: four large warships were burnt and the *Royal Charles* taken as a prize. In addition five lesser ships, captured earlier from the

Henry Bennet, Earl of Arlington. A member of the Admiralty Commission from 1673 to 1679, he received his distinctive wound on the nose fighting for the King during the Civil War. Bennet had Catholic sympathies and served King Charles as a signatory to the secret Treaty of Dover which allied England and France in a Third Dutch War. A pragmatic Catholic, he was happy to follow the King's example toward religion and converted to the Catholic Church on his deathbed. *Author's collection*

Dutch, and a couple of others were sunk as block ships. On top of that three other large warships were sunk to prevent capture, which later had to be raised and restored. For the Dutch, it was their proudest moment, one which modern historians readily accept as a brilliant action.

Charles II was of another opinion, for him it was a dastardly surprise attack on a peaceful fleet in harbour. He had been deceived while peace talks were in progress. It was the seventeenth century equivalent of the Japanese attack on Pearl Harbor. Samuel Pepys heard that Charles damned the Dutch and called them cowards[2]. He was determined the Dutch would pay, but for now he would have to bide his time to recover the Navy's finances. The peace Treaty of Breda was signed in July. It allowed territories gained during the conflict to be retained, while the Dutch gained the islands of Pulo Run and Surinam. The English gained the American territories of New York, New Jersey, Delaware and Pennsylvania.

Jean-Baptiste Colbert, the French Secretary of State for the Navy, who was responsible for the dramatic increase in the size of the Navy of Louis XIV. *Author's collection*

A scene from the Four Days' Battle of 1666. Collection of Frank Fox. *Oil on canvas by the author.*

Thomas Osborne, Earl of Danby. He was a member of the Admiralty Commission from 1673 to 1679 and Lord Treasurer. As a staunch Protestant he favoured the Dutch and served King Charles by brokering the end of the Third Dutch War. On the back of popular sentiment toward the Dutch he managed to persuade James, Duke of York and the King to agree for James's daughter to marry her cousin, William of Orange, in 1677. *Author's collection*

In spite of losing some fine ships at Chatham and having the indignity of seeing the *Royal Charles* carried off, the gains made under the terms of the Peace of Breda do not seem to accord with a defeat. In fact medals were struck in celebration. Forgetting the costs of battle to each side, it's worth looking further into the results of the two significant and damaging attacks each side made on the other. The lesser-known Holmes's Bonfire caused a million pounds worth of damage to the cargoes of the Dutch merchant fleet. But how much was a million pounds worth at the time? To put it into perspective, the thirty new ships of 1677, of which the *Anne* would be one, cost £600,000, including stores and guns. Ten of these ships were bigger than anything the Dutch had ever produced and the remaining twenty only matched by two or three of their largest. At these known costs, a million pounds would pay for a fleet of 50 very large ships almost the size of the *Royal Charles* and bigger than anything the Dutch had ever owned. On the other side, the losses suffered by the English during the more famous Dutch raid on the Medway cost about the equivalent of six or seven of these ships. On top of that was the cost to the Dutch of replacing at least 115 merchant ships while the English losses did not include guns or sea stores. The Dutch loss was at least ten times that of the English. No matter the size of losses suffered by each side, it was not to be the end of the matter.

The Third Dutch War

Following the Peace of Breda, Charles II grimly began plotting the downfall of the Dutch. His first act was to go along with a convenient Triple Alliance between England, Holland and Sweden. He then began a long series of negotiations with Louis XIV that eventually resulted in the secret Treaty of Dover in May 1670. The French were to attack the Dutch Republic by land while the English and French fleets were to be joined to fight them at sea. The French were new and powerful entrants in the naval arms race thanks to the efforts of Jean-Baptiste Colbert acting on Louis's behalf. To stop Charles being too dependent on Parliament, the French agreed to a subsidy that amounted to £600,000. Controversially, Charles agreed to declare the truth of the Church of Rome as soon as the welfare of his kingdom would permit. Of course, the welfare of his country never did permit his declaration, at least, not until he lay dying many years later.

The war began and soon the French were making good progress on land forcing the Dutch to open their dykes. The naval war began early in 1672 and during the next eighteen months a series of four inconclusive battles ensued. The Dutch, fighting for their existence, managed to avoid defeat using local knowledge of their shoaling coastline. They were brilliantly led by De Ruyter while the French skilfully managed to leave the fighting to the English. The war and France became deeply unpopular in England and with so much damage done to the Dutch, Charles made peace with them in February 1674. France fought on and although the Dutch avoided the total defeat planned for them, the war was a disaster. Their trading links were disrupted and burdened by the huge cost of war the economy collapsed. The magnificent Dutch Golden Age is best exemplified by the art and science it was able to support. Now, artists could no longer sell their paintings; Vermeer, as an example, lost everything, fell into poverty and succumbed to an early death. The Van de Veldes, famous for their marine paintings, emigrated to England to receive a retainer from Charles to paint and draw English ships. On land the war continued, further draining the economies of both the Netherlands and France.

Willem Van de Velde the Younger. Perhaps the greatest marine artist that ever lived, he emigrated to England during the Third Dutch War, along with his father and other members of his family. Both father and son are buried in St James's Church, Piccadilly. As if to emphasise their duel allegiance they lie within feet of a magnificent example of the carved arms of William III, which shows the English Stuart arms impaled with the arms of Nassau. *Author's collection*

Parliamentary approval for the thirty new ships

Although both his rivals suffered, the war left Charles II's Navy in a sad state. Many of the surviving warships had fought in more battles than those from any other era in the long history of the Royal Navy and were in need of repair or rebuilding. King Charles II received an income to carry out the work, but it was not nearly enough. Adding to his worries, the Dutch still had a strong fleet and the French were building new ships. As an absolute monarch, Louis XIV decided how much money would be raised and spent on increasing the size of his Navy. Charles II was not so fortunate; although he decided policy, he was restrained by Parliament who voted how much money would be raised by taxation. For shipbuilding and major repairs Charles therefore needed to rely on supporters to argue his case in Parliament.

In this he was fortunate in having Samuel Pepys, the eloquent master diarist who was also a Member of Parliament and Secretary to the Admiralty, the highest administrative post in the Navy. Raising taxes on the populace for ships was going to be unpopular as the last two Dutch wars had been hugely expensive. Opponents also observed the King's pleasures, which involved a number of costly mistresses who it was thought might somehow benefit from vast sums of money arriving at the Treasury. Faced with these difficulties Charles played another political masterstroke.

With the war he had engineered still going on between France and the Netherlands, he took the opportunity to let Parliament believe he would enter the war on the side of the Dutch. This appealed to Parliament and, after long delays and endless debates, the situation was at last resolved in February 1677. It went along with Pepys's arguments to vote for an Act raising the sum of £584,978 2s 2½d for the building of 30 ships of war complete with guns and rigging. With a supposed war threatening, the Act also

Samuel Pepys, Secretary to the Admiralty. *Author's collection*

Part of the Act for building thirty ships of war showing the rate and tunnage of the one first-rate, nine second-rate and twenty third-rate ships that were to be built. *Author's collection*

A model at the Science Museum showing an Admiralty Board meeting with Charles II at right considering the design of a ship. Samuel Pepys is at the far left taking the minutes. *Author's collection*

stated that the ships had to be completed within the space of two years. It was the final act by Charles in a series of extraordinary political and military manoeuvres initiated by the Dutch raid on the Medway.

The new fleet of powerful ships just about doubled the strength of the Navy. Within fifteen years of the Act being passed, Charles's fleet was transformed into the world's leading maritime power. His country would remain unchallenged in this position for the next 250 years. After Holmes's Bonfire, the attack on the Medway proved too much of a temptation for the Dutch. Their failure to realise the long-term consequences and the reaction of Charles would, in the end, be their undoing. They suffered the same fate as the Japanese 275 years later for a surprise attack on a nation they really should have left in peace.

The money for the new ships was to be raised as fairly as possible by a land tax. In a typical small town such as Heacham in Norfolk, as an example, a typical gentleman such as Samuell Gurlyn paid 3s 7d for land and 3d for stock while his lady paid 1s 6d for her land and 1d for stock. Less well off, the widow Houghton paid 1s 11d for land and 1d for stock while a poor person such as Thomas Large only paid 1d for land.[3]

Planning the new ships

The Act was deliberated by the Admiralty Lords, Prince Rupert, and Charles at the next Admiralty Board meeting. Also invited to attend were the junior naval administration officers of the Navy Board. They debated the ships' dimensions, shipwrights' draughts, supply of timber, and where they were to be built[4]. During this important period, indeed during most periods, Charles attended more meetings than any other Board member, which were generally held at an interval of one or two weeks. The enormity of the project now meant that meetings were taking place every few days. The merry monarch or '*Old Rowley*' as Charles's critics liked to call him, did indeed have his pleasures, but they rarely mention the Navy was at the top of those pleasures. Another duty he enjoyed was attending ship-launching ceremonies, especially those he could easily reach from Whitehall. He became popular for mixing with ordinary workmen such as boat builders[5] and became so informal with the shipwrights at Chatham that he was known to take off his wig for comfort.[6] Part of his popularity came from the expense on '*diet and drink*' given to everyone attending, which resulted in Admiralty enquiries and warnings to Master Shipwrights who organised the events.[7]

The Admiralty came up with many sensible ideas for building the new ships, such as having standard sizes for the masts and spars to make it easier for them to be replaced when lost during storms or battles. Charles also had the idea of having longer keels and more upright stems. This would have the effect of increasing buoyancy at the bows to reduce pitching in heavy seas as well as being stronger. When one of the ships, the *Captain*, was sent out for sea trials, she proved a great success and Pepys recorded that Charles would tell everyone whom he thought would understand, the triumph of his invention.

Charles also had the foresight to realise that a future enemy would probably be the French and the conflict would be further afield than against the Dutch in the North Sea. Not having the depth of his understanding, Parliament had voted for just enough money to build ships of the same size as those built during the last Dutch war. Charles realised that if the new ships

King Charles attending the launch of the third rate *Lenox*, the first of the thirty new ships to be launched on 12 April 1678. He is shown in the barge alongside accompanied by his mistress, the Duchess of Portsmouth, and their son Charles Lenox, the first Duke of Richmond and Lenox. *Author*

would be longer at sea they would have to be larger to carry more stores. This in itself did not conflict with the Act – which gave a minimum of 900 tons for third-rate ships. Charles considered the new third rates, which of course the *Anne* was to be one, should be 1,100 tons. Parliament had not allowed for an increase in size and cost of 20 per cent, which caused alarm and fear among the Admiralty members, no doubt remembering the Ship Money tax that had helped cause the downfall of the King's father, Charles I.

In spite of their pleas, Charles insisted on larger ships and only managed to placate them by saying that any extra cost would be paid for out of his own purse. The Admiralty knew the King had neither the intention nor the money, to carry out his promise, but he had absolved them from any blame should Parliament happen to find out. To help prevent that awful eventuality, a new method of calculating the tunnage was devised. Part of the established calculation involved the keel length. The longer keel lengths introduced by Charles were used as a reason to change the formulae to make the ships appear smaller. Charles helpfully added that the matter was beyond the comprehension of Parliament and they should not be told of it.[8]

Phineas Pett, Master Shipwright at Chatham

Charles II allowed his Master Shipwrights to make their own draughts according to the size and dimensions he and the Admiralty Board had decided. For his own general interest in understanding ship design, and to scrutinise the proficiency of the Master Shipwrights, he had them attend him with their draughts. Among those he saw most, and enjoyed a good relationship with, was Phineas Pett, the Master Shipwright at Chatham. There were many members of the Pett family had worked for the King as shipwrights, dating all the way back to Tudor times. Among them was Phineas Pett I (1570–1647) who became famous for building the first three deckers, the *Prince Royal* of 1610 and the *Sovereign of the Seas* in 1637. In 1677, Phineas Pett at Chatham – who was to build the *Anne* – was 42 years old, five years the King's junior. Confusingly, another Phineas Pett was active at the same time; he was the Master Shipwright at Woolwich responsible for building another of the ships, the *Captain*.

Our Phineas learnt his trade at Deptford Dockyard under his father, Peter, the Master Shipwright. He would have served a seven-year apprenticeship learning how to mould timbers, hew keels, set up frames as well as a multitude of other everyday tasks. All shipwrights were required to do the same as a '*servant*' to an experienced man. The '*master*' to whom he was apprenticed received the apprentices' wages but was responsible for their

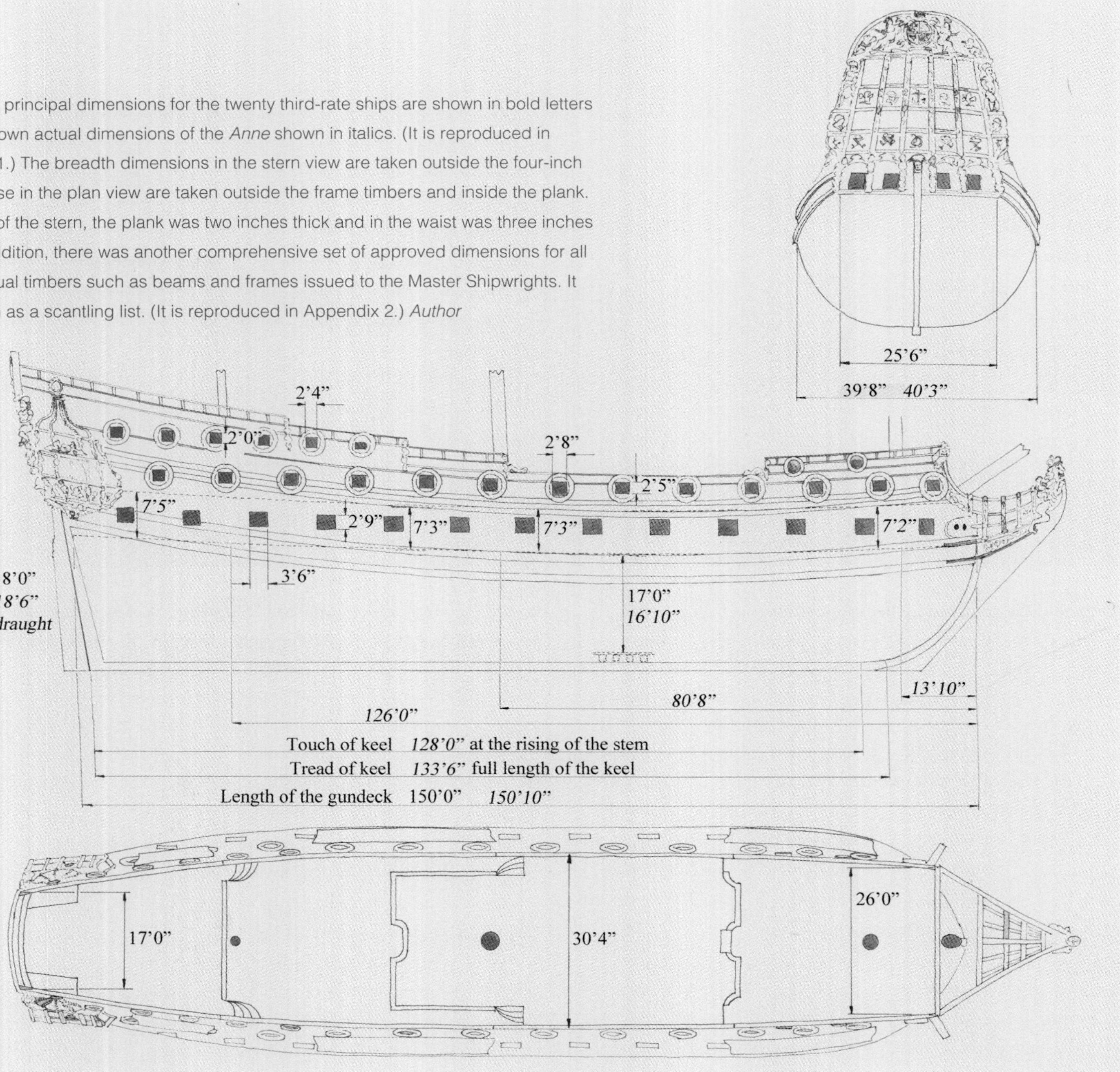

The official principal dimensions for the twenty third-rate ships are shown in bold letters and the known actual dimensions of the *Anne* shown in italics. (It is reproduced in Appendix 1.) The breadth dimensions in the stern view are taken outside the four-inch plank. Those in the plan view are taken outside the frame timbers and inside the plank. At the top of the stern, the plank was two inches thick and in the waist was three inches thick. In addition, there was another comprehensive set of approved dimensions for all the individual timbers such as beams and frames issued to the Master Shipwrights. It was known as a scantling list. (It is reproduced in Appendix 2.) *Author*

lodgings and welfare. On completing their apprenticeship they would have qualified to earn 2s 1d a day, plus overtime, making them very well paid by the standards of the day. As well as being able to carry out every day practical skills Phineas would also have learnt the jealously guarded '*shipwrights' secrets*' of how to design ships. With customary nepotism Phineas became his father's Assistant Master Shipwright.

Peter Pett died in 1652 during the time of the Commonwealth, but happily for Phineas's future prospects, decided to leave their employ and work for the Pett family ship building business at Ratcliffe, near modern day Limehouse. At the Restoration of King Charles II in 1660, his family's loyalty to the crown served him well and he was ideally placed to be appointed Master Shipwright at Chatham. Phineas successfully rebuilt the old *Victory*

and completed a new third rate. In 1668 he became involved in a scandal when he was found to be in partnership with John Bowyer in buying 90 loads of timber (a load is about the size of a tree) at 38 shillings a load, then arranging for another man, Robert Morecock, to offer it to the Navy. Phineas himself surveyed the 90 loads on the Navy's behalf and valued the timber at 48 shillings a load. After their first successful fraud the partners completed a second transaction involving 200 loads of timber. On being found out, Phineas's position as Master Shipwright was cancelled but with the help of friends and with the benevolence of the King he was reinstated after two months. Three months after this, Pett was accused of selling a boat and other stores belonging to the Navy. Samuel Pepys wrote in his diary that Phineas was 'a *very knave*', completely forgetting to mention his own indiscretions in receiving many presents and gifts of far greater value than any of Pett's frauds.

The most senior officer at Chatham was the Commissioner to whom the Master Shipwright answered. This had worked well enough when a relation, another Peter Pett, held the post, but he became a scapegoat following the Dutch raid on Chatham in 1667 and was dismissed. He was replaced by Captain John Cox and trouble between them soon followed. Cox wrote that Phineas was a '*liar and a perjurer*' and in another letter that he was '*too much the gentleman to perform his duty*'. Cox, being a captain, fought in the Third Dutch War and was killed at the Battle of Solebay in 1672. He was replaced briefly by Thomas Middleton but before the year was out, a fighting Captain, Sir Richard Beach, took over the post[9]. Beach was a disciplinarian who saw little difference between commanding a ship or a dockyard. The talents of Beach and Pett were very different and promised an eventful time at Chatham.

Because of his undoubted abilities, King Charles chose Pett to build the only first rate among the thirty new ships. This was a great honour and Pett settled down preparing draughts for the ship rather than worrying about what he was supposed to build first, the unnamed third rate that was to become the *Anne*. He did get Robert Lee, his assistant, to conscript shipwrights, an act known as pressing, and to look out for timber.[10]

A pregnant woman, Ann Maverly, whose husband was recently pressed to work on the ships at Chatham, wrote to the Navy Board during June 1677. '*Please for to order that my husband John Maverly, a caulker, may have a month's liberty before he goes into His Majesty's yard at Chatham being imprest last Wednesday in respect I am very big with child and look every day and having several things to do which I am not able to perform without my said husbands assistance. I humbly beg your Honourables compliance therein.*' As a result of Ann's letter and in harmony with the general tolerant attitude in the Navy during the seventeenth century, the Navy Board granted John Maverly one week's paternity leave.[11]

During the same month, Pett, having completed his draught of the three rates of ships, made a journey to London to attend the King and Navy Board. He was away for eight days and would later take two other journeys to London to see the King with his draughts of the first rate.[12] While there he met Samuel Pepys, and became aware of the King's intention to have the ships built with more upright stems and proposed another great alteration he thought would benefit the ships. This was to bring the draught of water two feet less than previously allowed for which he humbly sought the King's approval at an Admiralty Board meeting on 7 July. Phineas's idea did not impress other shipbuilding experts: Sir Anthony Deane and Sir John Tippetts thought the idea impractical. Charles entered the debate saying the depth of water given in his recent table of dimensions be strictly kept to and Mr Pett be directed to conform himself.[13] Showing just how independently minded he could be, Pett later told Pepys that from the beginning he didn't build his ships with such upright stems as directed by the King.[14]

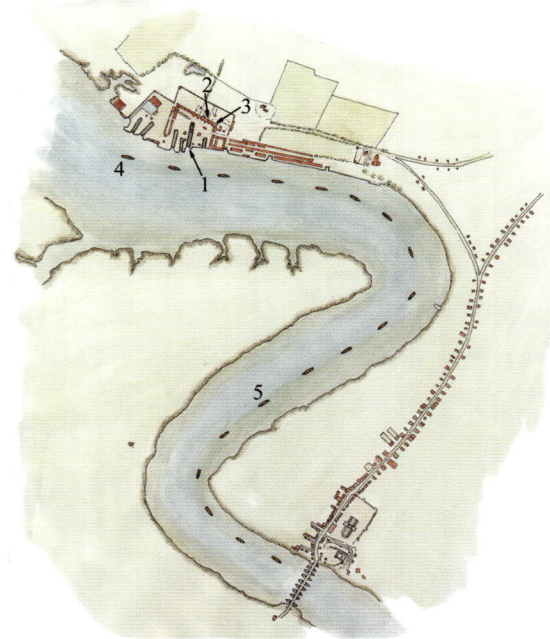

Chatham Dockyard. 1 The building place of the *Anne* at the head of the double dock. 2 The Master Shipwright's house occupied by Phineas Pett. 3 The Commissioner's house occupied by Sir Richard Beach. 4 The mooring place of the *Anne* after her launch in 1678. 5 The mooring place of the *Anne* in 1680. Author

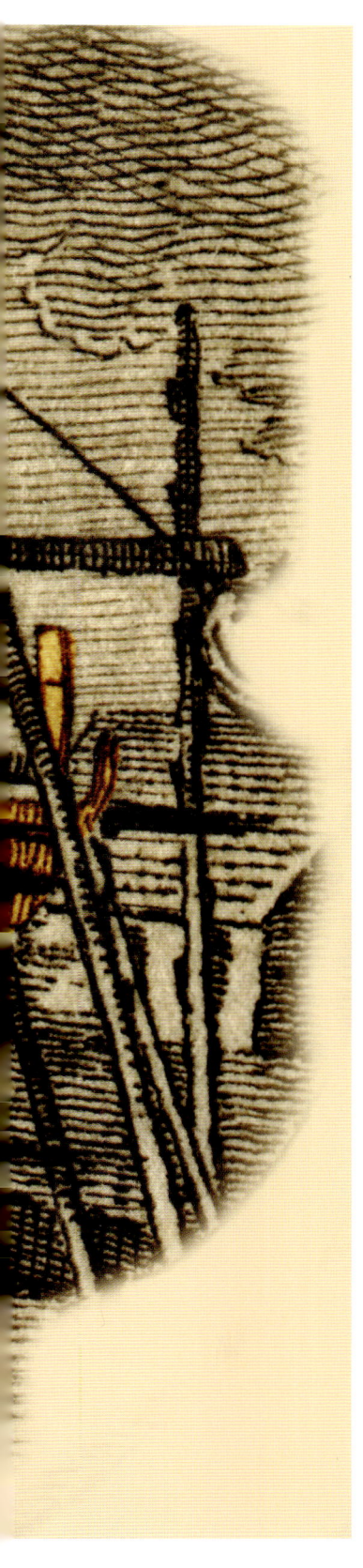

Chapter 2: Building the *Anne*

Preparations at Chatham

The *Anne* was to be the first of the four new ships of 1677 to be built at Chatham. After some consideration it was decided on 15 June to build her at the head of the biggest dock. This was the 335ft long double dock as measured from the wicket at the river end, to the stepped alter at the head. This would leave space astern for old ships of up to second-rate size to be brought in behind for repair. Before work started, measures had to be taken to make sure the money Parliament had provided to build the new ships was accurately accounted for, and not spent on anything else.[1] To do this, places had to be found in the dockyards where timber and other stores could be securely held. Phineas Pett and six other senior dockyard officers at Chatham '*accordingly advised together and although upon deliberation we conclude it is very difficult and perplexing task to perform as happily tis expected and consequently an intrigue for us to propose anything*'.[2] Shortly afterward Commissioner Beach, who was not present at the meeting, resolved their indecision. He wrote saying they were making room for the stores in houses or outside and that the Stores Comptroller would take care to keep a particular account in books relating to the new ships[3]. As part of the costing process, an estimate of £12,000 was calculated by Phineas for building the ship, which included her masts, painting, carving, joiners' work, iron work, plumbers' work and glaziers' work.[4]

This large straight oak from a plantation in northern Germany contains nearly three loads of timber and would be suitable for a stern post. *Author*

The keel

While he was taking his time working on a draught for building three, as yet unnamed, third-rate ships, Master Shipwrights at other yards were busy buying up timber, especially great pieces of elm needed for the keels. They were essential as the whole ship structure was built up upon them. For each ship Phineas would need four pieces, each 16in square and 39ft long.[5] But as he started rather late, he now found them almost impossible to obtain and on 22 June desperately suggested using oak as an alternative saying it would '*be as fit and serviceable as if they were made of elm*'.[6]

A shipwright 'squaring' a large oak. Vertical cuts were first made with a hatchet and plumb-line before a specialist squaring axe was used to finish the sides between them. The squaring axe head is bevelled only on one side and is angled to allow clearance for the shipwright's knuckles. Image created using actual seventeenth-century axes. *Author*

The problem remained unresolved and nearly three weeks later he wrote hopefully to the Navy Board saying '*Sir John Dorrill had a very good parcel of beech fit for keel pieces … standing near Maidstone if your Honourables approves of that sort of wood which by enquiry of several persons am informed it wears much better than oak and is as good as elm*'.[7] His suggestion for using an alternative wood for the keel of such an important ship was unsurprisingly rejected. Weeks passed and although the men were kept busy making frame pieces, the dock

remained embarrassingly empty as there was no keel to put them on. By 12 July Phineas had at last managed to obtain two elm pieces. One of them was the foremost piece, the forefoot, made with a scarphed joint to receive the lower piece of stem[8]. He was still missing half the keel's length and a solution had to be found. Not being able to wait any longer, Phineas was forced into a decision to make the keel from five pieces of elm rather than four.[9] In mid-August he forlornly wrote '*we having as yet but a keele for one ship (Anne) and that in so many pieces, being five in number which I could most heartily have wished might have been in four as I am informed ye other shipps that are now in building in His Majesty's yards elsewhere*'.[10]

Timber supplies

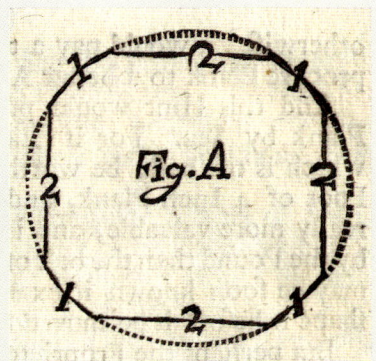

Figure 'A' from William Sutherland's *Shipbuilder's Assistant*, 1711 page 29. It shows squared timber, the wanes being 1,1,1,1 and the squares 2,2,2,2. The four wanes are equal to two of the squares.

The keel was not Pett's only problem. The quantities of wood needed to build the *Anne* were enormous. In all about 2,300 loads, were needed. A load consisted of 50 cubic feet of hewn timber[11], each weighing about a ton. Three-quarters of this amount was oak, consisting of about 735 loads of straight oak, 660 loads of compass or curved oak, 75 loads of knees and 250 loads of ready sawn straight plank imported from the Baltic.[12]

Many Master Shipwrights were very active and travelled the countryside themselves in pursuit of timber. Pett on the other hand relied to a great deal on his Timber Purveyor, Robert Eason. In September, he visited Squire Amhurst at Bay Hall and then, on to Sussex, where his timber lay. He found 80 ends of straight oak averaging two loads each that he judged were worth 52s a load. Smaller trees consisting of 150 ends, averaging one load each, worth 42s a load were also available. There were also 60 ends, about a load each, suitable for the frames worth 52 or 53s a load. It could all be delivered to Chatham although about 30 or 40 ends were shaken (split) or '*colty*'.[13] At the time most of the timber was not hewn or squared, but on seeing it later, he found it a little larger and suitable for clamps, wale pieces and footwaling while the compass timber would be good for frame futtocks.[14] Later on he viewed Mr Clark's oak timber and saw 154 loads averaging 60 cubic ft each; although it was shorter than ideal, there was also 30 loads of compass timber averaging 56ft a piece fit for clamps and footwaling forward on.[15] It was difficult finding so many large timbers and as early as 6 August, Pett was complaining to the Navy Board that he '*so extremely pestered with small straight timber it is my opinion that for the future (if possible to be procured) that no straight timber be served into these stores for the service... less than 60ft in a piece and to meet at two load in a piece one with another (average) and that no compass timber be served under 30ft in a piece and to meet at 55ft in a piece one with another*'.[16]

On one occasion Pett ventured out to survey timber himself and found a great tree from which to make the lower stem piece intended to be fitted to the front of the keel. Two teams of horses and a carriage were sent out to bring it to Chatham, but having taken it no further than a stone's throw the carriage sunk down to its axles in mud. They returned from whence it came and decided to save weight by sawing it to size on the spot. Having dug a saw-pit and fashioned the tree to shape they found it was defective and unusable, so all their efforts had been in vain.[17] Not only was the weather against Phineas, Sir Richard Beach had also begun complaining about him to the Navy Board, especially when he took some leave.[18] With all the delays, it wasn't until 13 September that the keel, stem and stern post were at last raised and set up in the dock on their blocks.[19]

Frame timbers

With the keel in place and many of her frame timbers already made, the *Anne* rapidly progressed. The lowest part of the framing, the floor timbers, were placed across the keel at right angles spaced at every 2ft 3in.[20] This was twice the width of the floor timbers, plus half an inch for clearance. The gap between the floors allowed the next frame piece, the lower futtock, to fit between with a suitable overlap.

Every other floor timber was secured by a vertical bolt that went through to the bottom of the keel. Bolts were not made of steel with a screw thread as in modern practice but made of wrought iron with a

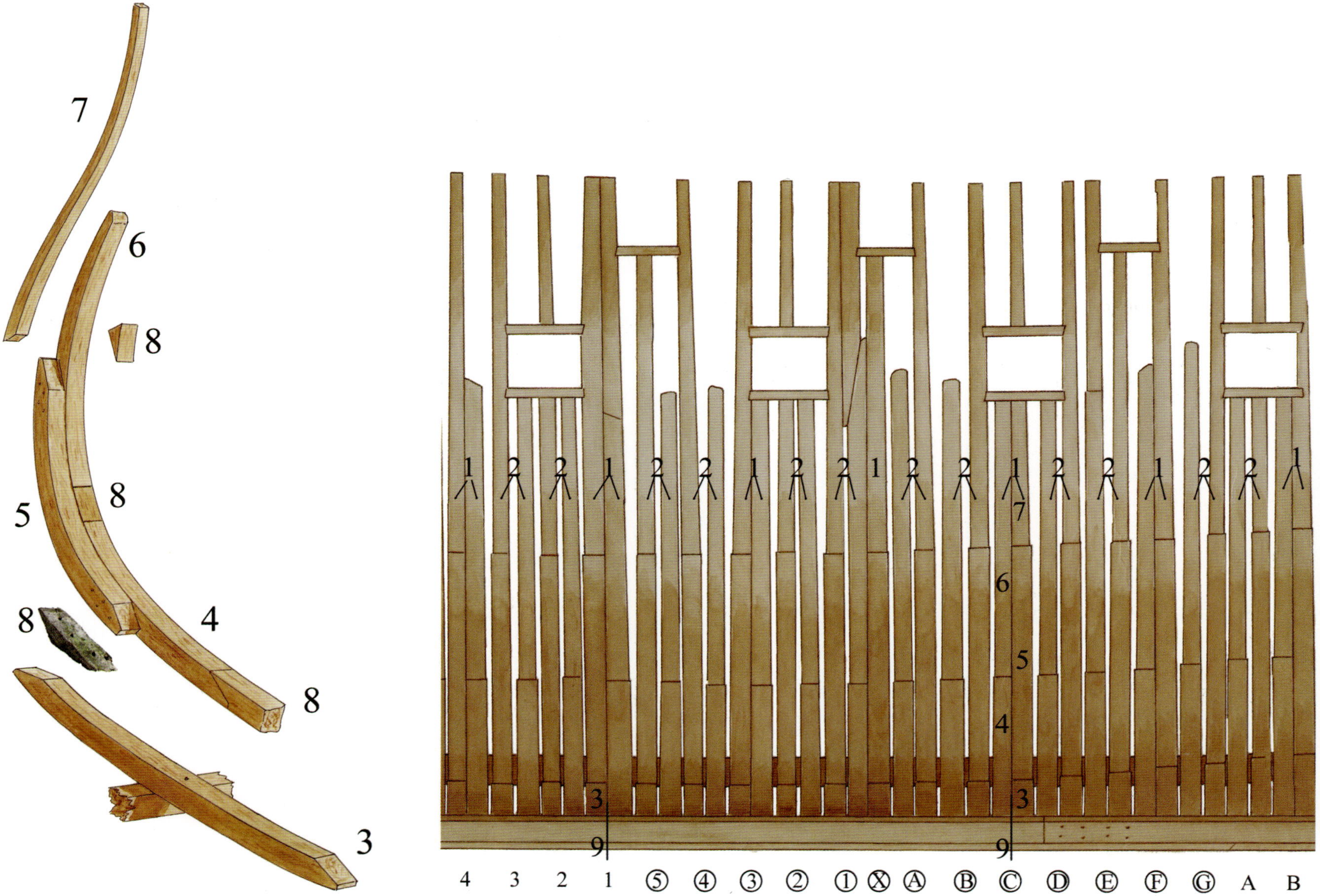

24 The Warship Anne

The arrangement of frames near the middle of the ship. 1 Frame bends. 2 Fill in frames. 3 Floor timbers. 4 Lower futtocks. 5 Middle futtocks. 6 Upper futtocks. 7 Top timbers. 8 Chocks. 9 Frame station. Every third frame was a master frame called a frame bend. They are usually the only ones shown on ships' draughts and to avoid confusion are identified by letters forward of frame 'X' and numbers aft. The largest frame amidships is frame station 'X' and those either side, shown inside a circle, are the 'flats'. As their name suggests, they were cut square as there was no need for trimming or 'bevelling' at this stage to follow the curvature of the hull. Once in place all the frames would be 'dubbed' with an adze before planking. Notice that half of a frame of timber has been dropped immediately aft of frame 'X' reversing the orientation of the frames about the frame stations. This results in the floor timber, middle futtock and top timber always facing toward the tapered ends of the ship from their frame station. This has the benefit of them being in the 'bevelled under' condition with material left on from the moulded hull profile, whether they are fore or aft of frame 'X'. The less important frame pieces, the lower and upper futtocks, are left with the awkward 'bevelled standing' condition. There were a number of ways the orientation of the frames could be made and this is just one example. This reconstruction fits the arrangement and number of flats as shown in the contemporary prints of one of the thirty new ships by Thomas Fagge. *Author*

Building the *Anne* 25

dome head on one end while the other was riveted over a washer known as a rove. As the hull shape narrowed toward the ends of the ship, the floor timbers had to curve steeply upward and these were called the rising timbers. At the extreme ends, the curve upward became so sharp it could not be made from a single piece of timber. Instead, additional fore and aft pieces, called the rising wood, were added to the top of the keel and a half timber bolted to it on each side. When all the floor timbers and chocks were in place, long pieces similar in section to the keel, known as the keelson, were placed over them. Then the alternate floor timbers that were not yet secured were bolted through the keelson, floor timbers and keel. The work did not progress in strict and logical order but only as suitable timber became available. Some floor timbers would have to wait many weeks before a piece of keelson was found to secure them in position. Even so, Pett built the frame of the *Anne* according to the accepted and usual seventeenth-century practice.[21]

The frame bends, spaced at every third frame station, were the next timbers to be erected in the ship. The lower, middle and upper futtocks that made up the frame bend for one station were laid together on the ground.[21] They were carefully lined up in their correct position as if they were in the ship and joined together with treenails. The assembly was then erected in its place and located with half of the length of the lower futtock fitting between the floor timbers. The frame bends established the shape of the hull up to the waterline. For now, temporary shores and ribbands on the outside of the hull made sure there was no movement. The inside was secured with crosspawls, nailed

The *Anne* as she appeared at the end of September 1677. Notice the sheer legs and lifting gear used to raise the first frame bends in position. Although dating from the mid-eighteenth century, a series of prints by John Cleveley show the same method of constructing used in 1677. 1 Keel assembled on the blocks. 2 Stern post. 3 Rising wood and knee. 4 Floor timbers. 5 Frame bends. Print by John Cleveley the Elder. *Author's collection*

A frame timber sawn to its fore and aft sided dimension and marked out ready to be cut to its moulded profile. *Author*

The floor timbers (nearest) with lower futtocks filling the gaps between. *Author*

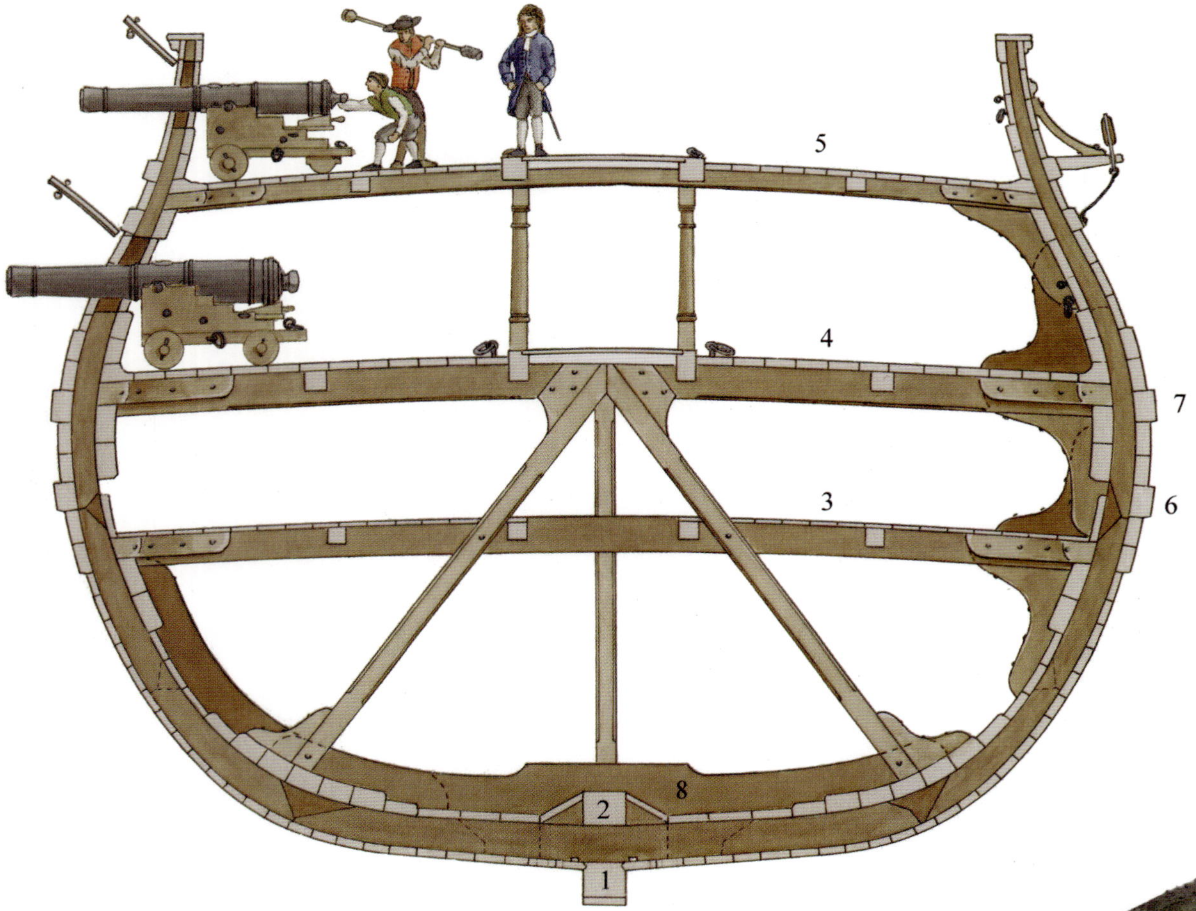

26 The Warship Anne

The midship section of the *Anne*. 1 Keel. 2 Keelson. 3 Orlop deck, situated just below the waterline and used for storage, anchor cables and cabins. 4 The lower deck or gun deck which carried the largest guns. 5 The upper deck. 6 Lower main wale. 7 Upper main wale. 8 Rider. Note the chocks between the frame timbers mentioned by Phineas in his report of 13 December 1677. Chocks allowed straighter timbers to be used for the curved frames. *Author*

A chock from the wreck of the *Northumberland* of 1677 that once fitted between the head of a floor timber and heel of a middle futtock. Notice the numerous 1¾ inch-diameter treenail holes.[22]

across each pair from one side to the other. Eventually, all the framing would be permanently fixed in position by the fore and aft planking. On 4 October, Phineas must have been relieved to be able to report, '*two thirds of her frame bends are up and most part of her floor timbers in and bolted and have set the frame to rights that is up and are hewing of timbers and fastening of her knee to the stern post and rising wood*'.[23] A week later '*she is filled up with floor timbers from the timber G forward to the 16 rising timber aft and have about half filled up that distance with lower, middle and upper futtocks*'.[24]

Pett reportedly fell '*very ill*' for the next few weeks, so ill that Joseph Lawrence, his assistant, wrote the progress reports for building the *Anne*.[25]. The final part of the framing, the top timbers, that reached to the top of the ships' sides were started shortly before 1 November when Lawrence sent the following progress report to the Navy Board.

	Timbers hewed and placed	Timbers hewn and moulded but not yet placed	Timbers wanting
Floor timbers	45	2	14
Lower futtocks	77	31	14
Middle futtocks	76	8	38
Upper futtocks	76	6	40
Top timbers	0	29	93

By adding up the timbers in each row of the table it shows the *Anne* was built with 61 frames. Shipwrights of the time often used the term '*timber*' to refer to any single piece of the frame.[26] Lawrence's next report a week later showed another frame, less the top timbers, had been erected. Meanwhile, at the bow of the ship he was trying to find a piece 26ft long that rounded 2ft 6in to make a false stem to overlap and strengthen the main stem.[27] For the rest of November, work continued adding the fill-in frames between the frame bends. The fill-in frames and frame bends both had the same number and types of futtocks. The fill-in frames were only different from the frame bends in that they were not joined together, or to any other part of the framing. They were simply laid in place supported by the temporary ribbands and would only be secured when the inside and outside planking was treenailed to them. The planking and the framing depended on each other for mutual support and strength. While the fill-in frames, especially the top timbers, remained unsecured they could be moved in the fore or aft direction for the convenience of forming the sides of the gun ports. This was necessary as the gun ports spacing was not co-ordinated with the spacing of the frames.

Planking

As soon as frames were in position, work would also have started planking the outside of the ship. The plank was vital in strengthening the floors as the whole of the rest of the structure was built upon them. The first ten feet or so underwater could be planked with four-inch oak, elm or beech plank, none of which would rot as long as they always remained wet. Pett favoured elm, writing, '*considering the long experience that hath been had of the usefulness and strength of elm plank underwater, more especially in the wake of the rabbits of the keels when grounding, being tougher than any other wood and also considering the ill consequences that hath lately attended His Majesties service by the working of East*

The floor timbers are in position and the frame bends erected. 1 Floor timbers. 2 Frame bends. 3 Stem. 4 Transoms. 5 Fashion piece. 6 Shores. 7 Ribbands. 8 Crosspawls. *Author's collection*

country plank on the London *and* Charles *by the sudden decay*'.[29] The rest of the outside four-inch plank was made of oak purchased from the Baltic or Northern Germany where trees grew tall and straight. It was sawn to thickness by water or wind-powered sawmills before transportation to England. At the ends of the ship, the severe curves at the buttocks and bows made it difficult to bend such thick plank by heat. Instead it had to be hand sawn to shape from English compass oak. The planks were secured by two 1¾in-diameter oak treenails at every timber. One went from the outside of the plank and through the frames, and the other through the outside plank, frame and inside plank[30]. Oak was better than iron nails for the task as it expanded to tighten the fixing when it became wet, and did not corrode.

Commissioner Beach

On 7 December 1677, Samuel Pepys wrote a letter to Sir Richard Beach which included an enquiry after Phineas's health. Unimpressed with the slow progress in building the *Anne*, Beach replied demonstrating an extraordinary ability in malicious letter writing:

28 The Warship Anne

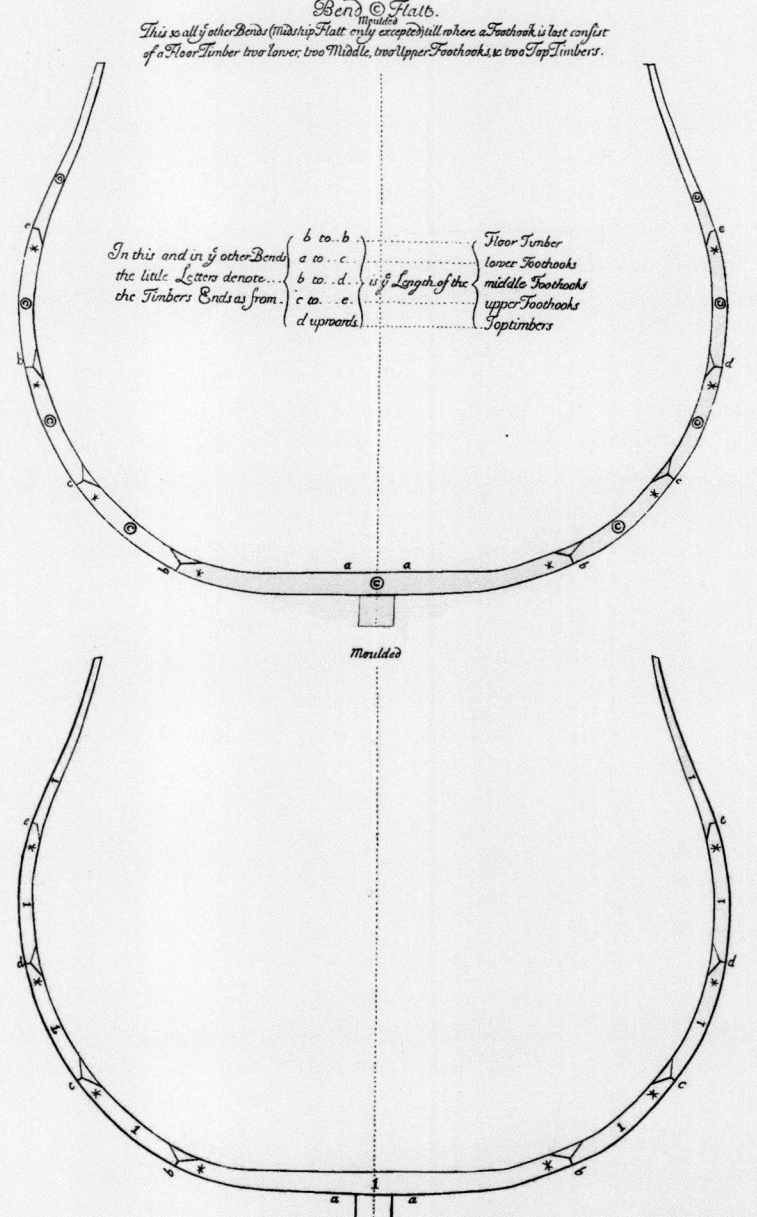

A remarkable series of prints by Thomas Fagge showing hull sections and the arrangement of frame timbers for a third rate of 1677. It is not dated but the prices given in the work for contract building of ships and the ship dimensions date the work from between 1677 and 1690. The heads and heels of the frame timbers and the sirmarks used to line them up in relation to one another are clearly marked. Notice how the frames R, Q, 25, 28 and 31 have a futtock fewer as the length they cover is less toward the ship's ends.[28] A contract for building a third-rate of the same specification as the *Anne* is reproduced in Appendix 3. *Private collection*

Building the *Anne* 29

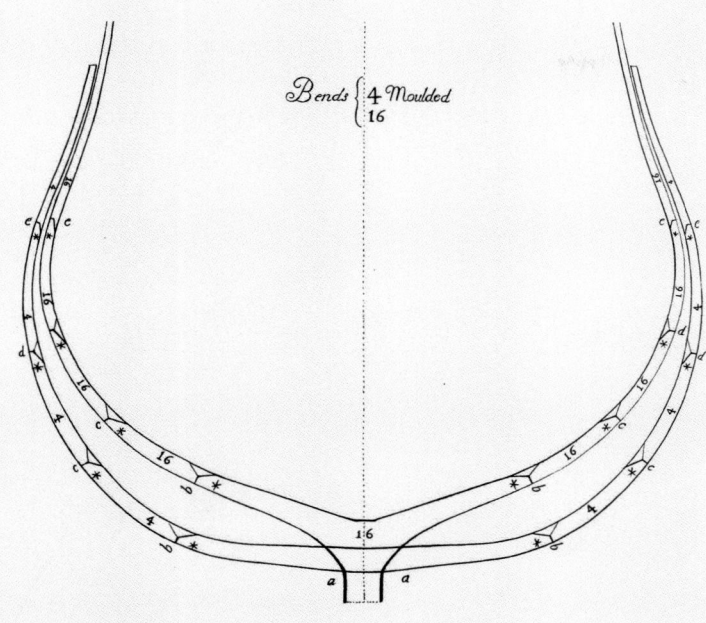

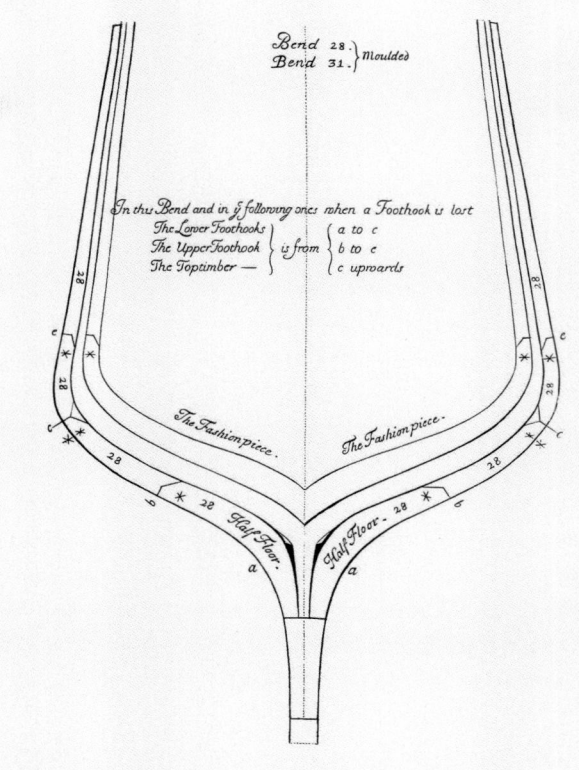

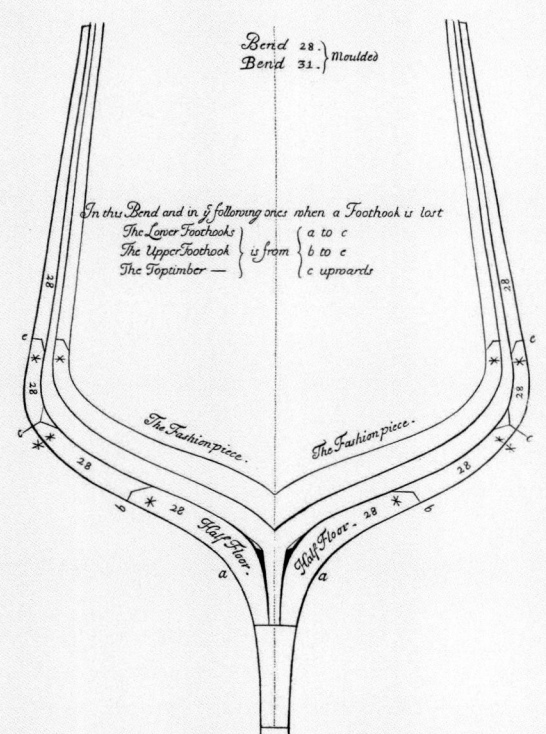

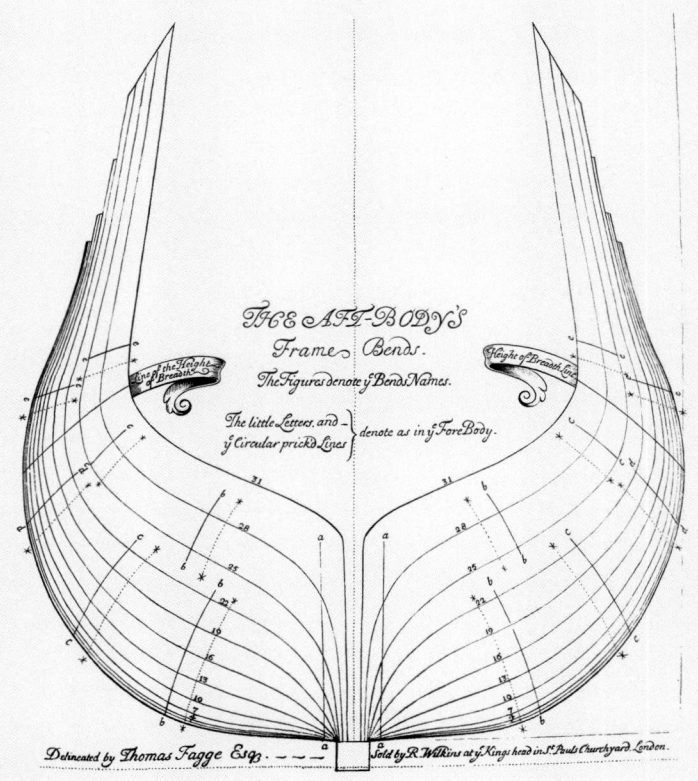

'But could wish your Honours had commanded a relation of the shipwright's indisposition from any other officer or person here in regard of the several differences that have happened between us since my being here (though all in reference to His Majesty's service) so that what I may write may seem to savour of too much malice or revenge. I shall therefore only relate what physicians and others that have had the honour of accosting him in his long pretended time of sickness report, vitz: That he hath been so transported with a passion of joy conceived of his great abilities in building ships and other vessels, particularly the Mary Yacht, that he had almost lost his sense. And by what have heard did expect his Majesty would have given him Honour (knighthood) as well as other shipwrights before him, which he was so confident of that he made some such promise to this last lady he hath married. [Pett was married a number of times.] But failing of his expectations it's supposed hath been a great occasion of his distemper and no small prejudice to His Majesty's service in regard he will neither mind his business himself relating to the new ships nor permit his assistant (Robert Lee) nor others to come near him … That he will hardly appear at Chatham Dock again this 4 months (going tomorrow to London in a coach with six horses).'

Beach then turned on Phineas's concerns for the welfare of his men: '... let us have an active able man here that would take care to reduce the workmen of this yard to their duties (which have been spoiled by the indulgence and carelessness of the Shipwright) … and too many boys entered for servants and old men introduced.'[31] Beach believed in naval discipline and his wish to 'reduce the workmen to their duties' and cut the number of apprentices and older, experienced men in the yard is in stark contrast to Pett's more empathetic and comfortable attitude. Pett, in common with other Master Shipwrights such as Jonas and John Shish at Deptford, carefully looked after their shipwrights[32]. An indulgence that meant knowing and being at ease with working men as a way of getting the best out of them. King Charles was also a famously indulgent and relaxed character; little wonder then, that Phineas was a favourite of his. But the Admiralty couldn't ignore Beach's letter and Pett duly received a caution and advice to look after the King's business with greater care and diligence than he had hitherto done. Even though he accepted this, Phineas thought '*false and malicious aspersions were laid to his charge*' by Beach. To speed up progress Beach made out a warrant for more men to be employed on the *Anne*. Pett duly took 30 shipwrights who were repairing old ships to work on the new. He also defended himself, saying that he had been out to procure timber and marked out large oak trees belonging to Sir John Dorrills but was refused permission to buy them. Another setback occurred when he bought some four-inch plank of good length off Mr Brown in Suffolk for the underwater of *Anne* but it was sent to Deptford instead.[33]

The decks

Apart from worrying about his relationship with Sir Richard Beach, Phineas Pett's attention was now drawn to putting decks into the *Anne*. The first stage

The main gun deck structure. It was massively strong in order to carry the *Anne*'s 65 tons of iron cannon. 1 Frame bend. 2 Frame timber. 3 Clamp upon which the beams rest. 4 Gun deck beam. 5 Fore and aft lodging knee. 6 Up and down hanging knee. 7 Carling. 8 Ledge. 9 Deck plank. 10 Waterway. *Author*

in making the gun deck was to bolt large fore and aft timbers called clamps to the frames for the beams to rest on. To carry the weight of the 2½-ton guns, the gun deck beams measured 1ft 4½in wide and 1ft 3¼in deep. When fitting in position they were let down into the clamps by an inch. One was placed under every gun port and one between, an exception being just forward of the mainmast where they were eight feet apart to allow for the main hatch. It would be very difficult to find the necessary trees of such size to make the 22 beams that Phineas actually used on the *Anne*.[34] Not only were they rare but trees that had grown to such a size had often become too old and were beginning to weaken and rot.

The problem was overcome by joining or scarphing two smaller, younger and stronger trees together.[35] Each end of the beam was attached to the ship's side by two knees, a vertical hanging knee and a horizontal lodging knee, both of which were bolted to the beam and through the frames. Lodging knees were always made from the cheaper, stronger and more open, raking knees. To make this possible they were placed at the aft side of the beam forward of midships and on the forward side aft of midships. Knees were the most expensive timber bought for ship construction, raking knees cost £3 10s a load against £2 16s 3d for ordinary straight oak. Square knees were even more expensive costing £4 10s a load.[36]

As Beach wrote his letter of complaint, the *Concord* merchantman belonging to William Nutt of London arrived at Chatham laden with plank and knees fit for the new ships. Phineas found it contained 50 very good knees, half of them containing ten cubic feet in each knee and suitable for binding the gun deck beams to the ship's side. The other half, of six cubic feet, good for the upper deck.[37] The loads imposed by the masts to the beams in front of them was spread to all the other beams by fore and aft carlings. There were four carlings between each beam and those in the wake of the hatches were in a continuous length, lying partly between and partly above them. Parallel to the beams were smaller ledges to support the four-inch thick deck plank. Each upper deck gun weighed a ton less than those on the gun deck, allowing all the deck structure to be made proportionately smaller. The beams were not only smaller in section but they were also shorter in length, made possible by tumbling in of the ship's side. On 13 December Phineas was able to report '*The first 3rd rate ship* (Anne) *in the double dock hath 83 carlings hewed-dubbing* (trimming with adze) *the frame and chocking the heels of the timbers. Two gun deck beams hewed and moulded and also four orlop beams.*'

During the depth of winter, in February 1678, 15 gun deck beams had been hewed and moulded but not placed. At the same time, all the futtocks and 84 top timbers were up in place. Fourteen other top timbers were hewed and moulded and ready to go up, but timber to make the remaining 24 was still wanting. The frames were strengthened on the inside by ten strakes of planking near the keel, called footwaling. On the outside, the lower main wale was treenailed in place on each side at the widest part of the ship. A little later, during March, there were 117 men working on the *Anne* and 30 each on the other two ships. In all, 56 pressed men were working on the three ships.[38]

The main wale being examined on a modern replica of a ship the same size as the *Anne*. Author

Anne as she would have appeared in early 1678. Work has started putting up the top timber frames that reached to the top of the sides. Author's collection

The progress on the *Anne* had slowed toward the end of 1677 as Phineas started work on the two other third-rate sister ships. The ship that was to become the *Berwick*, launched on 29 May 1679, was built on the boat house

All the frame timbers are up and the gun ports cut out. The frame timbers were not spaced or co-ordinated for the convenience of the gun ports but cut out where needed and local arrangements made to the frame timbers to form the gun port's sides. The port nearest the stern has sills fitted between adjacent frame timbers. *Anne* was in this stage of completion about March 1678. Author's collection

By June 1678, all the major work is complete with only the lighter upper works to finish. *Anne* remained in this state for some months waiting for timber to complete her. *Author's collection*

old slip, and the other, *Pendennis*, launched on 25 December the same year, was built on the lower slip.[39]

The shipwrights

As they were only paid at three-month intervals, shipwrights working for the King always suffered from a shortage of money. This was bad enough for men working on the *Anne* and the other new ships when money raised by Parliament was readily available. The pressed or conscripted shipwrights working on the repair of old ships had to wait longer as the King's revenues for this work lagged far behind the money spent. They got to hear of the injustice and went round to confront Commissioner Beach with their complaint. Very unhappy at the visit, he responded by blaming Pett. He took the matter further by writing to the Navy Board accusing Pett of sending the men round to his house.

A ship ready for launch with the ways laid and a cradle attached to the hull to enable her to slide down into the water. Once the ways were laid and cradle fitted, the blocks under the keel that had taken the weight of the ship during the building would now be cut away so that the weight of the ship would be transferred to the cradle. 1 Ways. 2 Cradle. 3 Blocks under the keel. *Author's collection*

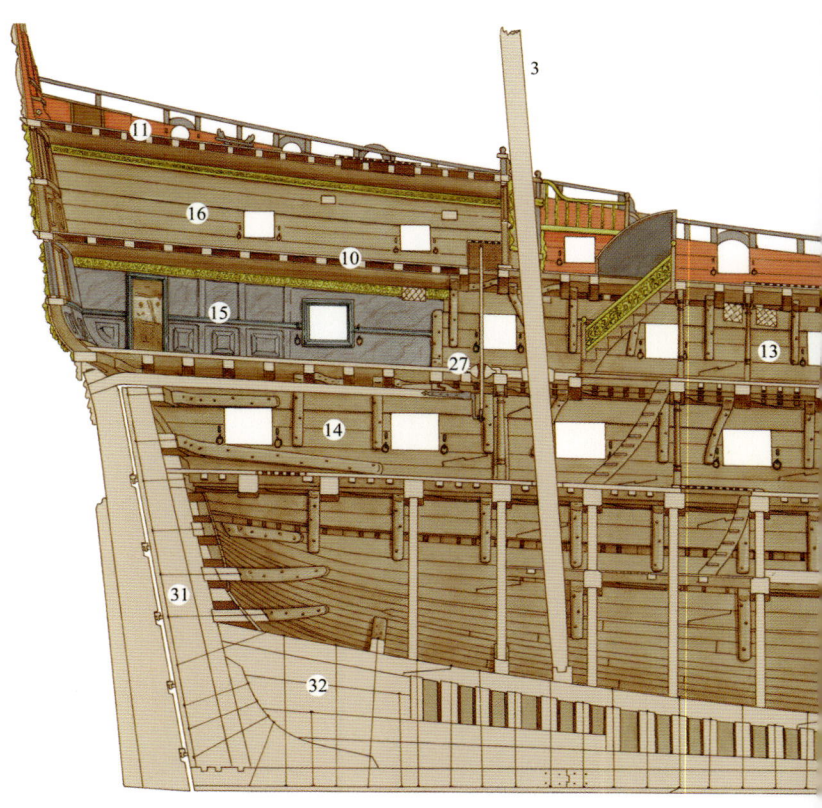

Building the *Anne* 33

To defend himself Phineas wrote to Pepys arguing the contrary, saying Sir Richard had sent the pressed men to him, in a tumultuous manner, where they crowded in at the doors. He persuaded them with '*fair language*' to calm down and allowed two or three of them in to air their grievance. Once inside they told Phineas that Sir Richard had sent them. What's more, Sir Richard had informed them he had made out a warrant to Phineas for them to be employed on the new ship (*Anne*). In reply, Phineas told the shipwrights that he had received a warrant from Beach sometime earlier and that 30 shipwrights had been transferred from the old to the new ships but that was all the men he could use at the present until more timber came in. He also promised that if they peaceably got on with their work he would bear them in mind. He must also have explained why shipwrights working on the new ships had been paid promptly. With that, said Phineas, they thanked him on behalf of themselves and the others and went away satisfied.[40]

With the coming of spring in 1678 and the lengthening days, Sir Richard Beach spoke to Phineas Pett about having the men work overtime in order to complete the *Anne* more quickly. Traditionally, over a long period of time, shipwrights had been able to add to their daily wage of 2 s 1d by working one and half hours overtime for which they received an extra six pence. This was

A section through a third rate of 1677. 1 Main mast. 2 Fore mast. 3 Mizzen mast. 4 Bowsprit. 5 Hold. Contains ballast, beer, water and food casks. 6 Orlop deck. Storage for anchor cables, sails, cabins and cartridge-filling room. 7 Gun deck. 8 Upper deck. 9 Forecastle deck. 10 Quarter deck. 11 Poop. 12 Forecastle. 13 Steerage. Cabins for many officers. 14 Gunroom. Quarters for the Gunner, Surgeon and midshipmen. 15 Captain's great cabin. 16 Roundhouse. Lieutenants and other officer's cabins. 17 Seat of ease. 18 Manger. Water drain area for anchor cable. 19 Riding Bitts. For securing the anchor cables, the second is a spare. 20 Pissdale 21 Cook room. Two cauldrons called furnaces, for boiling and a range for roasting. 22 Jeer capstan. The everyday capstan for raising masts, yards and anchors. 23 Chain pumps. One each side. 24 Well. 25 Shot lockers. 26 Main capstan. Used for heavy lifting. 27 Whipstaff. To steer the rudder, it moved sideways through a pivot called a rowl. 28 Keel. 29 Keelson. 30 Stem. 31 Stern post. 32 Rising wood. 33 Head. *Author*

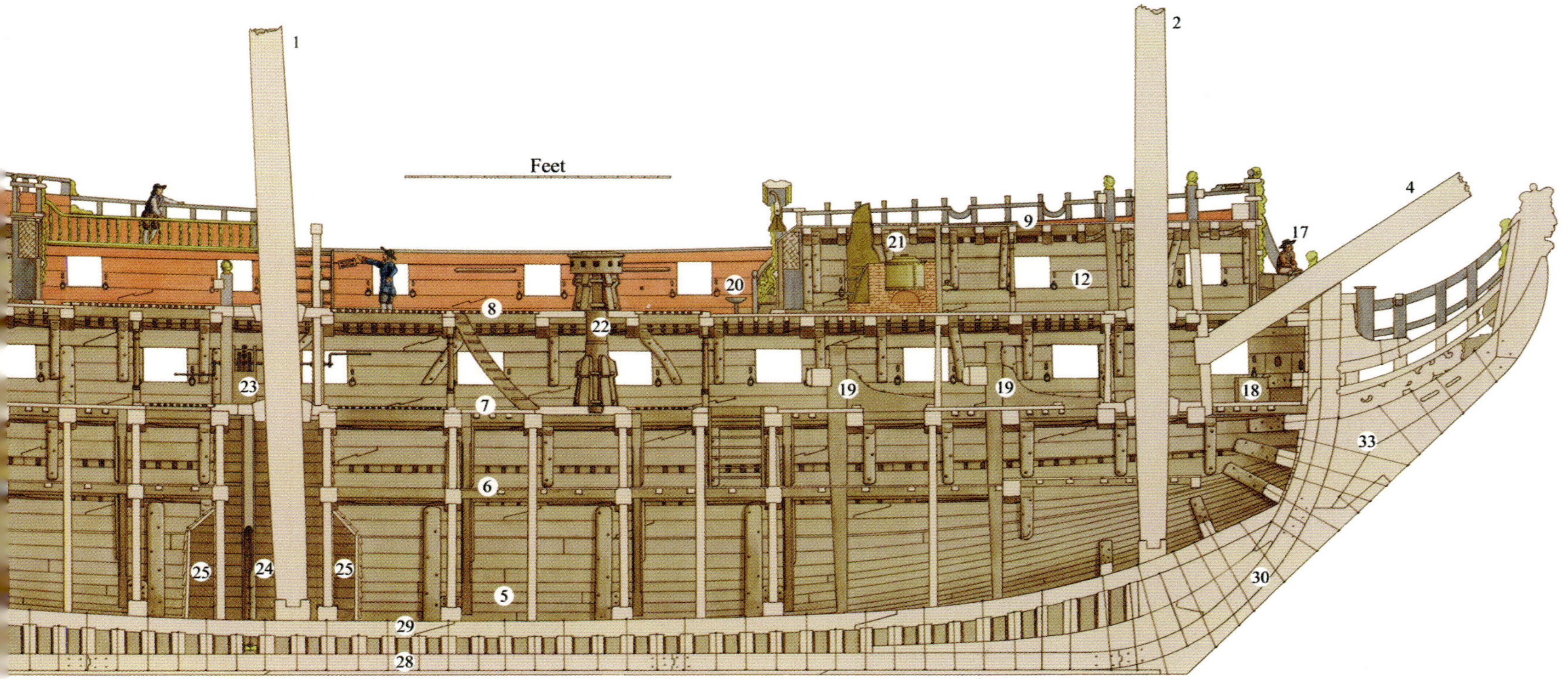

The only known contemporary image of the Anne *by Willem Van de Velde the Elder. Pencil 31 5/8' x 125/5'. Probably made on the occasion of a Royal visit to Chatham. Boymans-Van Beuningen Museum, Rotterdam, MB1866/T327*

historically known as a '*tide*'. Beach told Phineas that the shipwrights should now work two hours for a tide instead of the one and a half hours. But, he wrote, the Master Shipwright '*will not nor dares not oblige himself… nor will the men hear of working two hours for a tide extra upon the said new ship*'. Not willing to face the shipwrights himself, Beach had no option but to abandon his idea. Even so, he still thought the ship could be launched toward the end of June to make room in the double dock for building the first rate ship.[41]

Finishing works

By 5 June the upper works, quarterdeck and forecastle were being made ready for planking[42] but lack of Prussia deals began to hold up the work. Two weeks later progress temporarily almost came to a standstill.[43] Commissioner Beach became increasingly frustrated at the delays, complaining that he had sent the timber purveyor out looking for timber but he could find only one or two pieces. They couldn't be moved because so much rain had fallen it had made the ground too soft '*And the Shipwright is so infirm (or so he pretends to be) that it is not to be expected that he can travel the country to look for timber.*'[44]

The long-term complaints about travelling and the occasional reference to gout suggests Phineas possibly suffered from arthritis. July came and after six weeks waiting for Prussia deals to complete the upper decks, they had still not arrived.[45] Phineas himself wrote to the Navy Board asking for Prussia deals, large fir timber and the design and manner of the carvings, particularly those for the stern.[46] The ships of 1677 were among the most lavishly carved ships ever built, giving the impression the cost must have been enormous. But in a world where skills in carving were all too common, they cost only £160 out of a total build cost of £12,000.[47] (A copy of a contract for the carvings is given in Appendix 4) Eventually, by mid-July, Beach ordered that deals intended for repairing the *London* be used on the *Anne* to plank the quarterdeck, forecastle and poop. More positively he reported the upper deck was finished and caulked. The upper deck was often finished before the lower gun deck in order to keep the weather out.

Important fittings, the pumps, capstans, whipstaff steering gear, stairs, cook room, quarter galleries and windows would have been started during the summer. At the end of August, the three stern lanthorns were ordered from Mrs Stains, one of the specialist suppliers to the Navy.[48] The two copper furnaces or cauldrons for boiling meat in the cook room was ordered from Mr Taylor, the Brazier at Chatham. The larger was 41in diameter and 30½in deep and the smaller 30½in diameter and 26½in deep. In addition, a copper chimney, hood and funnel were also ordered.[49] Another important fitting was the scuppers for which Phineas wrote a specification for their supply.

Scupper specification for the *Anne*

Deck	Diameter	Length	Number
Lower Deck	5in	2ft 6in	6
Lower Deck	4in	2ft 6in	24
Upper Deck	3in	2ft 0in	24
Quarter Deck & Coach	2in	1ft 4in	8

The weight for cast scuppers was estimated to be 12lb per square foot for those between three to five inches diameter and 9lb per square foot for three inches downwards.[50] Their length was of course the same as the thickness of the ship's side. Most of the scuppers are for draining seawater back out to sea with the outer end sealed by a simple collapsing leather tube. The six large five-inch scuppers were distributed with one each for the two pumps with the other four in the manger, at the bows, to drain the water off the anchor cables.

No internal cabins would have been fitted in order to allow air to circulate freely in the new ship. At the end of August, Phineas wrote a progress report for the *Anne*. The head was almost finished, as were gratings for the hatches. Using deals intended for the *London*, the quarterdeck, forecastle and poop were also finished. Most of the fir carvings were made, hollowed out and fastened. The main and fore channels, which took the main rigging for the masts, were bolted in position. The four stern gun ports lids were made but not yet hung. The bitts that held the anchor cables were fitted and the gun deck two thirds laid. All that was holding up her completion was the supply of a dozen knees, some large fir to make the royal arms for the stern and some canvas for covering the galleries. Sir John Tippetts, the Surveyor of the Navy, ordered they be supplied from Deptford.[51]

Although so very little work needed to be done to complete the ship, it was not until 19 October that Phineas gave a possible date for the launch. He suggested 7 November 1678, during the next spring tides.[52] He received confirmation of the date from the Navy Board and began to fit her for launching by making the ways and attaching a cradle to the ship.[53] To make sure she was ready for the spring tides, he had 181 men working on her. This number was made up by taking men off from building other new ships and from off those being repaired.[54]

The launch

The new third-rate ship was launched on the appointed day without mishap. She was the fourth of the new ships to be launched and preceded by two at Deptford, one at Harwich and another at Woolwich.[55] To ease the ships launching, Pett requested six firkin (54 gallons) of crown soap for easing the cradle,[56] which Beach thought '*a very extravagant demand*' which he referred to the Navy Board for their consideration.[57] To keep the weight down during the difficult and potentially disastrous operation, the masts

A typical launch scene and the beginning of the celebrations. Notice the launch flags in place of the masts and the cradle bolted to the ship's hull that now has to be removed. *Author's collection*

were not fitted but temporary flagpoles set up in their place. The ballast was also kept to a minimum with just enough to stop the ship rolling over. Only ten tons of shingle rather than two or three hundred tons normally used was put in the bottom of the hold. Without doubt there would have been the customary celebrations amongst the men who built her, involving considerable merriment and drinking. Usually the Lords of the Admiralty, the Navy Board and the King, who chose the ship's name, attended to join in the celebrations but without him, the new ship – for the moment – remained unnamed. Phineas reported the event, noting that she drew 9ft 9in afore and 15ft 3in abaft.[58]

The apparent lack of official interest in the launch was the result of a political storm that had just broken out in London. On 28 September, Charles attended an Admiralty Board meeting at Whitehall and afterward, a Privy Council meeting. Two characters were brought in, Ezrael Tonge and Titus Oates. Oates revealed a fantastic Popish plot to assassinate Charles and replace him with a Papist successor, the implication being this would be his brother

The launch cradle from *Blanckley's Naval Expositor* 1750.

James, Duke of York. Charles didn't believe a word of it, but unfortunately, everyone else did.[59] The poisonous plot became politically all-consuming, resulting in the Admiralty not sitting again for another three months.[60]

Shortly after the launch and hearing that Charles had named the ship *Anne* after his niece, later Queen Anne, Sir Richard Beach sourly wrote to the Navy Board: '*I was in hopes to have had the honour of some of your companies at the launching of the* Anne *and since for settling diverse affairs here and you might have considered of the body of the same ship which I fear will not be approved of so well as expected by the builder.*' He went on to suggest they change the framing of the two ships being built to the same draught before Pett was allowed to proceed any further.[61] It does appear that personal animosity began to rule Beach's rational judgement, for even the most impartial observer would question how an ex-sea captain would presume better knowledge of ship design than an eminent Master Shipwright. Perhaps he had also forgotten that Phineas had shown and discussed his draughts with the King and Navy Board and had their approval. The hull lines, or body plans, of one of Phineas's ships, the *Berwick*, built to the same draught as *Anne*, was recoded six months later by Edmund Dummer just before her launch.[62]

After the *Anne* was safely launched, some of the longest bolts that went through and secured the stem and head were fitted and bolted. This could not be done while the ship was at the head of the dock as there had not been enough room to do it. There was also some work to be done in the cook room, and the lower masts needed completion.[67] The topps supplied for the ship, which fitted to the head of the lower masts, were found to be too thin and weak for the task.[68] The final cost in wages for building *Anne* was £4582 9s 0d

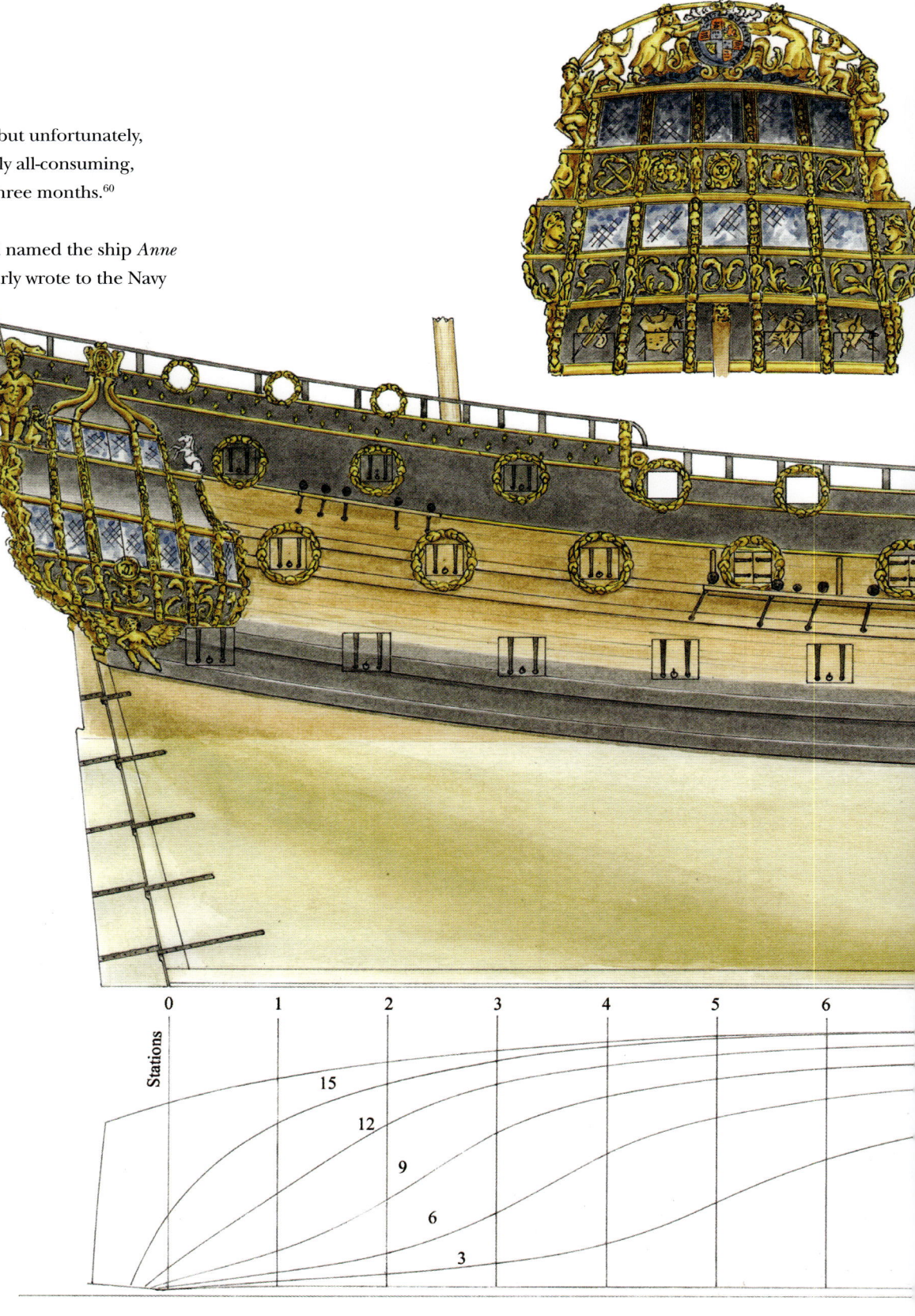

Building the *Anne* 37

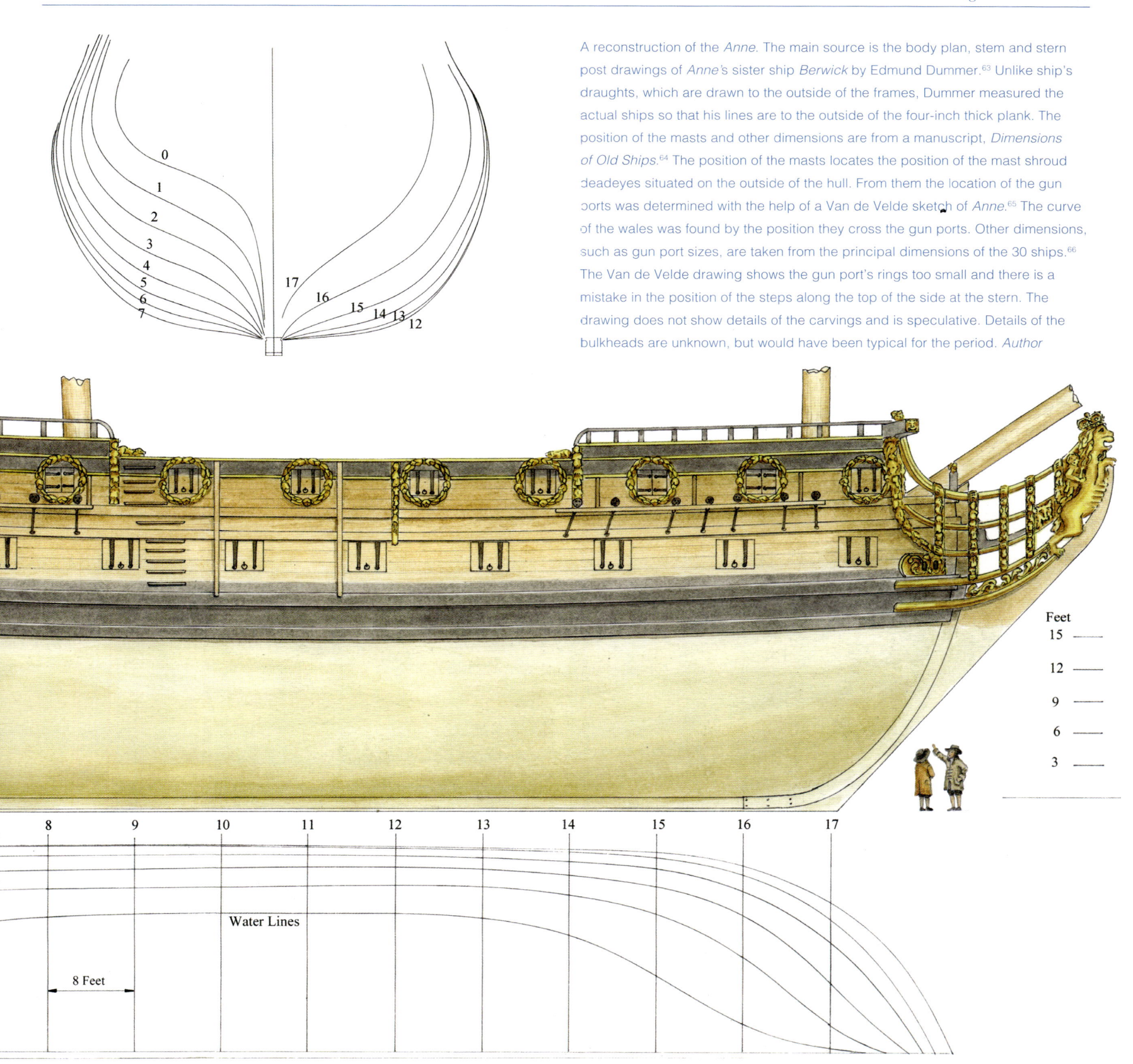

A reconstruction of the *Anne*. The main source is the body plan, stem and stern post drawings of *Anne*'s sister ship *Berwick* by Edmund Dummer.[63] Unlike ship's draughts, which are drawn to the outside of the frames, Dummer measured the actual ships so that his lines are to the outside of the four-inch thick plank. The position of the masts and other dimensions are from a manuscript, *Dimensions of Old Ships*.[64] The position of the masts locates the position of the mast shroud deadeyes situated on the outside of the hull. From them the location of the gun ports was determined with the help of a Van de Velde sketch of *Anne*.[65] The curve of the wales was found by the position they cross the gun ports. Other dimensions, such as gun port sizes, are taken from the principal dimensions of the 30 ships.[66] The Van de Velde drawing shows the gun port's rings too small and there is a mistake in the position of the steps along the top of the side at the stern. The drawing does not show details of the carvings and is speculative. Details of the bulkheads are unknown, but would have been typical for the period. Author

of which £3714 2s 0d was for shipwrights. Other notable amounts paid for workmanship was £468 13s 4d for joiners and £216 19s 8d for caulkers.[69] The actual cost of building her hull complete was £14,600,[70] £2,600 more than Pett's original estimate.[71] In 1687 the cost of the ship completely rigged with stores for 6½ months was put at £22,079 7s 4d.[72]

Phineas Pett's reckoning

As the final work on the *Anne* was being completed, Sir Richard Beach wrote a letter to the Navy Board complaining yet again about the Master Shipwright's '*great neglect of duty under pretence of sickness*'.[73] Unhappy with all the complaints, the Navy Board sent a copy of the letter, dated 14 January 1679, to the Admiralty. At their next meeting, with King Charles in attendance, they discussed the long disagreements between the men. Suspecting there may be faults on both sides, they decided that Mr Pett should be acquainted with the complaints made against him and that the Navy Board make an impartial report.[74] Afterwards, '*His Majesty be truly informed where the blame ought in justice to be laid and punished.*'[75]

Some months later, on 4 June, and presumably after the report had been delivered, Beach and Pett were summoned by King Charles to the Admiralty at nine in the morning for examination.[76] It must have been a stressful time for both men, particularly Phineas, as he was the junior officer and most of the complaints were against him. The odds were not good but after duly considering all the evidence, the King in Council directed that Sir Richard Beach be suspended as Commissioner at Chatham.[77] Quite probably Beach had made unsubstantiated remarks about Phineas's neglect of duty, after all, the *Anne* was not that far behind the other ships and he was preparing to build the great first rate and being responsible for the huge task of repairing most of the fleet moored at Chatham.

Another consideration in the judgement was Phineas Pett's good personal relationship with the King. Phineas revelled in his victory and became unbearable to the other officers who were his neighbours in Chatham Dockyard. One, Edward Gregory, the Clerk of the Cheque, and temporarily acting as Commissioner during Beach's suspension[78] wrote '*his behaviour which of late days I suppose hath scarce kept within the bounds of modesty even unto your Honourables and then I humbly leave it to you to judge what treatment his poor neighbours are to expect from him*'.[79]

Phineas Pett's greatest moment was yet to come. He petitioned the Admiralty, pointing out his long service of near twenty years '*at a salary too mean for the support of himself and family*', adding that during this time no ships he had built proved faulty, nor added to their cost by having to be girdled. He then pointed out his long suffering under the Commissioners who thought '*that they were the best judges of the nature of timber as to scantling and dimensions as well as price and goodness and all other naval particulars*'. The Admiralty and King were meant to notice these were, of course, the precise qualities Phineas himself possessed. He also reminded them that the King had promised him a higher position when a vacancy appeared.[80] In case he had not impressed

A nineteenth-century watercolour by an unknown artist. It is a copy of a lost oil painting with the frame bearing Pett's Arms. The sitter appears to be in his mid-forties and is wearing the style of clothing appropriate for 1680. The original may very possibly have been made the year Phineas Pett was knighted at the age of 45. *Courtesy National Portrait Gallery, London.*

them enough, he wrote again adding a list of the successful ships he had built that would perform to the good liking of His Majesty, they including the *Anne*, and the first rate he was building.[81] Rather surprisingly his shameless efforts bore fruit, and in October 1680 he was made one of the Principal Officers and Commissioners of the Navy acting as Comptroller of the Store Accounts. At the same time, he was knighted by the King.[82] One can almost hear the groans of despair from his colleagues.

He would, however, soon be brought back down to earth with a bump from an unexpected quarter. The new Lady Pett was also aware of her new and elevated status in life and ran up debts with Mrs Elizabeth Brooker, probably a seamstress or milliner. Mrs Brooker took to the law and petitioned the Admiralty for permission to prosecute Phineas. As Secretary, Samuel Pepys gave notice to Phineas and invited him to give a reason why he should not be left to the law. Phineas replied, perhaps saying he knew nothing and was innocent of his wife's indulgence. After considering his reply, it was decided that Mrs Brooker should be allowed to proceed and her solicitor be informed.[83] In those days there were serious downsides in being responsible for your wife. Phineas could easily end up in debtor's prison and languish there until his wife's debt was paid or he died.

Most people would be forgiven for wondering why '*that contentious man*', as Gregory called him[84], was ever given a knighthood. King Charles knew, as did others who knew about the art of building ships. One of them, William Sutherland, a shipwright himself and author of *Shipbuilders Assistant* of 1711 and *Shipbuilding Unveiled* of 1717, the only authoritative contemporary works on English shipbuilding, wrote:

'But King Charles the Second was much delighted in our art, being able to discourse and examine most of our principal shipbuilders and at length bestowed the honour of knighthood on three, which was Sir Phineas Pett, Sir John Tippetts and Sir Anthony Deane … but Sir Phineas was a great favourite of the King … I could never learn that Sir Anthony was much of a mathematician or a very great proficient in the practice but had the art of talking well … Sir Phineas was counted the greatest scholar of a shipwright that ever went before him and I am apt to believe as good as most that came after him and being encouraged by the King, he first began to invent something to reconcile and form our transverse lines [probably introduction of water lines] *and by the assistance of Doctor Wallis the famous Mathematician they made the cono-cuneus … I know they was handed down and is much admired by several material shipwrights at this day … However by all that I heard and by my own judgement, Sir Phineas was the greatest proficient since he produced what he did from rules … Indeed I must insist a little farther on what I observed of Sir Phineas, that his Britannia, also the Pendennis, Berwick and Anne, all 70 gunships of Sir Phineas was really as good as any.'*[85]

The closeness of King Charles and Phineas Pett was noticed by Pepys, who saw the original draught and dimensions of a yacht, either the *Fubbs* or *Isabella*, drawn by the King himself and built by Sir Phineas in 1682.[86]

Sir Phineas Pett's humiliation at the hands of Elizabeth Brooker must have caused amusement amongst his neighbours. Perhaps chastised by the experience and satisfied by his knighthood, he seems to have become more amenable to his colleagues. In 1686 Pett was at Chatham, acting as Commissioner, when Edward Gregory wrote in his diary for 26 October '*I and mine dined with Sir Phineas Pett*', and a week later '*Sir Phineas Pett and sundry other friends dined with us*'; the next month '*Sir Phineas and sundry of his friends unexpectedly supt with me*', then again a week later '*I dined with much company at Sir Phineas Petts*'.[87] Yet again, on 12 April 1687 '*I dined with Lord Dartmouth etc. at Sir Phineas Petts*'. It was also a happy outcome for Sir Richard Beach – shortly after being suspended he was made Commissioner at Portsmouth. Although far away and years later in 1690, he was still bearing a grudge, writing '*since it pleased God to visit me with this distemper, being afflicted as well in one of my knees as in my foot that rages so extremely that I cannot put my foot to the ground*'. He added, '*I am not like Sir Phineas Pett to make pretences of sickness when I am well.*'[88]

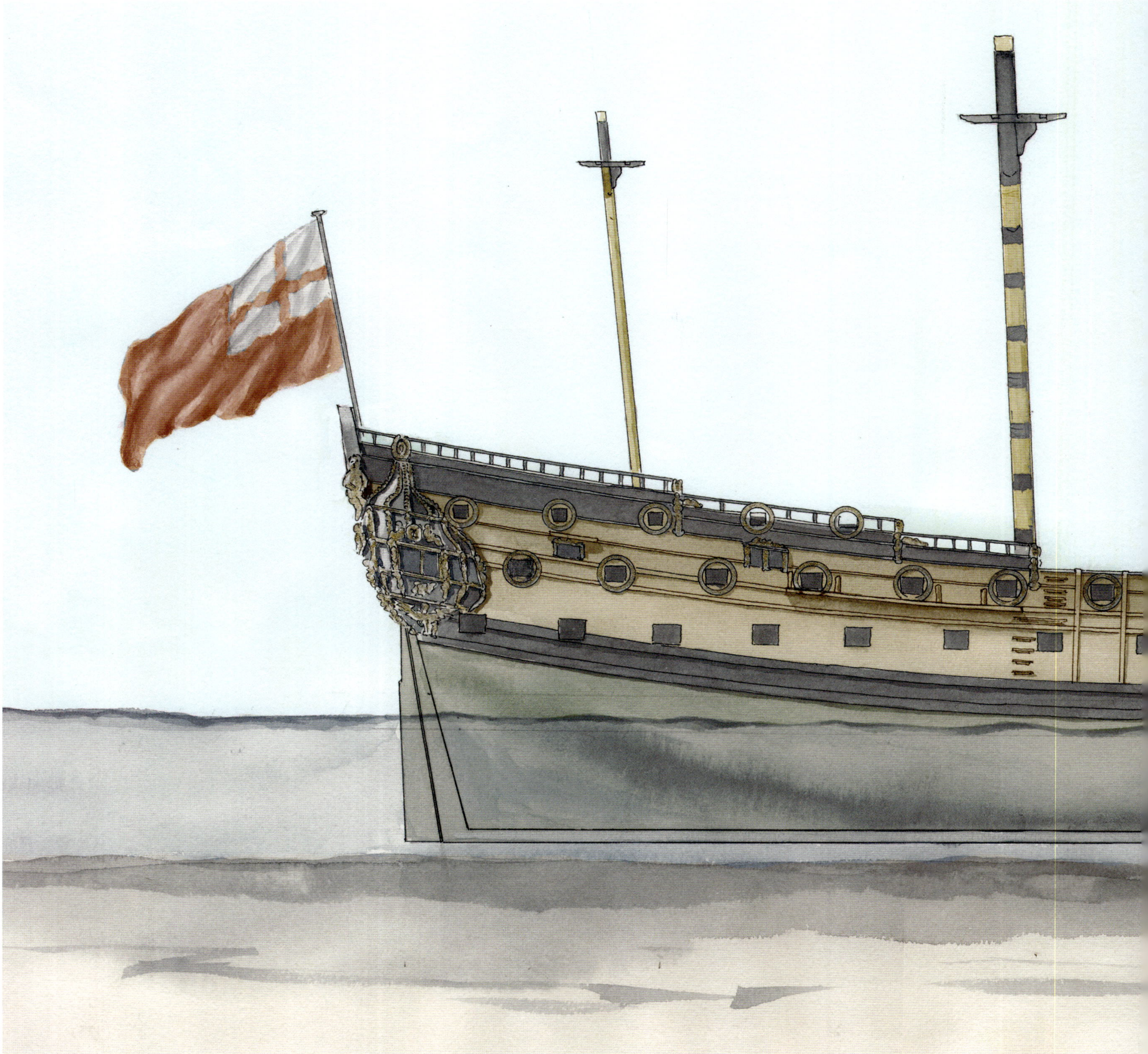

Chapter: 3 Laid up in Ordinary

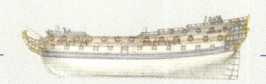

Moorings

With no wars in progress, *Anne* was moored in the Medway with many other large warships near Chatham Dockyard. There was still a small amount of work to be done. Permission was sought to make a main mast and a bowsprit, and a cost of £13 was estimated for the completion of the cookroom.[1] Ships laid-up were moored with two anchors at the bow so they could swing to face the tide or river flow head on. To avoid the cables crossing, they were joined by an iron swivel just in front of the bow. The upper masts, spars and rigging were not set up and if space

Previous pages: One of the new third-rate ships laid up in ordinary at Chatham and moored in the usual manner with only the lower masts set up. Two bridles lead from the hawse to the swivel from where two cables lead to the anchors. The flags were only flown on special occasions, such as a visit from the King. *Author*

Above: A model of a third rate of the 1677 programme in the Heeresgeschichtliches Museum, Vienna. It is shown here without perspective distortion and to scale as if it were a drawing. It has the specified number of thirteen gun ports on the upper and lower decks. The *Anne* and most of the other ships had the upper deck ports crowded forward. This ship has them crowded aft in the manner of the *Hope* and

was available, they were put in a storehouse ashore to keep dry. As this was not available, *Anne*'s rigging and top masts were all stored in her, below decks.[2] The consequences would reveal themselves years later. At the time it was estimated to get her ready for sea would cost only £60 for caulking and graving.[3]

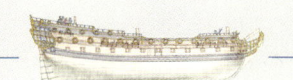

The River Medway at Chatham had gradually been silting up over a long period of time. This was probably caused by Rochester Bridge, built in 1391, which had large piers or starlings that slowed the river current. This had not been such a problem earlier in the seventeenth century, when warships were smaller and not so numerous. Now it was found that many of them were

Elizabeth, both built by William Castle in his private yard at Deptford. Some of the decoration is different from Van de Velde drawings of these ships, although the unusual quarter gallery supports and large royal arms at the quarterdeck bulkhead are the same. It is more likely to be the *Elizabeth* than the *Hope* as the *Hope*'s mizzen channels are different, shown by Van de Velde to be in two halves, one each side of a quarterdeck gun port. The space and room of the frames is a fraction under the specified 27in. The framing of model has been made in the usual contemporary stylised form with only one tier of futtocks each side instead of the actual three tires. In 1683 both ships were moored near the *Anne*, the *Hope* at the 13th and the *Elizabeth* at the 8th mooring from Rochester Bridge. *Author*

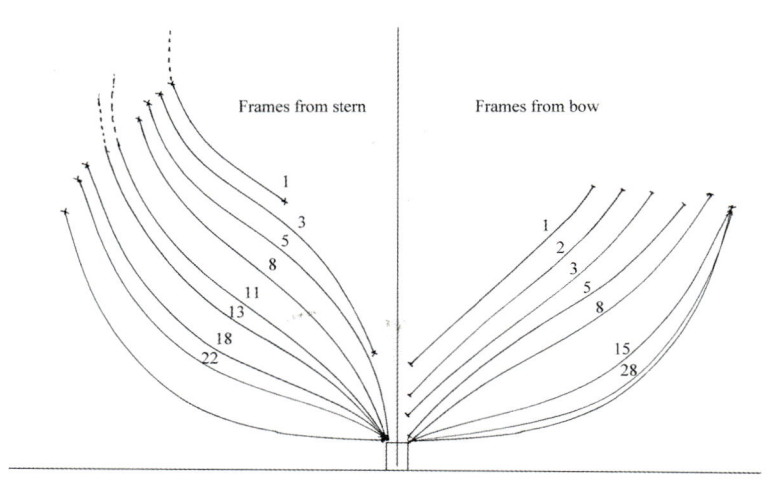

The frame lines from the keel to the lower edge of the wale traced from the model. *Drawn by Michael Wenzel and Willibald Mieschel.*

The head and beakhead bulkhead. *Photo Michael Wenzel*

The trumpeters cabin on the poop. *Photo Michael Wenzel*

The Stern. *Photo Michael Wenzel*

grounding in the shoaling river with not enough room for the new long-keeled third rates to '*wind*' or turn about their anchors.[4] A survey was carried out which found downriver from Chatham Key, at the first mooring, was the *Princess* with only ten feet of water to lie in when she swung with her stern to the Eastward. At the sixth mooring was the *Anne* and she grounded 16in.[5] A year later, on 24 September 1680, the *Anne* was moored at the sixth mooring

The quarterdeck bulkhead. *Photo Michael Wenzel*

The waist and jeer capstan. *Photo Michael Wenzel*

The roundhouse bulkhead. *Photo Michael Wenzel*

The forecastle bulkhead.[10] *Photo Michael Wenzel*

from the bridge downward and grounded six inches abaft on a bank with not enough space each side for her to swing at anchor.[6] At the time 39 large warships were moored at Chatham, of which 18 were part of the new 30 ship-building programme.[7] To overcome the problem of grounding, the ships were lightly ballasted and a revolutionary horse-powered dredger with paddle wheels built. The problem was not considered too serious as it was thought little damage would be done as the ships grounded on soft mud. By the end of 1680 it was estimated the *Anne* would cost £130 to complete for the sea, as she now needed caulking, graving and painting.[8] The mooring positions of the ships changed over time and in 1683 *Anne* would be found at the twelfth mooring from Rochester Bridge downward.[9]

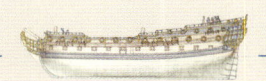

The Popish plot

Of much more concern to those in the dockyard were the implications of the Popish plot, with dark rumours of Catholic insurgents burning the ships in the river. The perceived threat was taken very seriously and a strict enquiry was made with the utmost authority to find out if any officer, seaman or workman was a Papist. None could be found, although one poor shipwright confessed that in his minority he was educated as a Roman Catholic but ever since was a Protestant. He was suspended for the present.[11] The plot even managed to implicate King Charles's Cavalier Parliament of having Catholic sympathies.

During the subsequent hysteria and fear, the naval administration came under suspicion and Pepys was thrown in the Tower for a while. In May 1679, a New Admiralty Commission consisting of political opponents was imposed. King Charles was reluctant to plead with a hostile Parliament for money,[12] fearful that a new Parliament would exclude his Catholic brother, James Duke of York, from the succession. For the Navy, which consumed more money than any other government department, the Treasury was now tasked with drastically cutting its budget. Charles undermined the new administration by failing to engage with them and sometimes bypassed the Admiralty and Navy Board completely, even to the extent of having a Master Shipwright build a ship without telling them anything about it at all.

The Warrant Officers

New ships were usually made and launched within a year or two from freshly cut, unseasoned timber. It required an enormous care and maintenance if serious problems of decay and rot were to be avoided. At the forefront of care were the five permanent warrant officers allocated to each ship. They were the Carpenter, Purser, Boatswain, Gunner and Cook, who were paid as part of the dockyard's '*ordinary*' and remained with their ship even when it was laid up. Seamen and commissioned officers, such as the Captain and Lieutenants, were only appointed when the ship went to sea. The warrant officers made themselves comfortable aboard, often berthing in the Captain's great cabin and causing damage to the carvings and decoration. They were usually men of great experience, and often of great age, whose primary duties were to generally look after their ship and keep watch.

To assist them in their duties they customarily had one or two '*servants*' or apprentices. They took it in irregular turns for leave ashore but with no senior officer aboard to enforce discipline, and being close to the shore, they were often tempted to abuse their positions. Especially now, as getting paid each quarter year would be uncertain and the King and his previous and efficient naval administration would not be visiting. Just before he was suspended, Sir Richard Beach wrote to the Navy Board, saying how sorry he was that there was little hope of getting money to pay the men. Understandably, this led to their neglect of duty and although only a few Boatswains were found to be absent, all the other warrant officers often were. They also came to expect every second week off to stay ashore days and nights. Beach made out a list of names of all those who had neglected their duty in spite of all the written and verbal orders, fair means and threatening he had given them. Of these men, he had only given leave to one man and he was the Purser of the *Anne* who was newly married. Apart from her Purser, during a ten-day period on the *Anne*, the Cook had been absent four times, the Carpenter once and the Gunner four times.[13]

Late one Tuesday evening in April 1681, Sir John Tippetts, Sir Richard Haddock and Sir John Narborough, all members of the Navy Board, made their way up the River Medway toward Chatham after viewing Stangate Creek. Passing the moored warships, they decided to check and make sure careful watch was being kept against any attempted sabotage by ill-disposed Catholics. Finding no one on the decks of *Anne*, they questioned the Gunner who was supposed to be on watch. He excused himself, saying he was not called by the previous watch keeper, who was John Russell, the Boatswain. He was suspended for going to bed without first calling the Gunner to replace him. Russell was not the only one in trouble; in all seventeen warrant officers from other ships were found to be in neglect of duty and all were suspended.[14] They were replaced by an able and diligent seaman from either the *Royal Sovereign* or *Princess*.

To help prevent such incidents happening again, orders were issued that a half-hour glass must be kept on watch and the bell struck each time the glass was turned. Neither was the officer on watch to leave the quarterdeck or poop until the succeeding officer was there to replace him.[15] The sudden action came as a huge shock to John Russell and the other warrant officers. A week after their suspension, and in keeping with the flamboyant language of the times, a '*humble petition*' arrived at the Navy Office saying:

'with great grief and sorrow of heart humbly acknowledge their great crime for which they stand suspended … and are commanded to wait on their Lordships next Saturday and having humbly laid themselves at their Lordships feet for mercy and pardon, your petitioners have nothing to offer in their vindication but do beg your Honourables notice their 20 years of faithful service in all wars with hazard of life and limbs and that this is their first fault … and favourably to move the Lords of the Admiralty to restore them to their employments wherein for life they will be double diligent and extra watchful day and night to charge their duty.' [16]

The warrant officers' petition was considered at the next Admiralty Board meeting with the Navy Board officers attending. King Charles was always susceptible to such sentiments and in pursuance to his pleasure their suspension was taken off. As a further warning to them, and other warrant officers, they were deducted a month's wages which were given to the poor chest at Chatham. Notices were also put on the gates of all the dockyards and on the bulkheads of the steerages of the ships, stating that if any officer committed the like offence they would face the severity of the law.[17] The lenient sentence of ten days' suspension was typical for King Charles's Navy but it did have an effect and afterward there were fewer cases of abuse reported. A survey carried out in September 1683 found that aboard the *Anne*, only John Standbury the Carpenter had been absent, but only because he was lame.[18]

Decay and decline

In January 1681, new Commissioner Sir John Goodwin and Master Shipwright, Robert Lee, noticed that the new ships were very defective in their works and in want of repair.[19] The problem was not unconnected to the conduct of the warrant officers, who should have been working hard to make sure their ships' unseasoned timbers were carefully looked after. When it rained they had a duty to close the hatches and gun ports to make sure water did not enter. The rest of the time they needed to make sure the gun ports were open and the hatches removed to allow the drying air to circulate.

During the summer, when the heat of the sun could dry exposed planks and cause splitting, they were supposed to water the ship's sides. The new naval administration, with less authority and even less money, found it difficult to enforce discipline. Just as damaging was the extreme weather of the so-called 'mini ice age', when the Thames frequently froze over during winter. The wet timbers became ice-filled and suffered serious damage-

when it thawed in the spring. The damaged timber then became extremely vulnerable to rot during the following hot summers. Goodwin made preparations for the forthcoming year by asking for 30 tons of blacking and ocum to caulk the new ships' damaged sides,[20] and as early as May he was complaining about the '*extreme hot weather*' and requesting caulkers to be sent down from Deptford to help.[21]

Shortage of money meant that repair and maintenance work progressed very slowly. To help preserve new ships they should have been graved once a year. The process involved burning off the old protective coating, probably consisting of oil, resin and brimstone, and renewing it. In August 1682, some of the new ships were being brought into dock for graving for the first time. On 25 August it was: *'found several of the new third rates very rotten in their plank and some of their (frame) timbers and at this time the* Anne, *now in the dock has seven plank of each side her buttock, perfectly rotten, also a large piece of her thick stuff'.*[22]

Alarmingly, after two days work on her it was found the '*Anne in dock proves more rotten in her plank than I could then give you an account of*'.[23] Two weeks later she was taken out of the dock and another ship entered in her room.[24] With so many ships to repair and not enough money to carry it out, it's doubtful if the repairs to the *Anne* were anywhere near as comprehensive as they should have been. Timber that is always wet or always dry does not rot but the buttocks, near the waterline at the stern, was the most exposed area of the ship as it was sometimes wet and sometimes dry. This area would be all the greater if the ship grounded with the tides. The news about the state of the *Anne* reached Samuel Pepys who noted it down for his proposed book about the history of the Navy[25]; it was all the more disturbing as she was less than four years old.

In March 1683, the lack of money for the Navy was causing other problems and letters started to arrive at the Navy Board. Rebecca Harming and Anne Lewis wrote a typical letter saying: *'We are the wives of Richard Harming and Henry Lewis, caulkers who were sent down from Deptford to Chatham. May it please your Honourables our husbands being at Chatham (while) us and our children are for want of relief ready to perish. Therefore we humbly pray your Honourables to consider our poor estates and be pleased to order that our husbands may be returned to Deptford yard to relieve their poor families.'* [26]

After receiving letters such as this the Navy Board informed the Admiralty *'The daily complaints which this Board receive from His Majesty's yards of the very great necessities which the workmen are reduced to by their wages being so long in arrears to the almost utter ruin of themselves and families, together with the want of almost all sorts of materials for carrying on the work now in hand.'* [27]

Recovery

By 1684 the hysteria of the Popish plot began to fade and hope sprang anew for the people and the ships. Charles gradually resumed control of his naval administration and began to appoint his own supporters. On 19 May 1684 he annulled the 1679 Admiralty Commissions patent and took control of the Admiralty himself; among the changes he made was the appointment of Samuel Pepys as Secretary for Admiralty Affairs.[28] The Master Shipwrights were tasked to exercise their minds in how to deal with the rotten new ships. This resulted in a discourse from Sir Anthony Deane[29] followed in April by a letter from Sir Phineas Pett[30] and another by Robert Lee and Daniel Furzer.[31] They tried and generally gave good advice for preserving ships while carefully absolving themselves from any liability.

Lee and Furzer blamed the use of East, or Baltic oak, an idea that Deane disagreed with, giving examples of its successful use. Deane also noted the lack of maintenance and regular graving, all necessary for the preservation and seasoning of newly built ships. One of the first acts of Pepys's new regime was to commission a survey of all the ships. The survey, dated 1 June, noted for the *Anne*:

'The breadroom to plate and the powder room to be lined. The foremast to be new; Some part of the bows and buttocks which appeared sound when she was last in the dock for repair we now find decayed and require shifting as also three or four planks between the channel wales. The bows to be lined for the anchors. With caulking, painting, graving and other small necessary works the sum of £532.' [32]

A shipwright working on the upper main wale with his feet resting on the lower. The two channel wales are those just above the gun-ports to which the channel is fitted. Note the decay in the upper main wale just underneath the middle gunport. Author

During the rest of the year only £24 10s 11d was actually spent on the ship for workmanship, showing the work could not have been carried out before then.[33] Some of the ships were now so rotten they were in actual danger of sinking. Unfortunately, at that time, the Treasury was only able to supply £12,000, a fraction of that needed to repair them all.[34]

King Charles died on 6 February 1685 and was succeeded by his brother James. Although James shared his brother's interest in the Navy, progress repairing the ships remained slow. Sir Phineas Pett, together with 13 other Master Shipwrights and Assistants were sent to Chatham to make reports. Pett's report, dated 12 May, complained that nothing mentioned in his previous proposals had been done. He did agree with Deane's earlier work and gave a list of advice related to drying the ships' timbers by keeping them clear of stores, gun carriages and rigging to allow the air to circulate. He also said the ships should be ballasted deeper to prevent hogging where the narrow and less supported ends of the ship sagged down in the water through lack of buoyancy.[35]

The other shipwrights' report of the same date broadly agreed with Pett but added '*there is no better way to preserve His Majesty's said ships of the XXX from future decay of this nature than with all possible speed to shift all such timber or plank as is now decayed on them*'.[36] On his return from Chatham, Pett wrote to Samuel Pepys complaining of the lack of care taken by just about everyone except himself.[37] The Navy Board noted that the *Anne* had already had one repair and it was proposed she would be the first to go in hand with a second.[38] A plan was made to repair 42 ships and by July 1685, eight had been completed, although the *Anne* was not one of them. The work had still not been carried out by January 1686[39] but she was listed as one of thirteen that was supposed to be repaired before July.[40]

With all the reports about what should be done and a sympathetic Parliament, a plan was put forward by Samuel Pepys. He proposed spending £400,000 a year to repair the ships and complete their stores. King James agreed and a warrant was signed for a Special Commission to start on 25 March 1686 and last for two years.[41] Pepys wanted to have people behind him upon whom he could rely to see the work was properly carried out. He managed to persuade his protégé, long-standing friend and Master Shipwright, Sir Anthony Deane, to join the commission. It included Sir John Berry, a naval officer with whom he had recently travelled to Tangier; Will Hewer, a lifelong friend and companion, and Balthasar St Michel, his brother-in-law.[42]

On 17 April, Pepys, the Navy Board and the Master Shipwrights held a conference with the main purpose of justifying the extensive use of foreign oak in the 30 new ships. Quite rightly and unsurprisingly, they found there was no alternative, as it was long and straight and best suited to the use.[43] On 21 May they visited Chatham and found the ships, especially the new ones, in an ill and dangerous condition with great numbers of boards and patches nailed to their sides, inside and out, and contrary to the rules of the Navy.[44] The second repair of the *Anne* was now estimated at £862, an increase in cost of £330 over the June 1684 estimate as a result of her steady deterioration.[45] This amount was marginally less than for most of the other new third rates.

Will Hewer. Samuel Pepys' closest friend and Navy Official. He was a man Pepys could totally rely on. *Author's collection*

The *Anne* appears to have been one of the first to benefit from the attentions of the Special Commission and all her repairs were completed before May 1687. Estimates for repairs were notoriously difficult to calculate as the planking hid any defects in the frame from view. The *Anne* was no different and actually cost £793 11s 1d for labour and £1279 5s 8½p for materials, two-and-a-half times more than the estimate and a sixth of her original building cost.[46] The money was well spent, for the *Anne* was now in very good condition, and ready for sea service with eight months worth of sea stores.

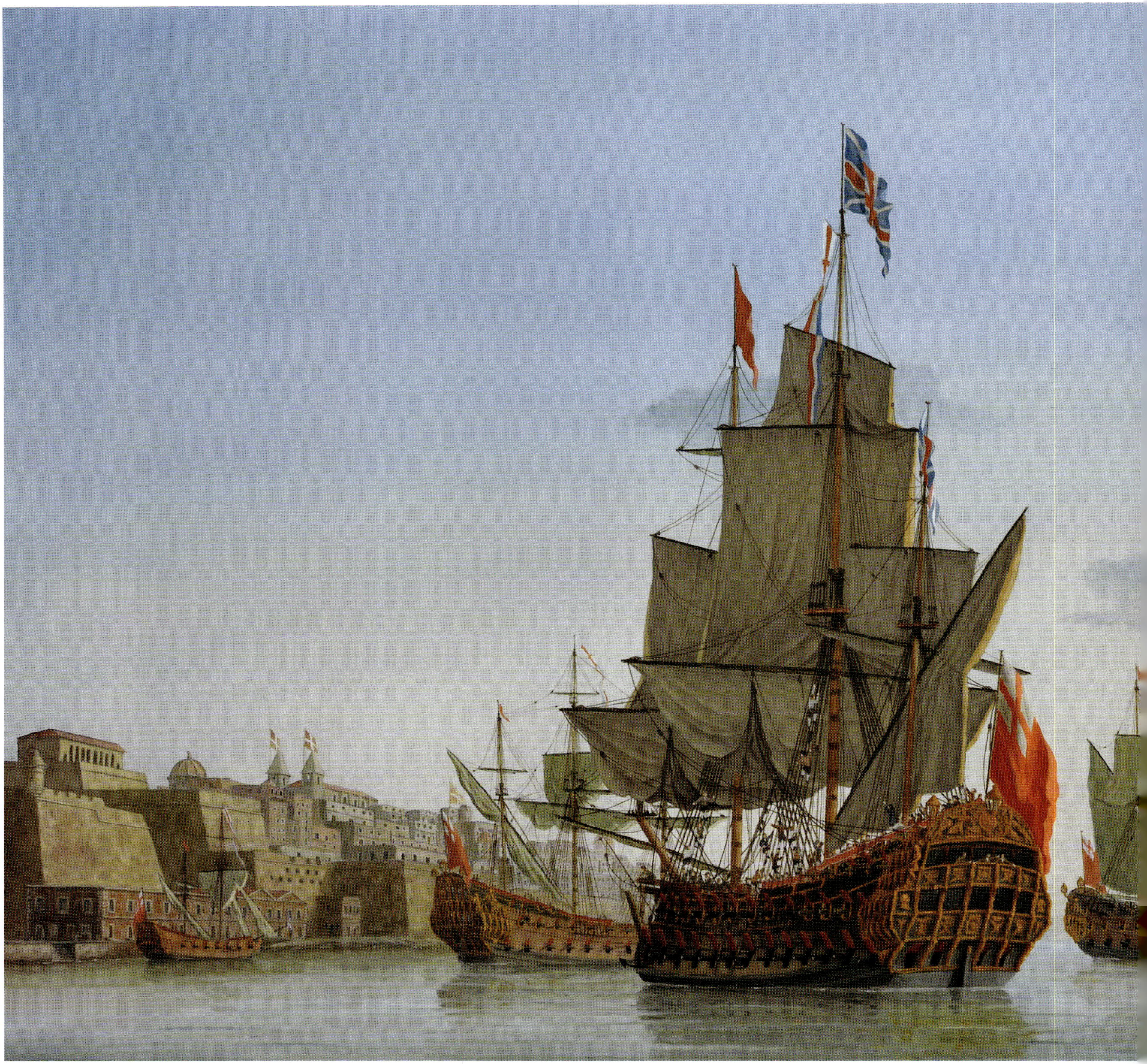

Chapter: 4

Mediterranean

The *Anne* and her fleet inside the harbour at Malta. Oil on canvas, *Author*

Choice of the *Anne*

James II. Author's collection

During the late 1680s a small squadron of ships was stationed in the Mediterranean for the protection of trade and to deter Barbary pirates. It generally consisted of about six ships of which two or three were fourth-rates and the rest fifth or sixth-rates.[1] An opportunity arose to send a powerful squadron to the area to impress the Barbary States and confirm peace treaties. Early in 1687, James II agreed to take the 20-year-old Maria Sofia Isabel de Saboia Neuburgo of Neuberg from Rotterdam to Lisbon to become Queen of Portugal. Her father was the Elector Palatine of the Rhine, who had 17 surviving children. She would be the second wife of Don Pedro II, whose first wife had died three years before, leaving only one child. With a precarious succession, Don Pedro II was attracted by the famous and extraordinary fertility of Maria Sofia's family. The negotiations resulted in a marriage contract being signed on 11 May 1687 and the marriage by proxy on 21 June. After considering the Navy Board's suggestion to use a three-deck, second-rate ship for the mission, on 5 April it was resolved that *'His Majesty is pleased to decline the making use of any of the great second-rates you propose for avoiding the extraordinary charge that will attend the same; and has therefore determined for making use of the* Anne *for refitting of which ship to the sea in the room of the Henrietta which will be left alone.'*

It appears the third-rate *Henrietta*, which had been on duty as a guard ship at Chatham with a crew of 80, had also been considered for the mission. She was less suitable than the *Anne* as she was much smaller and older.[2] For such a prestigious mission, James gave command to his 23-year-old nephew and King Charles's natural son Henry, Duke of Grafton. He had served at sea from an early age and had commanded the *Grafton* in 1683.[3] He lost no time in getting to Chatham to see the *Anne* arriving there on 16 April[4], even though his official commission as Admiral and Chief Commander for the summer's expedition wasn't made out until 5 June.[5]

Fitting out at Chatham

The Navy was not engaged in any serious wars at the time and the *Anne* would be the biggest ship sent to sea since her sister ship, the *Grafton*, went to Tangier in 1683. Proposals to fit out the *Anne*, appoint officers, and name several other ships that would join her, were made on 13 April. A new fourth-rate nearing completion was named in the list even though she wasn't launched until two weeks later.[6] The list of ships was confirmed by Admiralty orders a few days later. As well as the new fourth-rate, they included the fourth-rate *Hampshire*, the fifth-rates *Pearl, Richmond, Nonsuch* and the six-thrate *Lark*.[7] On Monday 2 May, the *Anne* was unmoored and put into the single dock for her underwater planking to be cleaned and payed with a protective coating. The following day King James visited to attend the launch of the new fourth-rate built by Robert Lee, and named her *Sedgemoor* after the battle fought two years before. The work on the *Anne* took two days after which she was launched and her place in the dock taken by the *Sedgemoor*. The launch cradle was removed and she was payed with protective 'stuff'.[8]

Both the lieutenants' logbooks survive[13] and record important facts from an operational and navigational point of view. The Master, Walter Barnaby, wrote as much in his logbook[14] as the two Lieutenants' combined works and its contents differ as he concentrates on the ship's technical issues. The four men each left a remarkable record of the *Anne*'s mission and cover the same subject in different ways. They are not referenced individually when used in the description of the mission. The logbook authors were inventive in their spelling of place names, inconsistent with each other, and even with themselves. This spelling has been adjusted in the text to follow that used on the images of the charts.

The handsome Henry Fitzroy, Duke of Grafton. He was the second son of King Charles II and his mistress Barbra Palmer, Countess of Castlemaine. *Author's collection*

During early May, the *Anne*'s five permanent warrant officers were joined by the commissioned officers. At the same time, the first crew members' names were entered on the *Anne*'s pay books. The Captain was 37-year-old Cloudesley Shovel. Unlike Grafton, Shovel owed his rank to Navy meritocracy having started his career as a nine-year-old cabin boy of humble origins. He had spent years on the Mediterranean station and would later become an admiral himself.[9] During his time in the *Anne*, he kept a letter book with copies of all the important correspondence received and sent.[10] For the mission to the Barbary States, Shovel was given a printed book of the treaties of peace and commerce agreements made with them. The first Lieutenant was an experienced officer, Captain Thomas Berry; he was first appointed lieutenant in 1672 and became commander of the *Success* in 1673.[11] The second Lieutenant was Francis Wivell; he became a lieutenant in 1682 and would later become the successful captain of a number of ships.[12]

Cloudesley Shovel in heroic pose painted some years after his time as captain of the *Anne*. *Author's collection*

54 The Warship Anne

Mediterranean 55

Mizzen mast and rigging	Mizzen topmast and rigging	Mainmast and rigging
1 Mizzen mast	19 Topmast	38 Mainmast
2 Yard and sail	20 Yard and sail	39 Runners and tackles
3 Sheet	21 Braces	40 Tackle
4 Shrouds and laniards	22 Lifts	41 Shrouds and laniards
5 Bowlines	23 Shrouds	42 Stay and Sail
6 Brayls	24 Halliards	43 Staysail halliards
7 Jeer	25 Back stays	44 Yard and sail
8 Peak hallyards	26 Bowlines	45 Jeers
9 Crossjack yard	27 Sheets	46 Sheets
10 Lifts	28 Clewlines	47 Tacks
11 Braces	29 Stay	48 Buntlines
12 Puttock shrouds	30 Crosstrees	49 Bowlines
13 Mizzen top	31 Cap	50 Braces
14 Top armour	32 Stump	51 Leachlines
15 The capp	33 Stay	52 Puttock shrouds
16 Crowfoot	34 Truck	53 Crowfoot
17 Stay and sail	35 Spindle	54 Lifts
18 Halliards	36 Vane	55 Top
	37 Slings of the crossjack	56 Top armour
		57 Top rope
		58 Cap
		59 Main yard tackles

Main topmast and rigging	Foremast and rigging	Fore topmast and rigging
60 Main topmast	81 Foremast	102 Fore topmast
61 Tackles	82 Runners and tackles	103 Tackles
62 Shrouds	83 Tackle	104 Shrouds
63 Back stays	84 Shrouds and laniards	105 Backstays
64 Halliards	85 Stay	106 Halliards
65 Stay and sail	86 Yard and sail	107 Stay and sail
66 Staysail halliards	87 Sheets	108 Halliards
67 Yard and sail	88 Tacks	109 Yard and sail
68 Braces	89 Braces	110 Runner
69 Bowlines	90 Bowlines	111 Lifts
70 Sheets	91 Buntlines	112 Braces
71 Clewlines	92 Leachlines	113 Bowlines
72 Lifts	93 Yard tackle	114 Sheets
73 Runner	94 Jeers	115 Clewlines
74 Buntlines	95 Puttock shrouds	116 Buntlines
75 Crosstrees	96 Crowfoot	117 Crosstrees
76 Cap	97 Top	118 Cap
77 Stump	98 Top armour	119 Stump
78 Stay	99 Top rope	120 Stay
79 Truck	100 Lifts	121 Truck
80 Pendant	101 Cap	122 Spindle
		123 Vane

A rigging plan of one of the 20 third rates of 1677. They were rigged to a standard pattern and the *Anne* would have been the same. The image has been altered to reduce some of the many errors in the original. It shows a bobstay which dates from a slightly later period. *Author's collection*

Bowsprit and rigging	Spritsail topsail and rigging	Hull
124 Bowsprit	134 Topmast	A The cutwater
125 Horse	135 Shrouds	B Stem
126 Yard and sail	136 Halliards	C Hauseholes
127 Lifts	137 Craneline	D Cathead
128 Sheets	138 Yard and sail	E Wastecloths
129 Clewlines	139 Braces	F Fore channel
130 Braces	140 Lifts	G Main channel
131 Bobstay	141 Sheets	H Mizzen channel
132 Top	142 Crosstrees	I Chestree
133 Top armour	143 Cap	K Entering port
	144 Jackstaff	L Head
	145 Truck	M Gallery
	146 Jack	N Taffarell
	147 Best bower buoy	O Poop lanthorns
	148 Cable	P Ensign staff
		Q Truck
		R Ensign

Manning ships like the *Anne* was an easy matter during a time of peace and very different to a time of war when thousands of men were needed. The first consideration for Captain Shovel was finding room for midshipmen, gentlemen volunteers and nobles, such as Henry Fitzjames, the 14-year-old illegitimate son of the King. Midshipmen were generally young men learning their trade as officers while volunteers were generally much less useful, being aristocratic friends and supporters of those in high rank. On such a prestigious voyage there would be many of them whom the Admiralty ordered should have cabins set up on the upper deck in the steerage. Toward the end of May, the Duke of Grafton sent down ten men for which Shovel complained was '*more can be found space for*'.

There was no need for pressing any of the crew, and Shovel was instructed to be very careful and enter only fit, qualified seamen so they would not have to be discharged if found wanting as this was a practice that caused resentment and discouraged others who wished to join. On 21 May, the men were mustered and conduct money, or travelling expenses, paid to volunteer seamen who had probably served under Shovel in the *James Galley* which had been paid off in December 1686.

By mid-May, there were enough men aboard the *Anne* to clear up the ship and start heaving out old ballast into a lighter. The first important stores to arrive was a hoy load of low-alcohol beer. It was much safer to drink than water and a generous daily allowance of eight pints was allowed for every man.

Before the month was out, the heavy anchors, their cables and small brass guns arrived, and were set up. The *Anne* would have had four main anchors weighing between 40 and 50 hundredweight each. The best bower and spare anchor were located on the larboard (left) channel and the sheet and small bower on the starboard. In addition there were smaller anchors stored in the hold, the kedge and stream anchors.

They were followed aboard by the Carpenter's and Boatswain's stores which were taken down to their places, forward on the orlop deck. The stores for six months service had been provided for the *Anne* when she was built, but how much survived and remained in good condition was questionable. The three masts were already standing but a new main top was fitted and the topmasts were raised. The Master suspected the mainmast to be faulty and had a fish, a strengthening piece, taken off so that mast makers could survey it. As they rigged the ship it was evident that a new main yard was required. It was becoming clear that much of the masts, yards and rigging that had been in store since the *Anne* was built were showing signs of deterioration. In spite of the problems, the sails were brought to the yards and loosed. Two days later, on 30 May, the *Anne* slipped her moorings and left Chatham for the first time, making it to the Buoy of the Nore by the afternoon. Most of the rigging and naval stores had been taken in at Chatham but to receive the provisions and ammunition from London, and the iron guns from Woolwich, she had orders to sail into the Thames.

Fitting out in the *Hope*

On 1 June, the *Anne* made her way up the Thames toward London and moored in the Hope against Tilbury Church. There she would spend the rest of the month completing her fitting out. First to arrive from Woolwich were ten of her great guns for the lower deck. They were delivered in batches of about seven guns every few days. Other gunners' stores, including 20 tons of shot, 240 barrels of gunpowder and small arms, were periodically delivered. Two of the chase guns were put down in the hold. Lighters and hoys brought 34 tons of beer, 404 bags of bread and 43 puncheons of beef, each puncheon being the size of two barrels. Thirty-four tons of beer sounds a colossal amount but the *Anne*'s crew would consume that amount in only 20 days. They would soon run out on the long voyage and then have to rely on getting fresh water.

Mediterranean

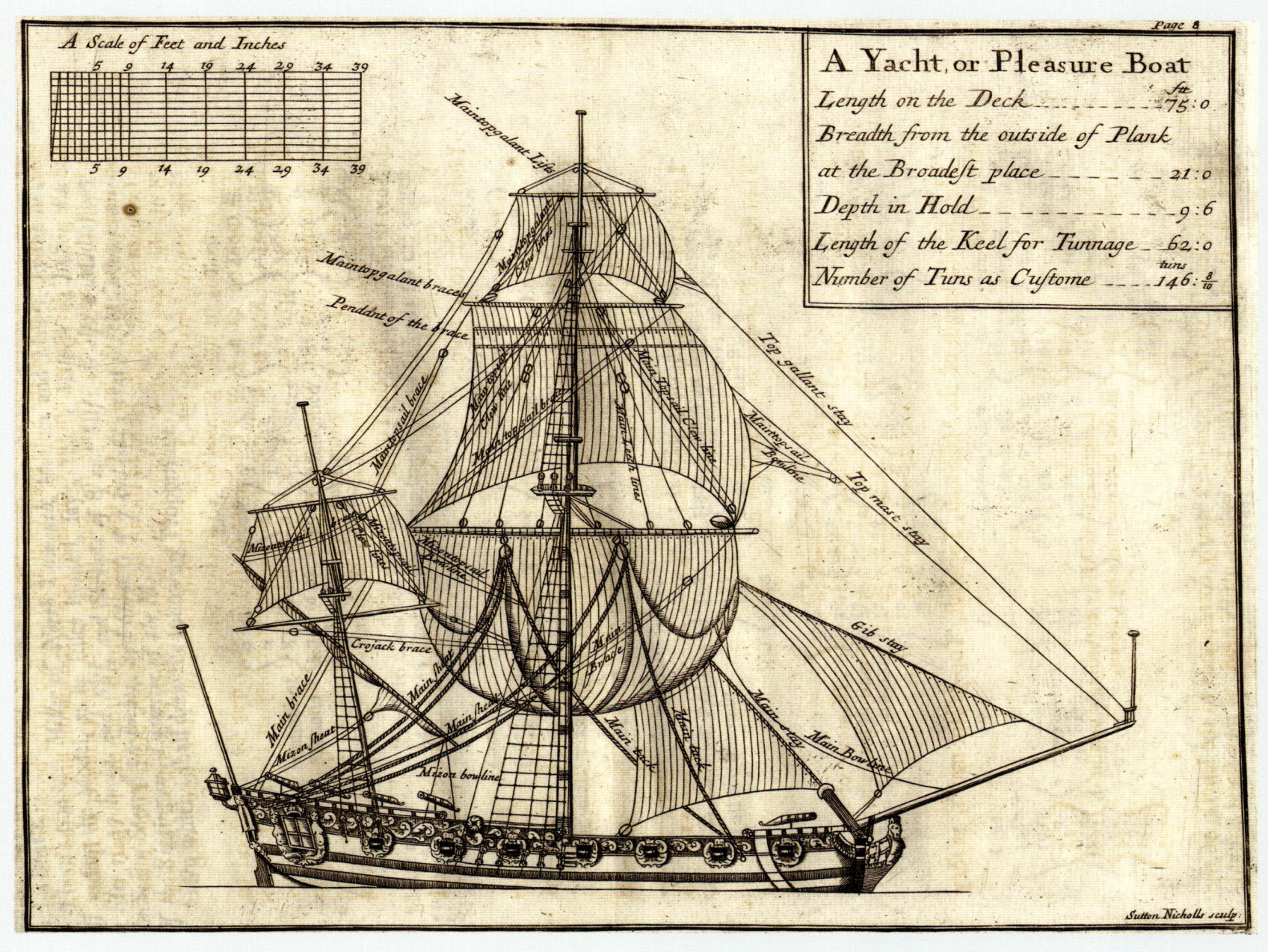

A Yacht, or Pleasure Boat

	ft
Length on the Deck	75:0
Breadth from the outside of Plank at the Broadest place	21:0
Depth in Hold	9:6
Length of the Keel for Tunnage	62:0
Number of Tuns as Custome	146:2/10 tuns

All the ships in the *Anne*'s squadron had three masts and were ship rigged in a similar manner to the *Anne*. The exception was the yacht *Isabella* which, in spite of being described as a yacht, was ketch rigged in the manner shown above. To handle the more complex rig, her crew was increased from the usual 40 to 45 men. From William Sutherland, *Shipbuilding Unveiled*, 1717. Author's collection.

Next day sea stores of beef, pork, casks of water and a hoy load of firewood arrived. On 3 June oatmeal, butter and cheese arrived, followed a few days later by five bales of slop clothes. On 8 June, a hoy completed the sea victuals of bread, beef, pork, peas, butter, cheese and more oatmeal.

Concerns about the masts and rigging remained. The shrouds were reset; Captain Shovel measured the fore top and found it to be 13ft 10in in diameter, which he judged too small for the spread of the topmast shrouds. He thought it could be altered and made 18 or 20in wider but in practice the dockyard workers found it easier to fit a replacement. On 6 June, the men scraping the masts and blocks thought the mizzen mast might be rotten; it was surveyed by two mast makers from Chatham who confirmed their fears. Only a couple of days later it was replaced when they '*heaved out our mizzen mast and set a new one and rigged it*'. It was an operation that must have taken considerable ingenuity and seamanship to perform. The main and fore shrouds were set up again and the rest of the rigging sorted out and reworked. The rigging, the shrouds in particular, were showing worrying signs of stretching and becoming slack. On setting up the shrouds, three of the deadeyes broke, and it seemed all the others were unsound, having been exposed on the channels since the ship was built.

The Carpenter's stores included vast quantities of items such as oak plank of different thicknesses, spare spars, elm board, many types of bolts, caulking equipment, hinges, spikes, nails, rings and forelocks.[15] For six months' supply in 1687 the value was £115.[16] The Boatswain's stores included an even greater variety, among them, flags, canvas, hammocks, compasses, many time glasses, chains, crows, locks, mauls, hooks, tallow, tar and such like. It also included spare sails and the materials and tools to mend them. Added to that were 60 spare blocks, 20 dead eyes, vast quantities of cable-laid cordage from 3½ to 18in circumference and hawser-laid ropes from ¾ to 7½in.[17] For six months' supply they were valued at £440 in 1687.[18] The list of *Anne*'s equipment included 30 sails containing 7,186 yards of canvas valued at £499 1s 4d, cordage for the rigging at £372, cables at £708, anchors at £408 10s, and blocks, top and pumps at £139 16s. Other items, such as a spare tiller, whipstaff, sprit yard, oars and flags, one of which was a royal standard, were among the last items delivered. Most of the stores almost certainly came from the great storehouse at Deptford.

Cloudesley Shovel noticed some deficiencies in the tackle used for raising the anchors. The ship had two capstans, the smaller jeer capstan situated forward of the main mast and used for everyday tasks. The other, the main capstan, was situated further aft between the main and mizzen masts. For raising heavy anchors in firm ground the main capstan was used. As the anchor cable was too large to go round the main capstan, a smaller messenger hawser was used in an endless loop to pull it in. It was attached to the anchor cable every few feet by small ropes known as nippers. The nippers were attached to the anchor cable where it came in near the hawse and detached just before the anchor cable went down the hatch onto the orlop deck below where it was coiled.

Sometimes, when using anchors in soft ground or when the main capstan needed help, the jeer capstan was used. As the looped hawser was shorter it was called by a different name, the voyall. It was used in much the same way as the messenger but because the jeer capstan was forward of the hatch and had to pull the anchor cable past itself, the voyall hawser went through a large block, the voyall block, temporarily attached to the main mast. Shovel had written about the '*roundabout*' or endless looped voyall needed for the ship, and that the 6½in (2in-diameter) hawser, supplied as the messenger, was too small. His reference may be the earliest known mention of the messenger. Earlier, smaller ships did not need one as the smaller anchor cables were more flexible and could bend round the main capstan.

Two years later, the Lieutenant of another third-rate ship of the 1677 programme, the *Suffolk*, demanded he be issued with an 8in hawser and complained that his jeer capstan broke when heaving up the anchor. Edward Gregory, the Commissioner at Chatham, wrote, '*if our people will not make use of their main capstans to relieve them in heaving up their anchors, they will tear all the jeer capstans in the Navy to pieces*' [19]. Another of the ships, *Lenox*, broke her jeer capstan at the same time in the same manner.[20]

Another technical problem that Shovel had to deal with was King James's fascination with ships pumps. In June the previous year Sir Samuel Moreland, one of the great inventors of his age, demonstrated a sea-pump to the great satisfaction of James, who had it replace one of the *Charles*'s chain pumps[21]. Moreland was not the only pump inventor. Two months later in St James's Park, at seven in the morning, James saw the demonstration of another pump invented by Sir Robert Gourden. It was not successful and shown to need further development[22]. Yet another pump inventor, Robert Lodgingham, found King James enthusiastic to test his ideas[23]. A trial of the three pumps was arranged to take place at Deptford. Lodgingham didn't turn up, Moreland's pump was supposed to be tested on the *Portsmouth* but when he demanded a foot square hole cut through the edge of the gun-deck, another cut through the ship's side and the wall of the well taken out, the dockyard officers refused, saying they couldn't carry out such drastic work unless they received direct orders from the Navy Board.[24] By default, the winner of the dubious competition was Gourden. On that basis it was rashly decided that the pumps he used in the St James's Park trial were to be further tested on the *Anne* and the *Sedgemoor*.[25] It involved replacing one of each ship's two chain pumps.

Gourden seems to have become deluded, claiming his new invention was

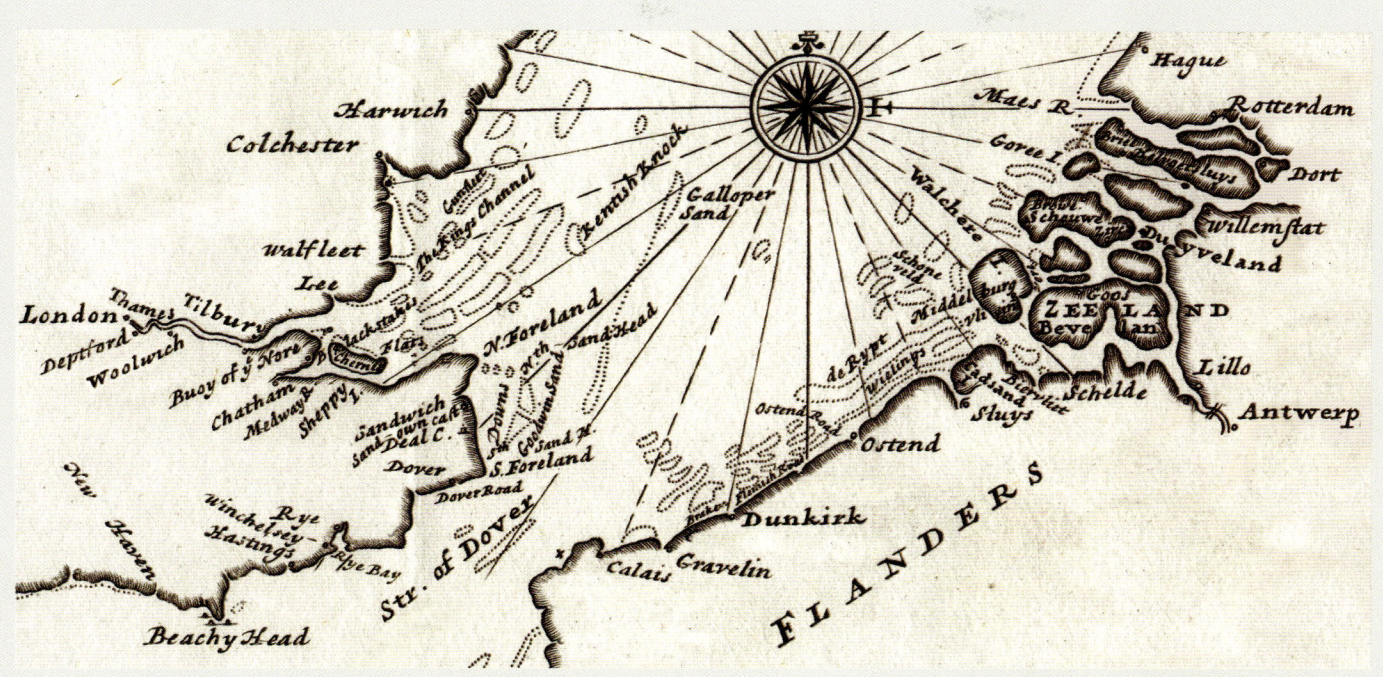

A contemporary map by H. Moll showing all the important maritime places visited when the *Anne* went to Rotterdam to collect Maria Sofia, Queen of Portugal. *Author's collection*

of utmost national importance, and that the French King had employed sinister persons to discover his secrets. John Martin, the *Anne*'s Carpenter, was sworn to secrecy when instructed how the pump worked. Cloudesley Shovel soon discovered there were problems. Gourdon's invention seems to have been a type of suction pump, for he described it as having two staves, a plug, two boxes and two small iron rods. These iron rods bent and broke and the pump couldn't be made to work with less than two feet of water in the hold. On examination, the *Anne*'s Carpenter thought the pump tube was damaged and needed re-boring with a 10½in bitt. In spite of Shovel's and Pepys's best attempts, they couldn't find Sir Robert Gourden or any of his workmen to help. Captain Lloyd on *Sedgemoor* said of his pump, '*it was so tiresome to the men as the whole ship's company cannot free so much water in one hour as may be done with ten men*' (on the other chain pump).[26] Just before they sailed, *Anne*'s pump was fixed, although they had no spares, and the Carpenter thought it wouldn't work in less than 30in of water.[27] In spite of these problems, the pumps were not replaced until the ships returned from their mission.[28]

On 9 June, a merchant ship, the *James and Mary* of London, arrived in the Thames with a fortune in gold and silver plate recovered from a wreck on the shoals of Ambrosia in the West Indies. For its security, 12 men were sent from the *Anne* to board her. Captain Shovel strictly ordered her commander, Captain Phillips, that nothing be meddled with or carried from the ship. Later, on 23 June, another merchant ship, all ablaze, caused a distraction as it drove down from the eastward. To avoid it, they heaved themselves away northward, presumably by hauling in the best bower anchor to the north.

Cloudesley Shovel noticed '*the extraordinary work to be done to the ship for the accommodation of the Duke of Grafton*' to make the cramped cabins on the *Anne* as stately as possible. On 15 June, two gentlemen came by the King's order to measure the stateroom for it to be hung with damask and to see what space was available for putting up a fine bed. This stateroom was probably just forward of the great cabin on the upper deck. They also noted what further work needed to be done to the great cabin, which had been varnished and supplied with four brass locks a week earlier. The great cabin would already have been panelled, wainscoted and painted. As a matter of course, all great cabins in the King's ships resembled the interior of a stately home. There were no hanging knees to spoil the elegance, instead the overhead beams were let down into a wide string at the sides which was carved to double as a cornice. Nor were the beams overhead visible, as they were covered with a ceiling of painted light boarding. The reduced number of guns carried by *Anne* left empty ports in the great cabin and stateroom.

They would have glazed windows fitted for which the carpenter made moulds. To complete the accommodation for Maria Sofia, two hoys brought goods and provisions supplied by King James.

The Earl of Sunderland mentioned to Grafton that the Portuguese Ambassador would need a convenient apartment. That would require a large cabin built in the middle part of the bulkhead of the lower coach. Among other details that needed attention were the replacement of a weak awning beam and provision of 20 iron stanchions. The beef room store scuttle needed work to accommodate several of the Duke's stores. Between decks, the powder room scuttle required a hanging lock and an iron bar to go across it. Work was also carried out on the fish room scuttle and the door to the cook room. They also needed tarpaulins and painted canvas to keep rain water out of the gallery, gallery bulkhead and the bulkheads of the coach and cuddie. The sides of the ship were scraped clean before being payed with a protective mixture of pine resin and tallow. The ship was then heeled and scrubbed as far down as could be reached.

By the beginning of June, it was clear the *Anne* was going to be overcrowded. Unfortunately no final orders had been received saying how many men would be allowed the Duke, who had just sent down some of his servants. Then orders were received for 16 passengers to be taken to Lisbon in the ships of the squadron, they including Gracia Logia and her three daughters, Francis Rodriguez with his wife and Antonio Villella with his wife and son.[29] Not all the men entered on the *Anne*'s books were as carefully selected as they should have been for, on 25 June, one of the Master's mates was found stealing from the Master's chest. Grafton ordered that he be whipt at the capstan then sent ashore.

The Duke himself left the ship to receive lengthy and detailed instructions for the mission and returned on 5 July. His instructions detail the complex alternative ship movements and what should happen if the peace negotiation with the Barbary States failed. (These are reproduced in Appendix 5.) Also essential for the mission was a set of fighting and sailing instructions. Apart from the *Anne*, copies of the fighting instructions were given to all the ships that would enter the Mediterranean. They were, in the order of battle, *Pearl*, *Charles Galley*, *Anne*, *Sedgemoor*, *Hampshire Mermaid* and the *Isabella Yacht*. They included such instruction as:

'*Sign for engaging* – As soon as you shall see me engage or make a signal by putting out a red flag on the fore topmast head you are to take the best advantage you can to engage the enemy according to the order of battle.'

The sailing instructions were in similar layout: '*Weighing by day* – As soon as I shall fire a gun & loose my foretopsail, you are immediately to weigh & being come to sail to follow ye flag' another example was '*If I would have you at any time give chase to any ship to windward I will put abroad your signal & a yellow & white flag on my ensign staff & if to leeward ye signal will be a red one there.*' The individual ships had their own identification signal. If Grafton wanted to signal the *Mermaid*, for example, he would fly a pendant at the fore topsail yard.[30] Shovel also went ashore to receive instructions regarding looking after the Queen of Portugal.[31]

To Lisbon

On 3 July, a detachment of 52 soldiers arrived to complete the manning of the *Anne*. The rigging was set, topsails loosed and the ship unmoored. The Duke came aboard two days later and together with the *Fubbs* and *Isabella* yachts, sailed as far as Lee Road. They made their way up the King's Channel to the Gunfleet where they were joined on 7 July by the *Bristol*, *Hampshire*, *Sedgemoor*, *Pearl*, *Richmond* and *Henrietta Yacht*. The next day the whole squadron departed, sailing close to the wind heading eastward. At midnight it appeared that the *Anne* was in grave danger of running aground on the Galloper Sands and was forced to bear away southward to anchor at the Sands' southern end. By 10 July, Middelburg was observed to the south-east, four or five leagues away, a league being three nautical miles. The following day, they passed Schouwe Island and anchored that night off Gorée Island, which they observed to the south-east three leagues away. At four o'clock in the afternoon of 12 July, they reached their destination, anchoring near Briel at the entrance to the River Maes.

On 13 July, the Duke of Grafton left with the three yachts to sail up the Maes to Rotterdam to meet the Queen. While he was away the shrouds were set up yet again, the rigging fixed and the ship cleared. While they waited, the long boat brought fresh water, and two hoys brought some of the Queen's goods aboard the *Anne*. The Queen herself arrived on 17 July with the Ambassador, a great retinue and her baggage, much of which had to be distributed amongst the other ships. They didn't delay long and set sail the

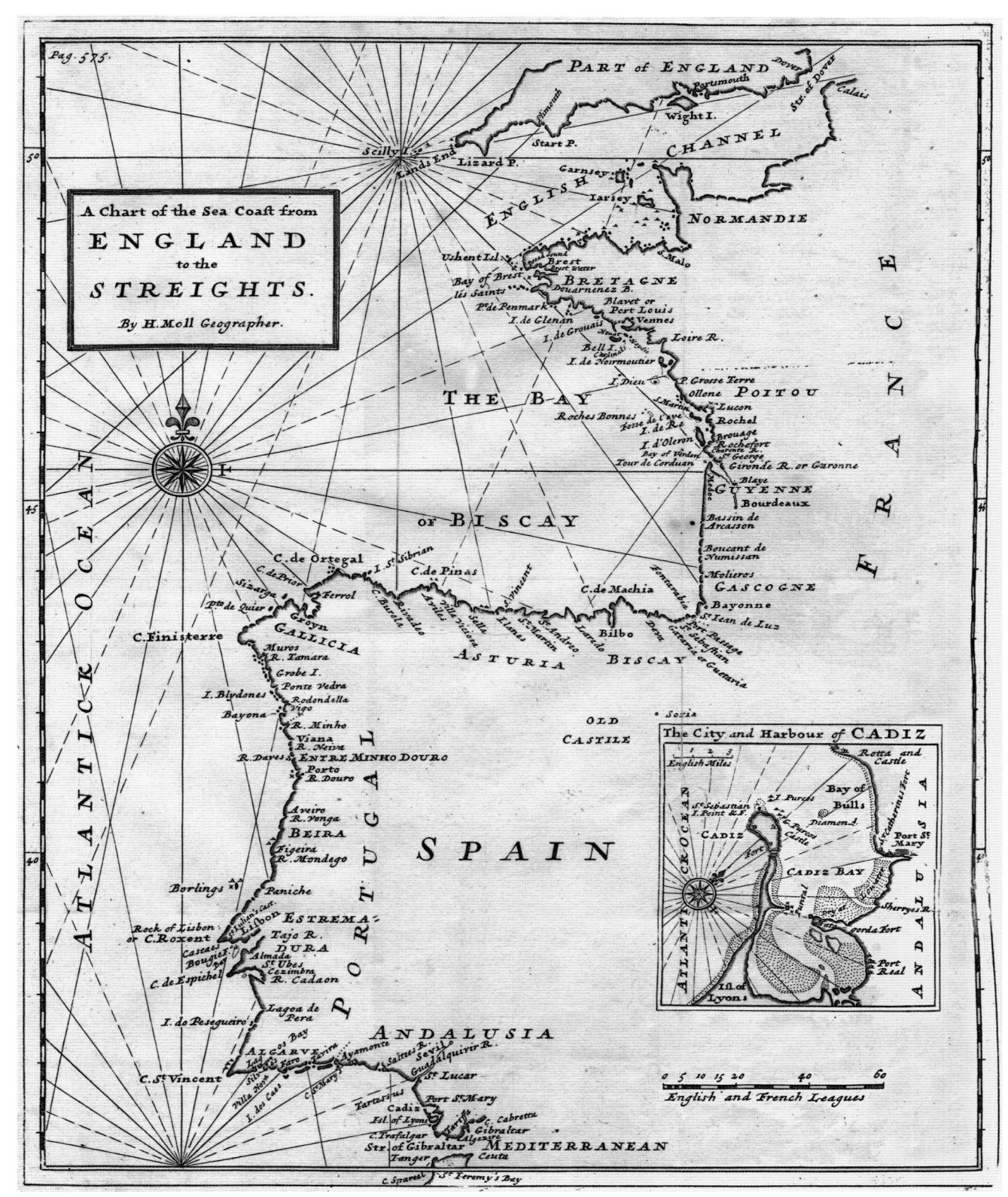

England to the Streights by H. Moll. With the weather in their favour, the *Anne* and her squadron completed the voyage from Plymouth to Lisbon in only eight days. *Author's collection*

62 The Warship Anne

The *Anne* near the English coast. Collection of the Nautical Museums Trust. Oil on canvas, *Author*

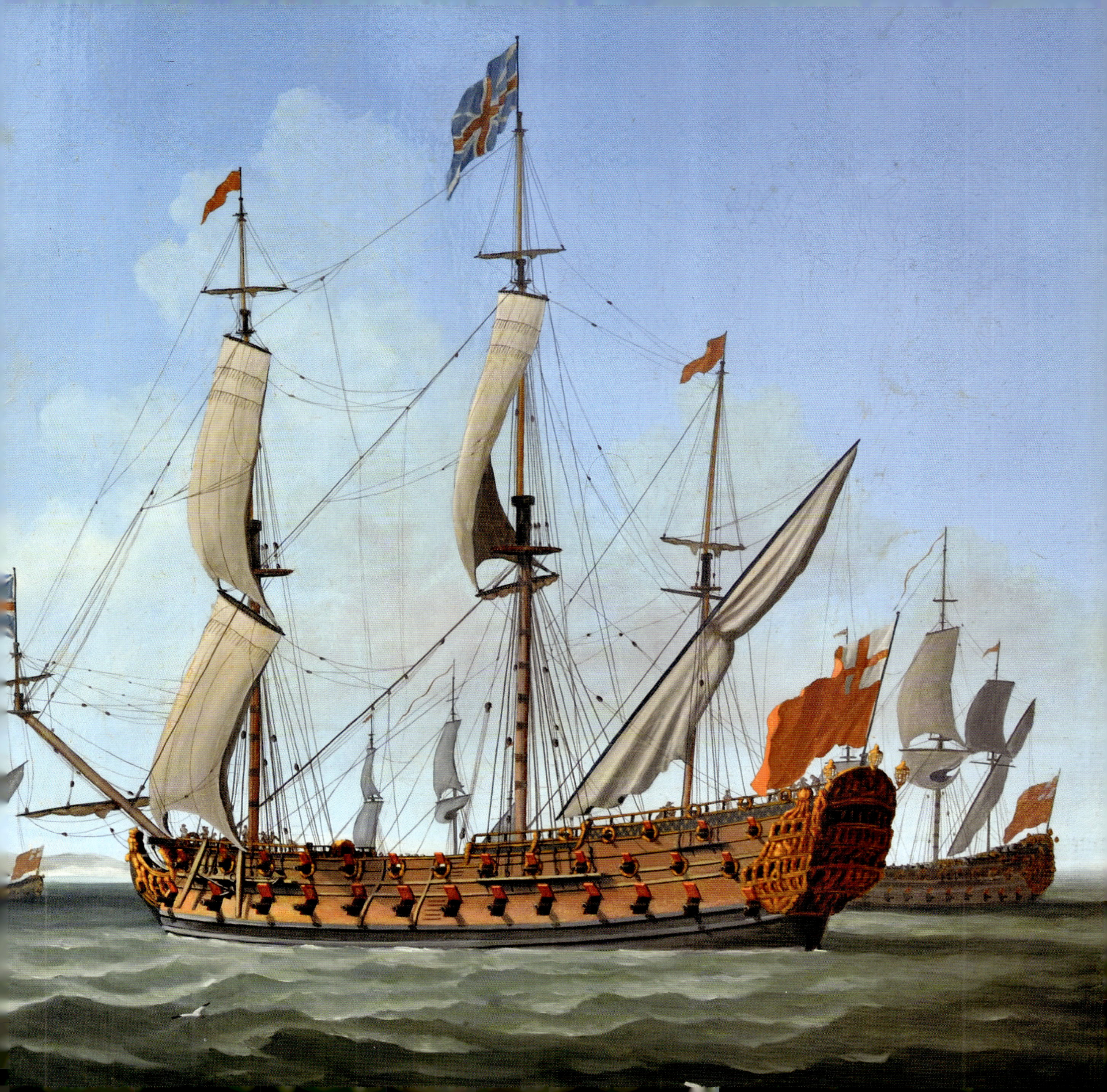

next day for the North Foreland, all that is, except the *Fubbs* and *Henrietta* yachts which departed on separate missions.

The food provided for the Queen and her retinue was truly lavish. For dinner on her first day aboard, the Queen was served capon, sirloin beef, veal ragout, mutton, geese, chicken, pullets, turkey, quail, steak, gammon with tongue, artichoke, salmagundi, eggs, olives and mango. There was almost as much for supper. The Ambassador was served almost the same while the ladies, ship's officers, King's servants and others were given a more modest fare. The same amount and quality was served up every day they were aboard. The Queen had a table to herself but there was a second table at which sat five dressers, three priests and a physician. At her third table were five ladies' women, a page and six maidservants, while at the fourth were three cooks, a butler's boy, a cooper, an apothecary's servant and four footmen. Eleven people sat at the Ambassador's table including the Duke of Grafton and Captain Shovel. In all 101 people were catered for.[32]

The squadron passed through the Downs on 19 July and over the next four days made their way westward observing Beachy Head, Cape Hague and Start Point. On 23 July in rainy, dirty weather, with the wind blowing very hard, they sensibly bore up and anchored for shelter in Plymouth Sound. Next day the weather turned fair and they took the opportunity to take in more water. Just before they departed that afternoon, the *Phoenix*, with Edward Barlow aboard, arrived from the East Indies, and he recorded seeing the *Anne* in his journal.[33]

Making good progress, they were off Lizard Point on 25 July and in four days crossed the Bay of Biscay to be within 14 or 15 leagues of Cape Finisterre. They were blessed with fair wind and weather and two days later they were four leagues off the Borlings where they saw an Algerian 40-gun warship, the *Orange Tree*. She was chased and caught by the *Hampshire* and the *Sedgemoor*. On inspection they found she had a pass signed by the English Consul, so they left her in peace and exchanged salutes.

On 1 August, the squadron arrived at the Cascaes at five in the morning. Taking a pilot aboard, they made their way up to Lisbon and were saluted along the way by the castles firing their guns. *Anne* and her squadron moored before the City of Lisbon in the early afternoon and were soon visited by many of the Portuguese nobility, eager to meet and pay respects to their new Queen. Getting onto and out of a ship like the *Anne* involved a rather undignified scramble, hanging onto small treads on the outside of the ship. The Ambassador had thought of this and, while in Holland had some special stairs made, that were now fitted by the seamen to the outside of the ship. The operation took three hours and when completed, at about five in the afternoon, King Don Pedro came aboard from his barge. He stayed about half an hour before returning to the palace with his Queen. As they left, all the ships saluted them by firing their guns. After the deafening roar, the couple went to the quiet of the palace chapel to receive a benediction.

The *Anne* then began to discharge the Queen's retinue and baggage. That night, the Portuguese ships and houses ashore were illuminated. More celebrations had been planned, but the *Anne* arrived earlier than expected, before they could be completed. The Duke of Grafton was invited ashore to an apartment, but declined, wishing not to leave his ship overnight. On 4 August, the Duke and others of high rank from the squadron went ashore in one of the King's barges for an audience amid great pomp and ceremony. That night, as they were being entertained, presents of fresh provisions and wine were sent and distributed amongst the ships. A few days later, Grafton received the present of a sword and cane set with diamonds. Jewels were also given to others of rank, including all the ship's Commanders, while diamond rings were given to several others. Their duty done, preparations were made to leave as all the empty casks were washed and filled with fresh water. Knowing a long cruise lay ahead, the men were put on short rations. On 10 August, the Duke went ashore to take his leave of their Majesties,[34] an event recorded by Captain Shovel, who wrote to Samuel Pepys: '*yesterday we cleared our ship of all the Queen's baggage. Today the Duke of Grafton took leave of their Majesties and intended to sail tomorrow, though much desired to stay till the King's marriage is consummated, which will be done the next week with great solemnity, nothing else to trouble your Honourable with at present.*'

In spite of its dignity, the marriage was more like a breeding programme for prize cattle than anything to do with love and, to be sure, that pretty much is what it was. It must have been difficult for the young Maria Sofia to have sex with someone she had only just met. It demonstrates the high price of being born into a royal family. She performed her duties admirably but died shortly after the birth of her eighth child in 1699 at the age of only 33.

The City of Lisbon as Maria Sofia would have known it. The city was largely destroyed in the great earthquake of 1755. *Private collection*

Repairs at Gibraltar

The Mediterranean Sea. Author's collection

On 11 August, the squadron made ready to sail for Gibraltar but, as there was little wind, they used the tide to take them out. As soon as they were clear of land, the *Bristol* and the *Richmond*, carrying members of King James's household departed to return home. By the afternoon of 14 August, the remaining ships, *Anne, Hampshire, Sedgemoor, Pearl* and *Isabella Yacht* sighted Cape St Vincent, six or seven leagues to the south-south-east. On 16 August they were off Cape St Mary, and next day passed St Sebastian Point to anchor four miles off the town of Rotta, at the entrance to Cadiz. The next day they weighed anchor, but off Cape Trafalgar it began to blow fresh and as they reefed the sails to shorten them, the *Anne*'s mainmast cracked at the head, splitting in two or three places. The weakness in her masts, which had first been noticed while she was fitting out at Chatham, was now becoming very evident.

A charming seventeenth-century view of Gibraltar, though its accuracy is somewhat dubious. Author's collection

Then, as the wind continued to blow hard, the fore topmast split in three places below the cap. The strong Levant wind, blowing from the east, prevented them heading toward Gibraltar and forced them south to Cape Spartel. There they anchored and spent some days continually setting up the stretching shrouds. On measuring them it was found they had reduced by an inch, from seven to six inches circumference, since they left Chatham. On 22 August, they found themselves off Tangier, and as the wind eased managed to reach Gibraltar at seven in the evening, where they found three English warships, *Leopard*, *Mermaid* and *Swan*.

On 24 August, the *Anne* came to the head of the new mole and moored. Gibraltar was still held by the Spanish but used as an English base where many naval stores were kept. Grafton expected to meet some ships already on the Mediterranean station to give them fresh orders. Waiting for them would give him two weeks, during which time the deteriorating masts could be repaired and almost all the rigging replaced. The work was essential if the *Anne* was to continue her mission. On the first day, the fore topmast was unrigged and taken down. It was found to be split and splintered from the fid hole (a hole in the heel of the mast through which the fid, or pin, is pushed to secure it in position) to the cap, a distance of several feet. The lining as well as the heel was split in pieces.

The problem was not a complete surprise, for when the *Anne* was being fitted out at Chatham, Cloudesley Shovel reported that the heel of mast was rotten. All the mast makers did at the time was cut out the rot and repair it with a two-inch thick plank lining. Now it was beyond repair and had to be replaced with the *Leopard*'s main topmast and the old split topmast left ashore at Gibraltar. Earlier in June, just after the rotten mizzen mast was replaced, Sir Phineas Pett, acting as Commissioner at Chatham, wrote that after the *Anne*'s masts, yards and tops were defective, he instructed Robert Lee, the Master Shipwright, to survey the masts of other ships. Initially Lee said they were all good, but after pursuing the matter Pett discovered that 27 of them had to be repaired.[35]

Details of the *Anne*'s main and fore mast heads. *Author*

1 Lower mast
2 Topmast
3 Cap
4 Top
5 Paunch
6 Cheeks
7 Jeers. For raising and lowering the yard
8 Top rope. For raising and lowering the topmast
9 Fid. For securing the topmast
10 Yard
11 Lower mast shrouds
12 Topmast shrouds
13 Deadeyes and lanyards
14 Puttock shrouds
15 Stay

With a new fore topmast in place, the stretched fore shrouds were unrigged and new ones served. All the other rigging that was amiss on the mast was secured or replaced. With this done, the main mast and main topmast where unrigged and new shrouds served in place of the old and other rigging replaced where necessary. It could not all be completed until the cheeks of the split and damaged head of the main mast was strengthened. This would be done by having two iron hoops made ashore which were intended to bind it together. It took a number of days before they were finished and fitted in place, then the main topmast was got up and the mast's rigging finished. The main yard was considered too small for the ship for it bent a great deal in an ordinary gale. This resulted in it becoming sprung, or split in two places. It was taken ashore to have a 40ft-long strengthening strip, a fish, attached to it. With the repair work done, the masts and yards were scraped and the yards blacked. The ship's sides were also scraped and payed with tar. Finally the ship was heeled as far as possible each way and the exposed underwater surface scrubbed.

When the *Anne* arrived at Gibraltar, the Duke of Grafton, following his orders, sent the *Pearl* and the *Hampshire* to cruise off the Atlantic coast of Africa for a week in pursuit of a war with Salley. The *Garland* arrived at Gibraltar on 25 August and two days later went into the harbour to be careened as the *Swan* came out. The *Swan* was sent home carrying letters, including an account by Shovel about the state of the *Anne*. Then, as expected, the fourth-rate *Charles Galley*, commanded by Lord Berkeley, came in. She was specially built for operations in the Mediterranean, being a fast, lightly armed ship that could be rowed. She was followed in a couple of days later at the beginning of September by the old fourth-rate *Dragon* and the fifth-rate *Sapphire*. During the same period a number of French warships also arrived.

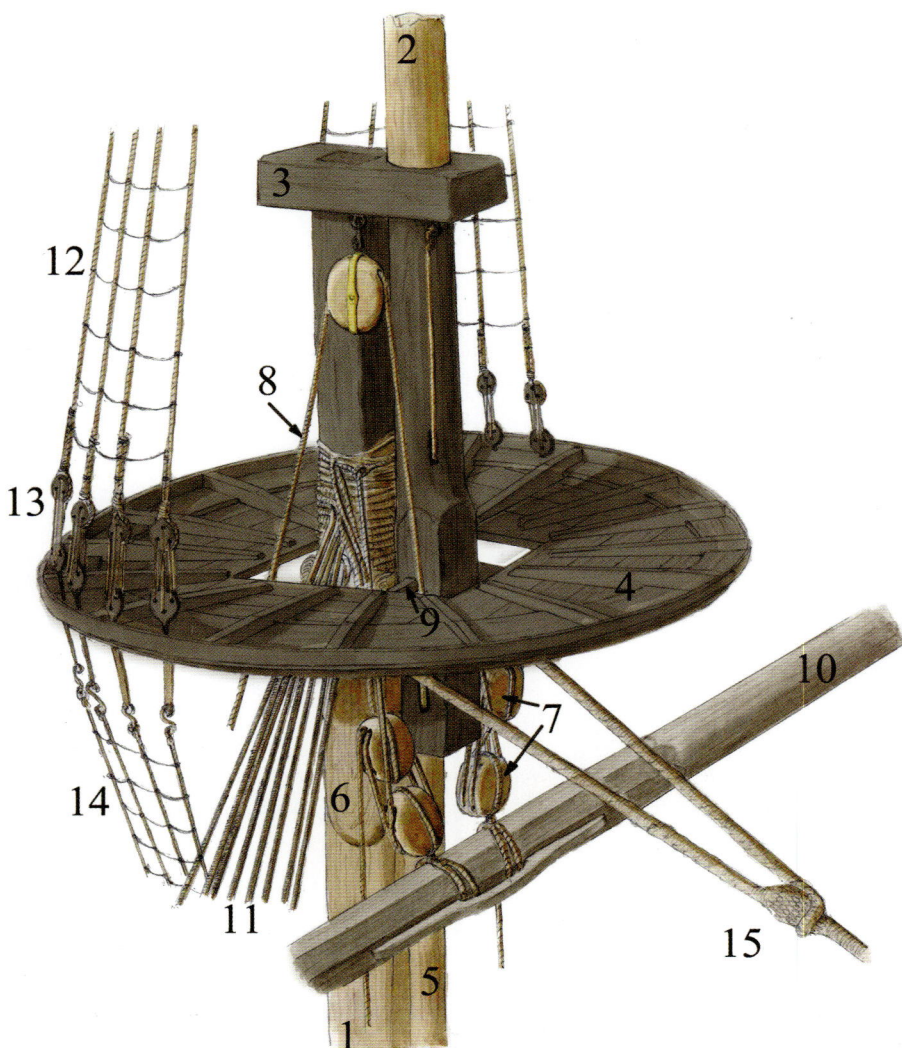

The letter carried by the *Swan* relating to the state of *Anne*'s masts and rigging would cause considerable embarrassment to Pepys and his administration when King James heard about it. Pepys had been loudly proclaiming, for some time, how he had repaired the fleet and what good condition it was in. It is no exaggeration to say he considered himself the saviour of the Navy. But Pepys knew how to handle situations like this, especially as the complainant was a long way away. He would organise his own enquiry. Sir Phineas Pett, acting Commissioner at Chatham, was consulted, and in complete contrast to what he said before, was persuaded somehow to change his story.

He agreed that when the *Anne* was fitting out, Cloudesley Shovel complained of the sappiness of the main mast. Together with Robert Lee, he went on board to inspect the mast and ordered that it be well secured with a strengthening paunch. He now alleged they found no defects in the cheeks or anything else and that '*never in my lifetime knew more care taken in the fitting out any ship than was upon the* Anne *and* Sedgemoor'.[36] A testimonial was written by senior officers in the dockyard, saying that the rigging being new, and the ship so portly and stiff, it would be strange that by crowding of sail the rigging would stretch. They asserted that the masts and yards had been viewed and searched several times and as far as any man's eye could discern they were all very good and serviceable. They added that the heel of the fore topmast '*was only a little sap rotten at the square which was dubbed off and lined with oak as hath been usual and well secured … cannot apprehend how any ship could be better fitted*'.[37] No mention was made of the rotten mizzen mast that had been replaced.

Before the *Anne* and her officers returned home, the Chatham officers went further. They said the rigging was new when the ship was completed in December 1678 and of the best quality.[38] It probably was, but they didn't say it had been stored aboard the *Anne* since then and been affected by the same damp conditions that caused the timbers to decay.[39] They added that when they visited the *Anne* at the time she was fitting out, the sea officers aboard told them there was '*nothing to find fault with, everything was well*'.[40] The testimonies were obtained for Pepys's enquiry by his two closest associates, Anthony Deane and Will Hewer, who added a note: '*We send you transcripts of them herewith, hoping they will satisfy His Majesty in the groundlessness of those* [Shovel's] *complaints.*'[41] Such distortions of the truth are not at all typical of the seventeenth-century Navy but they are of Samuel Pepys.

The young Duke of Grafton had other duties to attend to. On 3 September he held a court martial with his senior officers to decide the status of a ship called the *Lemontree*. On 6 September another court martial was held on board the *Anne* with all the senior officers, including Grafton, Berkeley and the ships' captains. They were to adjudicate on a charge of wilful murder against John Shaw of the *Pearl*, just returned from her mission off Salley. There were three main witnesses, Thomas Crannys and John Westcombe, who were in their hammocks near the bitts, and Roger Lampeere, who was sitting on the main deck near the entrance to his cabin door, also by the bitts.

From their evidence it appears that at about 3 o'clock in the afternoon of 25 August, John Shaw was drinking with Allan Leeds, his mess mate, near the main hatch, just forward of the main mast. They were arguing about who was the better man, with Shaw swearing he was undervalued in the ship. Leeds must have disagreed, causing Shaw to become enraged. After some persuading, Shaw enticed Leeds, who was carrying a drinking can, to go with him forward of the bitts, presumably as there was a little more privacy. Shaw led the way, ducking under the hammocks, swearing he would have his '*frollick*' out with Leeds.

Once there, they sat down on a chest arguing to the same purpose. After about a quarter of an hour, Leeds asked Shaw what he had to say to him, Shaw swore he would stab him, and immediately after he said those words, was seen pulling his knife out of Leeds' stomach. He then left with the knife in one hand and Leeds' drinking can in the other. Leeds cried out that Shaw had stabbed him. Roger Lampeere, who was sitting by the cabin door, got up asked Shaw what had he done. Shaw replied he would do the same to him, or anyone else who undervalued him. Shaw then went aft, wiping the knife as he went. The evidence was damning for John Shaw, who must have deeply regretted losing his temper in a drunken rage. Although he pleaded guilty to the charge, the court martial had little alternative but, sentence him according to the 28th article of war. He was sentenced to be hung by the neck at the yardarm of his ship, the *Pearl*, until he was dead.[42]

After Shaw's court martial another was held the following day; John Lewis, Carpenter of the *Charles Galley*, was accused of selling a coil of inch rope and about three rows of pitch to a Spaniard. Lewis confessed to giving away 20lb of pitch but denied selling the rope. The court ordered that he should have £10 stopped out of his wages and the money given to the seaman's charity, the Chest of Chatham, as a punishment.[43] Another man found guilty of an unrecorded offence was the Boatswain of the *Sapphire*; he could have been hung for his offence but as was common practice at the time, he had the hangman's halter put around his neck and taken from ship to ship where his crime was read out. He was then sent ashore in disgrace. The court martials held by the Duke of Grafton were taken very seriously and the judgements seem very sound and reasonable for the time. The punishments would become a lot harsher during the next century. On 9 September, at 11 in the morning, John Shaw was hung from the yardarm of the *Pearl* according to his sentence. At three that afternoon, the refitted squadron that Grafton was to take up the Streights, the *Anne*, *Hampshire*, *Sedgemoor*, *Charles Galley*, *Pearl*, *Mermaid* and *Isabella Yacht*, began to unmoor. At five in the afternoon they weighed anchor and made ready to sail.

Negotiations with Algiers

By 11 September 1687, the squadron was five miles off Malaga on their week-long voyage to Algiers. As they sailed, they saw the Island of Alboran bearing south-east by east three leagues distant. On 16 September, Cape Tenes bore east ½ south, four or five leagues away and by noon the next day were anchored in Algiers Bay in 32 fathoms of water, a fathom being 6ft. The following morning, the squadron was greeted with a salute of 27 guns. The salute was in excess of that prescribed by the peace treaty and taken as an important act of acknowledgement. As a further act of friendship, boats brought presents of fresh provisions from the Dey. The English Consul, Erlisman, came aboard the *Anne* to consult with Grafton and prepare for the negotiations. Then Cloudesley Shovel, the Consul, and Grafton's secretary went to meet the Dey to deliver a letter from King James concerning the continuation of the peace. This he was happy to agree to. They got down to business on other matters. They argued '*with much heat*' about seven Scots who sailed from Rotterdam in Dutch ships but had been taken by Bustangee from Algiers, who sold them in Salley. The Dey argued that when Bustangee was in turn taken by English ships, eight Christian slaves were aboard, but his men were not returned and therefore the score was even. The Dey also denied any slaves were sold at Salley but took it very kindly that the Duke agreed to return Bustangee and his ship back to Algiers.[44]

He released others who were all taken from another Dutch vessel, a Mrs Eleanor Browne, her daughter Rebecca and a Negro, Sampson Ironside. He was an English subject born in Barbados. Grafton must have taken a liking to Sampson Ironside for he was entered on the *Anne*'s pay book as belonging to the Duke's retinue and paid the same amount as an able seaman. When they were finally back to England, he left the ship at the same time as the Duke. Eleanor and Rebecca Browne would also return home in the *Anne*. Once they reached the Downs they left for London in the *Isabella Yacht*.[45] As for the restitution of baggage taken from English passengers on Dutch ships, the Dey argued that the English plundering of Bustangee was an equal fault and ought to be forgotten.

The difficult negotiations were put at risk on 23 September as a result of an incident involving an English merchant ship, belonging to a Mr Appleby, that was moored at the mole head. Her Master was detained ashore, which so alarmed the crew that they cut her cables at the hawse to escape and join the *Anne*'s squadron. The next morning, a boat with the Consul and Captain Shovel was sent ashore under a flag of truce. After some tense negotiations, they were able '*to adjust the differences*' and agree the whole episode was a '*mistake*'.

Proceedings then returned to other matters. A 60-ton pink, the *Portugal Merchant*, laden with tobacco, was chased by an Algerine galley off the coast of Spain. The crew of the *Portugal Merchant* abandoned ship and, firing at the galley, killed two men. The pink was taken back to Algiers and its contents distributed there. The Dey claimed that the pink had been abandoned as a wreck and having no colours or pass, legally belonged to him. Grafton made it clear he believed the pink was known to be English and persuaded the Dey to return it. At the time she was still in their harbour, a third laden with Indian cane. As compensation for her previous and more valuable tobacco cargo, the Dey agreed to return four English slaves. The *Portugal Merchant* pink would stay with the squadron and be used as a store ship. Another merchantman, the *Endeavour of Weymouth*, was taken by Salley and sold at Algiers. At the time of the sale, a young man from the vessel was given by the Salleymen to the Dey. The Dey now returned the young man to the Duke and promised that he wouldn't allow such a thing to happen again.

There were other small matters to be dealt which resulted in some other slaves being given up. Then, on the night of 1 October, seven slaves escaped captivity and swam to the ships. The Dey demanded the return of them but as Captain Shovel said, '*the best answer we had for them was showing them the 11th article in our peace* [treaty] *which plainly tells them they ought not to make such a demand*'. But one of the slaves happened to be a valued shipwright who escaped with the help of the boat's crew of the *Hampshire*. His situation was not covered by the peace treaty and the Dey demanded his return. Eventually it was agreed that compensation of 300 pieces of eight be paid for him.[46] As all the business was nearly completed, Captain Shovel received a letter from the Dey to give to King James. The squadron made ready to leave, first drying their sails for a day and letting loose their topsails the next. The returned slaves seem to have made their sufferings well known to the men in the ships they had joined. Their stories, and knowing some others were still being held as slaves, prompted an outpouring of sympathy. A collection was made amongst all the ships to pay for their redemption.

The next day, their charity resulted in the slaves' release, amongst whom was an English woman. She was Sarah Hawkins, who was entered on the *Anne*'s pay book so the Purser could keep an account of victuals she was given. In all, ten men were entered without pay but five others were found employment and paid.[47] The following day the squadron left, as Shovel put

Algiers as it would have been at the time the *Anne* visited. *Private collection*

it having '*set all things to rights*'. The Dey promised to faithfully maintain the articles of the peace treaty and added they would never have peace with France, as they were mightily vexed at the taking of some of their ships.[48]

72 The Warship Anne

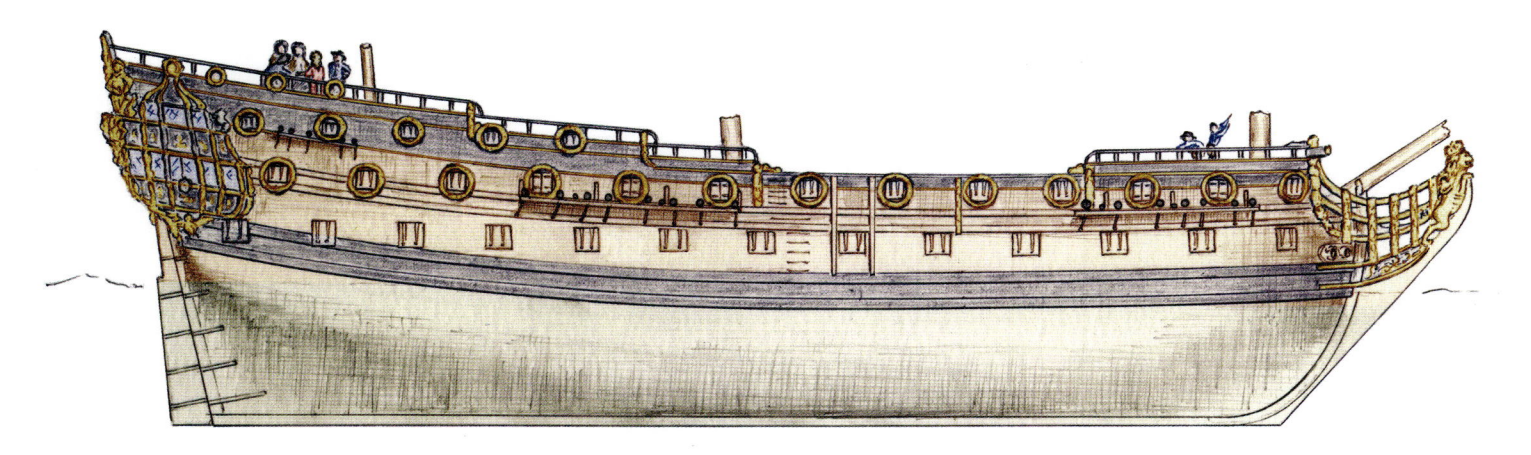

Above: The third rate *Anne* with the Queen of Portugal and the senior officers on the poop deck. She was the flagship of the squadron and her firepower made her unassailable by any ship belonging to the Barbary States. Author

The *Isabella Yacht*. She was contemporarily described by William Sutherland as 'not only counted beautiful but their lower bodies was admired … the *Isabella* was well known to be an excellent sea boat. Author

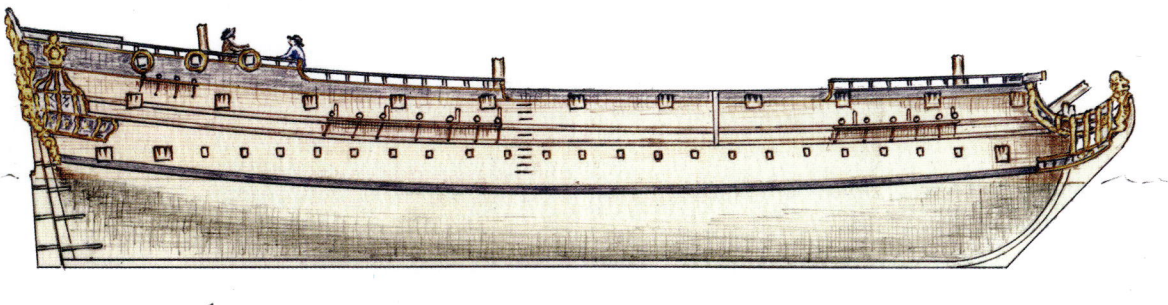

The *Charles Galley*. A ship specially designed for use in the Mediterranean against the fast-sailing Barbary pirates. Lightly built with extremely narrow proportions and lightly armed, she was very successful. Author

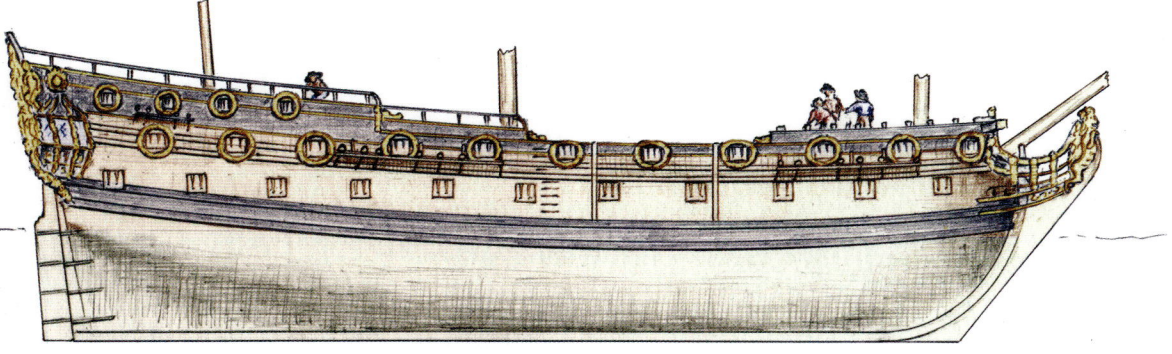

The *Sedgemoor*. A new fourth rate launched as the *Anne* was fitting out. Author

Feet
10 20 30 40 50 60 70 80 90 100 110 120 130

The ships of the Duke of Grafton's Mediterranean squadron

The 50- to 60-ton pink, *Portugal Merchant*. A very common type of merchant ship that carried the bulk of trade. *Author*

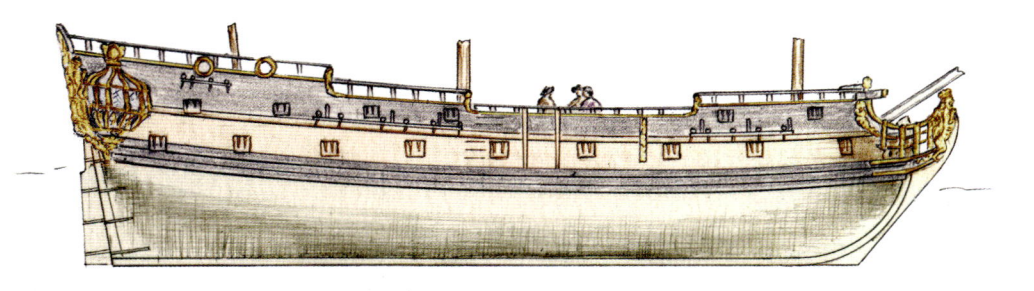

The *Pearl*, an old fifth rate built in 1651, that must have been repaired many times over the years. A successful design, she still had many years of service ahead of her. The near-identical *Mermaid* was built in the same year. *Author*

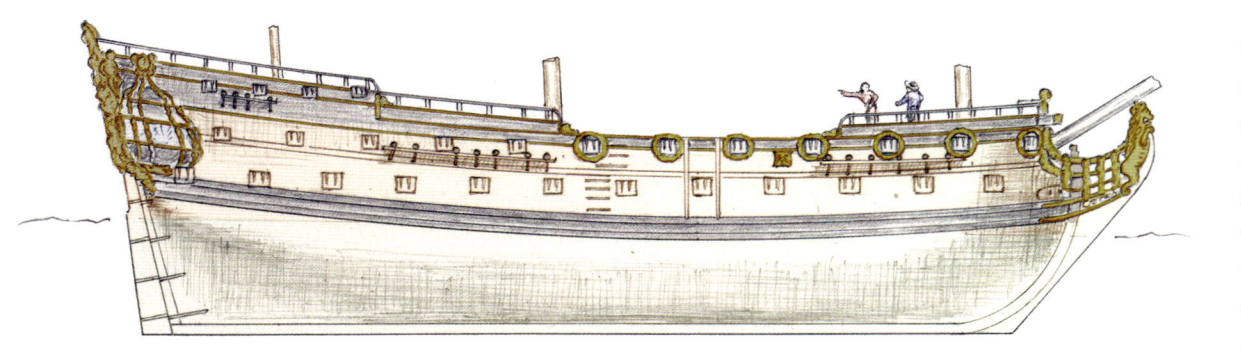

The *Hampshire*. An old fourth rate built in 1653. She had fought in many battles and had been repaired many times over her long career. A midship bend drawing of the ship survives upon which this drawing is based. She survived until 1697, when she was sunk in action near Fort York in Hudson's Bay. In all probability, her remains are preserved in good condition in the cold waters. Her full story is told in *Mariner's Mirror*, February 2005. *Author*

Grafton, in his own hand, wrote informing the Admiralty of the negotiations, saying with some understanding that he expected the good relations would remain only as long as they had war with France, after that, the situation could suddenly change.[49]

Kind and civil Tunis

At midday on 6 October, the squadron together with the *Portugal Merchant* pink set out from Algiers Bay, exchanging a 21-gun salute in respect to each other as they left. By 4 o'clock they were three leagues off Cape Matafuz but made slow progress into an easterly wind. On 7 October they passed Bugia, bearing south-east at a distance of three leagues. A day later it was still in sight to the south-south-east eight leagues away. Tacking and often handling their sails, they headed toward Sardinia, which they first saw on 11 October. Two days later they had made their way into the Bay of Cagliari intending to take in some of its famously fresh water. They anchored half a mile offshore in ten fathoms, half a mile from the watering place at the '*fire tower*'.

Disappointingly they found the water too brackish, which Shovel thought was caused by the sea breaking into the river. They sought another place further up the bay against the town but this was also unsuitable. The next morning, they weighed anchor and made their way back out to the fire tower. Sending the long boat ashore they, at last, found good water at the outermost watering place. Mr Fitzjames '*and others of quality*' visited the town and were invited by the Viceroy to a great entertainment and a ball. Grafton, who was also invited, declined the offer as a strong north-east wind started to blow that evening, ideal for sailing south toward Tunis.[50] Setting sail, they made good progress, anchoring two miles off Porta Farine at dusk. The following morning, 16 October, they made their way into Tunis Bay, and were safely anchored by midday.

The town of Tunis and the squadron saluted each other with 21 guns, then the Consul of the place came aboard while the longboat went ashore for water. As before, Grafton's representatives and the Consul went to meet the Dey. Shovel wrote of the meeting '*at Tunis we find the articles of peace religiously observed and the people of the country very kind and civil*'. The only demand made by Grafton was the payment of a debt due to the Consul and some merchants for monies taken from them to help pay for a civil war. The Dey had partly

An eighteenth-century print of Tunis. *Author's collection*

BANKES'S *New System of* GEOGRAPHY *Publish'd by Royal Authority.*

...TY of TUNIS *the* CAPITAL *of that* KINGDOM *on the* COAST *of* BARBARY.

paid some of the debt and promised to speedily pay the rest. Another topic of discussion was the promise to reduce the customs for passing wine to three per cent, which the Dey announced had already been granted. While there, Shovel also noticed they had only five men of war that carried between 40 to 50 guns each. There were also three galleys that had rotted and sunk since the civil war.

The squadron now took the opportunity to take in water. It is noticeable that those aboard the *Anne* were always scrupulous in cleaning and scraping water casks. On 19 October, an English merchantman from Algiers arrived, followed a few days later by a French warship whose officers boasted of their success in beating an Algerine 30-gun ship which they had taken to Toulon. The diplomatic business was finished, but before they could leave a storm blew up. To secure their anchorage, more of the best bower cable was veered out, knowing that an anchor had much better grip on a longer cable. The yards and the topmasts were lowered and not raised again until 25 October. A merchantman, the *London Merchant,* sailed out bound for Alexandria. The following day they lay the fore topsails loose, unmoored and heaved in the cable to half a length. They finally weighed anchor on 27 October and came out of the bay bound for Tripoli. By midday, Cape Bona bore east by north ½ north as their pink, *Portugal Merchant,* was sent on ahead to Livorno.

Difficulties off Tripoli

The first day out, the squadron rounded Cape Bona and the next they headed south, passing within two miles of the Island of Pantelleria. Continuing on course through the night, the island bore west-north-west seven leagues at 8 o'clock the next morning. Due to calms and contrary weather ,it took another six days before they supposed themselves to be east of Tripoli, which could not be seen through the hazy weather. Their navigation proved accurate and at noon the next day they anchored before the town, one league from the great castle. The Consul came out to them and they were greeted with a 25-gun salute. The Duke was given a horse as a present, although finding accommodation for it must have caused some problems.

Then the weather changed as it began to blow fresh and squally. On 10 November it blew very hard, causing them to lower their topmasts and drop the biggest anchor, the sheet anchor, to assist the best bower they were already riding by. The wind eased the next day and although there was a '*great sea*', the sheet anchor was brought up and the best bower cable hauled in. Deciding it prudent to berth further off shore, they weighed anchor but as evening fell the strong tide took them four leagues out to the east. Next day, the wind blew so hard it split both topsails as they tacked north against the strong current. Then a main shroud broke and in spite of their efforts to get closer, they found themselves eight leagues east of Tripoli. The *Sedgemoor* and the *Pearl* managed to join them but the next day they split another fore topsail, obliging them to sail under the main and fore courses. On 15 November, the *Anne* managed to ply toward the shore but broke some fore shrouds.

They tacked toward Tripoli and got within four leagues, at which point the *Sedgemoor*, being a good sailing new fourth-rate, was sent in to meet a boat from the shore with despatches. Now only the *Pearl* was with the *Anne* as the other ships in the squadron had lost contact in the bad weather. Next day, the stormy conditions claimed a victim when William Hutchins, an Able Seaman, fell into the sea and was drowned.

Captain Shovel wrote that he had no complaints against the government but was concerned that they changed their king two or three times a year. They expressed great friendship with the English and resolved to keep the peace. The only dispute arose when the Bagshaw '*pretended*' a Captain Daniel owed them 600 or 700 dollars. Shovel observed that during their great days of pirating they had ten warships but now had only four of between 24 to 40 guns each. They had a great deal of corn the previous year and had shipped it in English vessels. He reasoned that while the French were at war with Algiers, there was further opportunity for English merchants to expand their trade in the Mediterranean. After the *Sedgemoor* returned with the dispatches from Tripoli, the three ships set course for Malta. It was the rendezvous for the squadron and where the ships could take in water and refit. In all, the diplomatic mission had been a great success, and demonstrates the importance of maintaining contact with the Barbary States.

Tripoli. *Author's collection*

Shortening masts at Malta

Under favourable sailing weather, Malta was seen only a day after leaving Tripoli. Unfortunately, they could not weather the eastern end of the island and had to tack to the west. While swinging the yards round some of the parrel ropes, the ropes that keep the yards to the mast, broke. Then, on 18 November as they stood to the south, the topsails split. The shrouds were again givin‚g way and to help relieve the strain, a preventer rope was rigged to every shroud on the larboard side and most of the foremast shrouds on the starboard side. The straps of the main and fore jeers, which hauled up the yards, also gave way probably, reasoned Shovel, because they were made of bad hemp. Eventually they weathered the east end of Malta at 4 o'clock in

A Perspective View of the Town and Fortifications of MALTA.   Veüe Perspective de la Ville et des Fortifications de MALTA.
Published 1st May, 1794, by LAURIE & WHITTLE, 53 Fleet Street, London.

The Grand Harbour at Malta. *Anne* and the rest of her fleet moored in the left bay where the majority of ships are shown. *Private collection*

the afternoon of 19 November, and together with the *Sedgemoor* and the *Pearl*, anchored before the harbour entrance an hour later. They found the rest of their squadron had already arrived.

At daybreak the next morning, they unmoored and went to work warping the *Anne* into the harbour. This was done by taking a cable and securing it, probably to a bollard, then hauling themselves in with the capstan. By 10 o'clock they were safely anchored before the city, which saluted them with 80 guns. Lord Berkeley, Mr Fitzjames and the Duke of Grafton took it in turns to visit the Grand Master. Although not mentioned in Grafton's orders, the visit to Malta was important diplomatically. It expressed support from Catholic King James II to the Knights of Malta as an ally against Ottoman expansion into Europe. Although the Duke of Grafton was Protestant, the King's son, Henry Fitzjames, was Catholic and was royally received by the Grand Master Carafa, receiving a cross of diamonds. He was later given the nominal title of Grand Prior of England.[51]

During their eight-day stay, the water casks were taken ashore, trimmed and filled with fresh water. Much of the *Anne*'s sailing gear was again in need of urgent repair. The main and foremast were unrigged and all the sails taken ashore for mending. The head of the main mast, which had already been repaired at Gibraltar with hoops, was again breaking apart and the cheeks, just under the cap, found to be very defective. They were left with little alternative but to cut off 14in from the top and secure it with two new and more substantial iron hoops. The main topmast was also in poor condition and shortened by 4ft. To suit the shorter topmast, the main topsail was shortened to the upper reef.

At sea, most of the sails had given way and split at the boltrope, the rope that runs round the edge of the sail. This, Shovel thought, was caused by the tar on the boltrope burning through the twine and canvas, as they had both given way next to the tarred rope. They cut off the tabling in its vicinity and re-tabled the sails. The shrouds for the most part were taken down and the bad ones replaced. It was also considered the main and fore lower yards were too small and would break in a gale. They were taken ashore and strengthened with fishes. When all this work was completed, the masts were re-rigged. The problems with the *Anne*'s masts and rigging was much greater than would normally have been expected and was not repeated on other ships.

While this work was going on above deck, the hold was cleared and new stone ballast brought in over a period of several days. The ballast was changed for cleanliness as the areas near the bilges became very unhygienic and stank. This was caused by unknown decaying organic matter collecting at the bottom of the ship. Some of this was deposited by the men aboard, when they found it unpleasant to relieve themselves in the heads at the bow, as they were exposed to view and the weather. Not long after, new instructions were issued for all ships which had not had their ballast changed for some time. The upper part of ballast was to be thrown away and '*for airing the rest by heaving it ashore as the ships shall come into the dock to be cleaned*'.[52]

The *Anne* was then healed and the underside washed as far as they could reach. By 26 November, the watering was complete, the ship fitted and ready to sail. In the afternoon, the fore topsail was loosed in readiness for the following morning, when the fore topsail sheets were hauled home and the ship unmoored. They hauled short on the best bower anchor but as they found it impossible to sail out, the boats were used to tow her instead. A hawser had to be cast from a stern port, probably to keep her heading toward the harbour entrance. It wasn't until 6.30 in the evening that they were safely outside the harbour and anchored in 31 fathoms.

Victualling at Livorno

Cloudesley Shovel was now able to say the *Anne* was in good condition for the sea and '*thank God our fleet is very healthy*'. On the morning of 28 November, the squadron weighed anchor bound for Livorno to re-victual for the voyage home. They stood over for Cape Passaro at the eastern end of Sicily and next day headed north, passing under Mount Etna. After being delayed by contrary winds, they passed through the narrows and anchored by the best and small bowers off Messina at nine in the morning on 2 December. Here they found the fourth-rate *Crown* under Captain Neville, which had been to Turkey to bring back Lord Shandon, the Ambassador. He was flying the same flag as the *Anne*, which the Duke of Grafton ordered be taken down, as there should not be two of the same likeness. Then, following his instructions, Grafton ordered the *Crown* to continue on its voyage. The squadron stayed until 6 December, airing their sails, setting up the shrouds and taking in water. Getting under way again, they passed to the west of Stromboli, the most eastward of the Lipari Islands. Continuing north, they passed Naples on 10 December, but then strong winds split the main topsail two days later. The following day, Montecristo was observed to the north, Elba was passed the next and they anchored in Livorno Roads on 15 December.

Livorno was a very busy port with many merchant ships coming and going. Among them were the *Crown* and the pink, *Portugal Merchant*, released earlier from Algiers. The squadron would spend over three weeks gathering the two months' provisions necessary for the voyage home. As soon as they arrived, the water casks were cleaned, trimmed and filled with fresh water. During their stay, getting fresh water would be an almost daily occurrence. Fresh provisions were frequently brought from ashore and a Mr Searle was hired to go out in the country to find beasts, probably beef, which turned out to take a week longer than expected. The *Crown* was fully provisioned by 25 December and sent on her way with the pink. Among the provisions received on the *Anne* were 2,600 bags of rusk, or ship's biscuit; not so welcome was a consignment of cheese that was surveyed and found defective. During the early days of January 1688, the last of their beef and other provisions arrived. The masts and rigging were still in good order, for once sparing the crew the task of mending and repairing them. The second Lieutenant, Francis Wivell, was sent to Florence to see the English Envoy with an express letter.

Waiting for them at Livorno were letters from Samuel Pepys concerning Shovel's report about the state of the *Anne*'s masts and rigging at Gibraltar. Pepys, wishing his administration to appear faultless, made it known his enquiry found Shovel's report groundless. Shovel was having none of it. He replied saying he was surprised Pepys found fault with him for having masts and rigging that have proved unfit for purpose. He went on to say: *'I am obliged only to take notice [of them] in my survey book … as the goodness of the rigging is no thanks to me, so the badness is no fault in me, you were pleased to speak to me to give you a particular account of all things relating to His Majesty's service, which command I have justly and punctually obeyed and will make it my business to perform my duty to the utmost of my ability.'* Shovel was not at all concerned by Pepys's rebuke and the same day wrote another letter to the Navy Board giving all the horrifying details about the state of the masts and rigging and the further repairs made to the *Anne* at Malta.

It was 1688, the year of the Glorious Revolution, when naval men would very soon have to side either with King James or William and Mary. The cracks were already starting to show and Shovel's relationship with Pepys was one of them. Shovel's support for William and Mary would see him advance to become a famous admiral who would end up in Westminster Abbey. For Pepys, the year marked the end of his career and even a short time in the Gatehouse.

On the morning of 7 January, they made ready to leave and loosed the fore topsail. They began to unmoor their small bower cable but in taking off the stopper ropes that secured it to the deck forward of the bitts, a '*mistake*' was made and the whole cable ran out of the ship and was lost on the sea bed, six fathoms below. The cost of the cable and small bower anchor was about £200, a considerable amount of money. Not willing to leave them, they swept for the cable and finding it that evening, managed to get it to the hawse and secure it. As a result, it was not until the next morning before they managed to leave.

Return to Gibraltar

Outside Livorno, the boats were taken up on deck as the *Anne* waited for the other ships to join them for the voyage to Gibraltar. Now fully provisioned, the crew went to their whole allowance of food, for the first time since they left Lisbon in early August the year before. They sailed past Cape Corso then down the west coast of Sardinia for a few days before heading west. On 12 January, the eastern end of Minorca was estimated to be 25 leagues away to the north-west. The weather then turned against them, making any progress almost impossible. They tacked toward the Barbary Shore, then north, but after a week were still plying between Maiorca and Minorca. The problem of splitting sails reoccurred, although the damage was easily repaired as they went. The wind eased on 20 January allowing them, at last, to make progress. Two days later, the *Crown* and the pink, *Portugal Merchant*, surprisingly appeared and were greeted with gun salutes. The island of Alboran was seen the next day bearing south-west four leagues.

With the squadron in company, the *Anne* sailed close to the shore, anchoring at a watering place near Malaga to fill up the casks. They were saluted by the town's guns. The English merchants living there invited the Duke, Mr Fitzjames and the ship's commanders ashore. They were received by the Governor and the Magistrates[53] but did not stay long. By 27 January, were three miles off Fuengirola Castle and at midnight only a mile from Gibraltar. The next day they moved into the bay where they found the *Dragon*. As they moored by the best bower anchor, the cable suddenly parted 25 fathoms from the clench, supposedly cut through by the flukes of another anchor. It was lost in 15 fathoms of water, forcing them to drop the sheet anchor. It took four days of sweeping by the boats before they got hold of the cable end. After attaching it to a buoy, and having the long boat on standby all night, the cable was finally brought to the bow of the *Anne* in the morning. During the week spent at Gibraltar, a month's provisions of beef, pork and some fresh water was taken in. Stores that had earlier been put aboard the *Portugal Merchant* pink were also taken back into the *Anne*. Sarah Hawkins and another freed slave, William Furmidge, left the *Anne* a day before she departed.[54]

Home

A strong Levant wind had been blowing for some time and not wishing to miss the opportunity to get past Gibraltar, Grafton ordered the squadron to set sail. As the *Isabella Yacht* could sail close to the wind, she was left behind to take in the final dry provisions. She was ordered to catch up and re-join the squadron at Cadiz. Setting sail on 3 February, the squadron passed Cape Trafalgar and anchored in the Bay of Bulls at Cadiz, where they immediately took in more water. As arranged, the *Isabella Yacht* arrived with 80 bags of bread, but she was then sent back to Gibraltar to fetch some packets and letters. The *Anne* was scraped, tarred and the hold cleared abaft the mast ready for a visit on 9 February by the Governor of Cadiz and some merchants.

Before they departed the following evening on the long voyage home, the boats were taken into the waist. Once clear of land, the *Sedgemoor, Charles Galley* and *Mermaid* fired salutes as they took their leave of the squadron to head south and join the war against Salley. Later, when the *Charles Galley* returned to Gibraltar, William Bourk the Purser sent Samuel Pepys a present of two half chests of Flourence, two boxes of essences and six flasks of orange flower water, on account of the great favours Pepys had bestowed on him. Bourk must have found his position as Purser very rewarding to send such presents. It is strange that Pepys made no attempt to hide or remove such letters mentioning the gifts he received.[55]

The *Anne* and the rest of the ships headed north and were 23 leagues off Cape St Vincent by 14 February. The next day the fore topmast cracked in the cap and had to be shortened. This mast was once the main topmast of the *Leopard*, which had earlier replaced the *Anne's* original split topmast. The weather was very changeable during the voyage, sometimes fair and sometimes a '*great sea*'. By 18 February, they were 24 leagues west of Finisterre, and at the beginning of March in the middle of the Bay of Biscay. They often sailed under topsails but also with only their main courses, depending on the weather conditions. Two merchantmen were seen at different times and opinions regarding their position exchanged. As they neared the Soundings, they started to heave the lead. On 6 March, they found themselves in 88 fathoms of water with white sand. Following this, they cast twice daily as the depth and type of sand was useful to knowledgeable seamen as an aid to dead-reckoning navigation. Finally, on 9 March, they saw the Scilly lighthouse, four leagues off, and later that day made out Land's End. The next day they came into Falmouth and found themselves aground for an hour before getting off and anchoring in deeper water. Since leaving Cadiz, they reckoned to have sailed 1,364 miles at an average of just under 57 miles each day. The distance for each day's sailing varied widely between a maximum of 104 miles to as little as six.

After so long in the Mediterranean, the cold and snow they now encountered was very noticeable. On the morning of 13 March, they left Falmouth to make their way to Chatham, leaving the longboat behind to be filled with firewood. That evening they anchored in Plymouth Sound. While there, a lighter of beer arrived, and empty casks were sent ashore. After being away for such a long time, the beer must have been very welcome. The yacht caught up from Falmouth, bringing the longboat filled with wood. Over the next four days they passed Start Point and Beachy Head, sometimes anchoring when the tide was against them. On 19 March, they were in the Downs where they stayed for four days. The Duke of Grafton took his leave for London. His belongings and other things followed in the yacht and his horses were put ashore.

On 22 March, a quarter master's mate, Robert Prince, fell from the mizzen shrouds into the sea and was drowned. He was only the second man to die, both in accidents, a remarkable achievement for a voyage to the Mediterranean where it was common to lose dozens of men, usually to dysentery, the bloody flux as it was generally known. It is noticeable how often the water casks were *trimmed* or s*craped* and filled with fresh water. The officers on the *Anne*, by their good care, were responsible for preserving the lives of many men. After leaving the Downs, the *Anne* made her way north to the eastern edge of the Gunfleet before entering the Thames with the aid of a pilot. On 30 March they were at Blackstakes, and, at 6 o'clock that evening, lashed against the *Royal Katherine* at Chatham. The rigging was then taken down, the sails taken ashore and the ship cleared up. The stores were put ashore and guns taken out, the last being her prestigious brass guns. Finally the Commissioner came aboard and paid off the men.

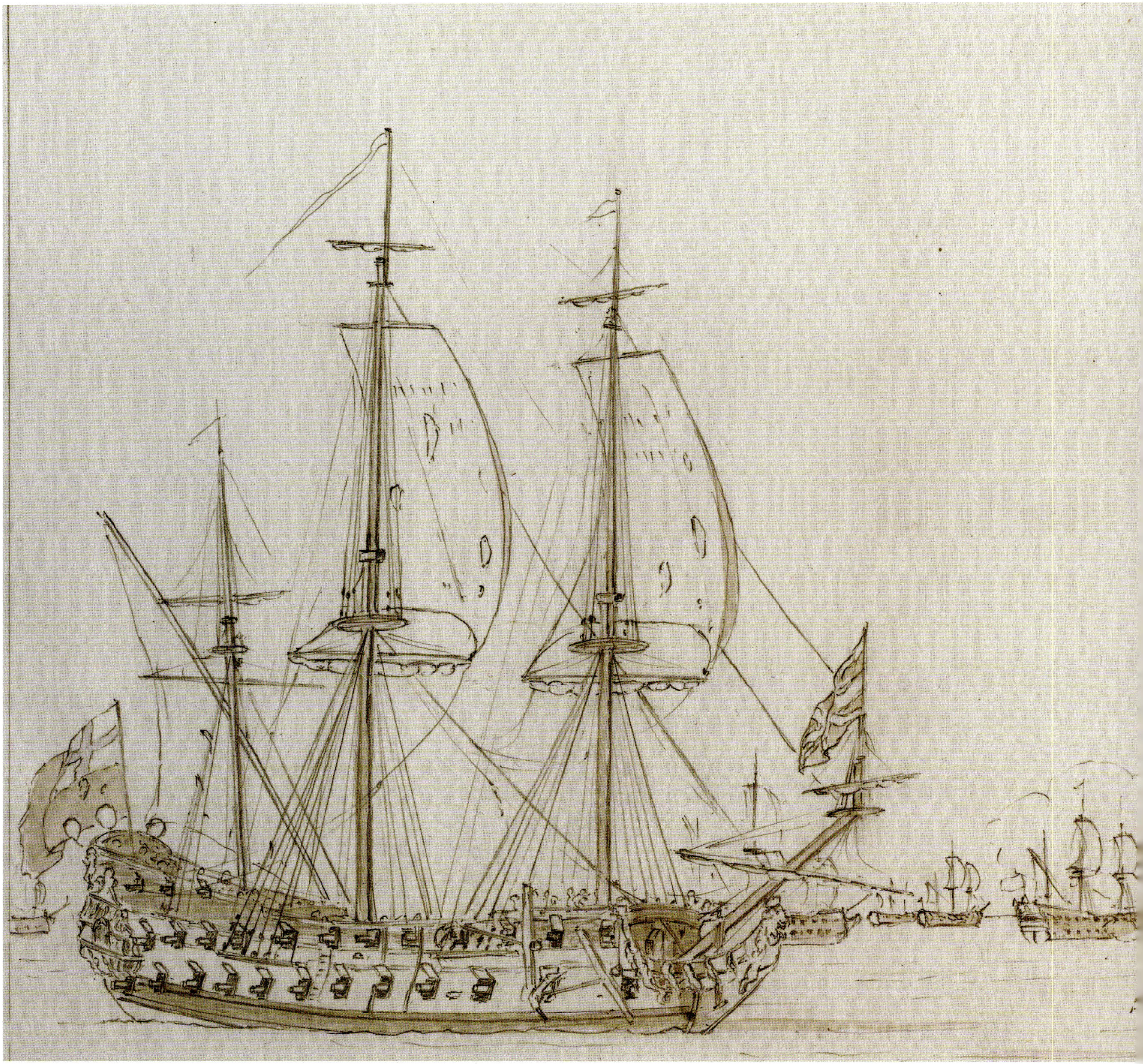

Chapter 5: The Battle of Beachy Head

The revolution of 1688

When the *Anne* returned home from the Mediterranean early in 1688, she was the largest ship in the Navy to be at sea. While she was away progress had been made repairing the fleet. Pepys's administration reported that nearly all the 39 third-rates in the Navy were completed. Only four were still under repair and three not yet started. It was a similar satisfactory condition for the nine first-rates, 11 second-rates and 42 fourth-rates.[1] At Chatham, the *Anne* joined 44 other large ships at their moorings and three others in dock. By 7 April, all her guns and stores were removed, the rigging taken down and the men paid off. The *Anne* became derelict apart from the five permanent warrant officers and their servants who must have felt the transition in lifestyle very strange. She was secured at the seventh mooring in West Gillingham Reach between the *Duchess* and the *Royal Oak*. The depth of water, measured from the swivel at the bow, was 23ft. She was ballasted to draw 14ft forward and 16ft 4in aft.[2]

The political and social situation had deteriorated in England since the *Anne* left the year before. At Chatham the men in the yard were about two years in arrears of their pay. Forced to borrow money, they were often at the mercy of their creditors and forced to pay extortionate interest-rates. Some were liable to be thrown into debtors' prison, even though they were owed more than enough to pay their debts. Some had even left the yard to become soldiers in order to prevent this happening.[3] Catholic King James had been popular when he succeeded his brother in 1685. He was supported by the Anglican Tories in Parliament and even by some Protestant dissenters and Whigs after he provided freedom of worship to them in 1687.

To maintain his popularity, James would have to rule with some sensitivity, as the vast majority of the general population was Protestant. Unfortunately for him, he proved blindly insensitive and gradually alienated everybody, not by a single act, but by a gradual and incessant advancement of his religion. A small example, which must have been noticed by those in the *Anne*, was the naming of the *Sedgemoor*. This was the new ship launched at Chatham by James himself on 3 May 1687, and which had gone to the Mediterranean with the *Anne*.[4] The Battle of Sedgemoor was James's victory over the Protestant rebellion led by King Charles's first born but illegitimate son, the Duke of Monmouth. It resulted in Monmouth's defeat, capture and execution. This was followed by the Bloody Assize of Judge Jeffreys, where hundreds of the

William Prince of Orange, Stadtholder of the United Provinces and King William III of England. *Author's Collection.*

rebels were hung by the roadsides, while others were transported abroad. James's naming of a ship after this brutality was typical, and he followed it up by appointing one of his staunchest Catholic supporters, Captain David Lloyd, as her commander who would later follow James into exile. Had she not been wrecked in January 1689, the *Sedgemoor*'s name would probably have been changed by William III.

In 1687, the Protestant Earl of Danby had been in contact with James's daughter, Mary, and her husband, William Prince of Orange, Stadtholder of the United Provinces. The moves against James increased, especially after the birth of the Price of Wales. Only two months after the *Anne* arrived home, many leading Whig and Tory nobles invited William to come over to England and save their religion. James was aware of the plots against him and began to prepare the fleet to oppose an invasion. The work at Chatham was to be carried out on the hulls, masts and yards of the warships under the supervision of Robert Lee, the Master Shipwright, for which he requested an additional 100 shipwrights. To have some of the ships ready very quickly, it was proposed to work on those requiring the least work while they remained afloat.[5]

At the time the *Anne* returned home, the *Monmouth*, *Royal Katherine* and *St Michael* were taken into dock. In early June the *Royal Katherine* was finished and the *Anne* was brought onto the ways in the dry dock to make good her hull. As the dock emptied of water, the considerable weed growth and damage by worm to the hull was exposed. This was made good by replacing any damaged pieces of four-inch-thick plank. Treenails were bored and the work caulked to make the joints watertight. After the repair work, the outside hull was protected by graving. Two weeks later it was found necessary to carry out more work and several other pieces were put in after the caulkers had finished. A pillar and cleat was needed for the awning beam. This was the frame that supported an awning which covered the quarterdeck as far aft as the poop. One of the gangways at the side, leading from the upper gun deck in the waist to the quarterdeck, needed repair.

As the month ended, the gun wales, plank sheers and the upper rails around the forecastle were also made good. A ladder was made for the gun deck and three brackets on the head fastened. By 7 July a new forecastle beam, new gratings for the head, deck grating and four new awning beams were fitted. With the work on the *Anne*'s hull complete, work began on her main yard in the mast house. Progress was then delayed as all the men were sent to fit out some of the ships ordered to join James's gathering fleet. The delay meant it wasn't until halfway through September that work began once again on her fore and main yards.[6] It took another two weeks before everything was complete and the *Anne* was once again ready for sea service. All she was missing was a longboat and a pinnace.[7] Shortage of boats for the fleet would remain critical well into the next year.[8]

By this time William's invasion had started. To oppose it, 11 third- and 21 fourth-rate ships were at sea. No three-deck first- or second-rate ships were commissioned as winter was not normally the season for war due to the expected poor weather conditions. The English fleet controversially appeared unenthusiastic to engage William's fleet, first the weather held them back in the Downs and then they became scattered once they got out. William landed at Brixham on 5 November and by Christmas James had fled to France. The *Anne* took no part in these events and remained at Chatham.[9]

1689 at Chatham

Catholic Louis XIV, the Sun King, still recognised James II as King of England. Catholic Ireland also supported James, who landed there with a French army, as a first stage in reclaiming his throne. The new French fleet, built by an absolute monarch under the supervision of Jean-Baptiste Colbert, was immensely powerful. It was paid for by the resources of a nation that had a population of 20 million, four times greater than that of England. Louis was even prepared to invade England for James and the Catholic cause. To do this, he would have to clear the seas by beating the English and Dutch navies.

Chatham Dockyard began taking on more men to fit out the fleet. Edward Gregory, the Commissioner, needed 50 extra riggers and 30 caulkers. Caulkers were particularly in demand to repair the seams of hull planking and he was delighted when 26 of them actually turned up.[10] Meanwhile at sea, an inconclusive battle was fought at Bantry Bay in Ireland. On 8 May, Gregory was asked which six third-rates could be soonest fitted for the sea. After consulting the Master Shipwright and the Master Attendant, they pitched upon the *Essex*, *Breda*, *Anne*, *Burford*, *Captain* and *Monmouth* as they could soonest be graved and rigged. It was now a year since the *Anne* was last graved and it was estimated she could be ready in four weeks.[11] A week later Gregory wrote saying they intended to dock the *Burford* and *Monmouth* for a tide or two '*then to have shut the gates upon the* Anne *and* Captain'. Before work could start he had to wait for official approval of his plan from the Navy Board.[12]

Delays were caused by high tides before the *Anne* was taken into the old single dock on 25 May.[13] While she was there having her hull cleaned and graved, Gregory wrote that no time would be lost in dispatching the ships. He added that as soon as the *Burford*, *Anne* and *Captain* were launched they would go in hand fitting the rest of the third-rate ships.[14] Of 12 ships being worked on at Chatham, the *Anne* was one of four that had now been ordered to be fitted for sea. They reckoned she would be ready to receive men and provisions as soon as she left the dock, and completely rigged four days later.[15] The dock gates were opened on 10 June and the *Anne* launched after spending 16 days in the dock.[16] While the dock gates remained open, the *Hope* was taken in to replace her. In the rather chaotic events, the *Anne* was in fact not fitted for service, although the dockyard officers wrote that if orders were received she could be fully rigged by 17 July.

Only nine men were aboard the *Anne* on 23 June. They could only have been her five warrant officers and their servants.[17] Three of the five warrant officers would stay with the *Anne* throughout the rest of her career. One, Thomas Adams the Gunner, was particularly interested in her and had meaningful conversations about her sailing performance with Robert Lee, the Master Shipwright. He told Lee:

'that her foresail never stood fair and that in a head sea she falls off a little … that when she turned out of Falmouth Harbour [13 March 1688] *on a leeward tide with the wind at WSW she never missed once staying which was so much taken notice of, that the neighbourhood stood admiring at it'.*

Lee wrote to the Navy Board quoting Adams's comments, adding that she wasn't one of the worst sailors and: *'though her main mast be very well & properly placed yet, her foremast being less than 12 feet from ye stem might be better, as we conceive, if carried 16 inches further aft. Which may be easily done, being clear of all ye beams'.* The cost of moving the mast would be about £10.[18] It was agreed to carry out the work and three weeks later the mast had been moved. The *Anne* was then reported to be completely repaired, graved and ready to receive men and victuals if occasion demanded.[19] From the dimensions mentioned by Lee, it would appear the foremast's new position should be in the region of 13ft 4in from the stem. In fact, it was measured and recorded as being 13ft 10in.[20] The *Anne* was one of the few new third-rates lucky enough to have been to sea so that any defects had been exposed and alterations made to correct them.

As the summer wore on, it was reported from Chatham that nine of the third-rates had been docked and '*all that could be thought needful to them has been done*'. The *Captain, Hope* and *Burford* were completely rigged and the *Anne* well-nigh in the same posture. Of the others, the *Restoration, Sterling Castle, Mary, Lenox* and *Grafton* were repaired and graved. The *Anne*'s rigging was completed and although eight or nine of the new third-rates went to sea with the fleet, she remained at Chatham for the rest of the year.[21]

Fitting out for war at home

The main concern at the beginning of 1690 was to prevent the French Toulon squadron sailing north and joining up with the fleet at Brest. To prevent this happening a powerful Mediterranean squadron under Henry Killigrew was fitted out for sea. The most prominent ship was the *Duke*, one of the nine, three-deck, second-rate ships built as part of the 1677 building programme. Realising that the forthcoming summer campaign would probably end in a decisive battle it was intended to fit out the whole fleet. In early January orders were sent to Chatham for the *Anne* and the other 13 large ships, still at their moorings, to be put in condition for sea with their

A contemporary romantic painting of Captain John Tyrrell leaning on a gun with ships in the background. It is inscribed Captain John Tyrrell, in the lower left hand corner. He was Captain of the *Anne* during the Battle of Beachy Head.

guns, stores and provisions. They were to be armed with their maximum complement of men and guns for war in home waters and to have four months provisions.[22] As part of the preparations, the *Anne* and the other ships were each taken briefly into dock to have any weed growth removed to make sure they would be in the best possible sailing condition.[23]

John Tyrrell joined the *Anne* on 19 February as her captain. He was an experienced, 44-year-old officer, whose first commission was as Lieutenant of *Resolution* in 1665.[24] He had recently commanded the fourth-rate *Mordaunt*, and 30 of her men, chosen by Tyrrell, were ordered to be '*turned over*' into the *Anne*. Turned over men were those who had served aboard one ship and then entered on the pay books of another, whether they wanted to or not. The *Mordaunt* was at Portsmouth and so the men were paid conduct money, or travelling expenses, to reach Chatham.[25] By the end of February, *Anne* had received four months' victuals[26] although there was only 40 men on her books.[27] The actual situation was even worse, for when mustered there proved to be only 29 actually aboard.[28] King William was growing concerned at the slow progress in fitting out the last 25 ships yet to join the fleet. He met the Commissioners for Victualling and the Duke of Schomberg, Master General of the Ordnance, in the Robes Chamber in Whitehall to progress the situation.[29]

When ships like the *Anne* carried their maximum complement of men, guns and provisions, their carrying capacity was severely reduced. To overcome the problem, small merchantmen were hired to attend and replenish them. The *Anne* was allocated the smack, *Dorothy* of 35 tons and a hoy, *Lewis & Cliff* of 70 tons. They were overworked bringing the guns, stores and men as the *Anne* fitted out.[30] On 6 March, Tyrrell met Ambrose Williams, Master of the *Richard & Samuel,* a ketch of 90 tons manned by nine men and carrying four guns. Williams offered his ketch to attend the *Anne* for £50 a month. Tyrrell wrote a note for Williams to take to the Navy Board explaining their arrangement, an arrangement which was agreed to.[31] The *Richard & Samuel* served the *Anne* for the next 75 days during the time she fitted out.[32]

Although lack of money was holding up progress, it was hoped the *Anne* would be ready to sail by mid-March.[33] James Smyth, a supplier of necessities for sick and wounded, was typical; he had not been paid and was in '*great streights*' finding himself unable to supply anything more.[34] Another ship fitting out at the same time was the *Grafton*, another new third-rate ship of 1677. The Duke of Grafton was commanding her and, seeing the *Anne*, remembered she had a splendid kersey awning fitted for the Queen of Portugal in 1687. He requested he have it again in his new ship.[35]

To Beachy Head

Toward the end of March, the *Anne* left Chatham and anchored at Blackstakes. She had 70 tons of beer on board and was receiving deliveries of her iron guns. John Tyrrell requested a new pinnace and longboat as the longboat recently supplied was so small that it could not carry the small bower anchor, even though the water was very smooth. Still needing men, he asked for orders to move up into the Hope, where he hoped it would be easier to press them[36] out of merchant ships. Pressing was the legal enlistment of mariners, more like the conscription of the twentieth century, rather than the violent kidnapping popularly associated with Nelson's time.

On 30 April, the *Anne* left Sheerness to join the gathering fleet with the *Royal Sovereign, St Andrew* and the *Duchess,* with Rear Admiral Rooke aboard. With them were the *Albemarle, Windsor Castle, Captain, Lyon,* and *Dolphin* fireship.[37] They stayed at the Nore until 4.30 in the morning of 22 May, when they and the *Sandwich, Royal Katherine, Grafton, Elizabeth, Defiance, Assurance* and some fireships left for the Downs. At five that afternoon they saw the North Foreland, and were safely in the Downs the next morning. They joined the *Coronation, Berwick, Suffolk, Edgar, Hope, Plymouth, Expedition, Hampton Court, Breda, Nonsuch, Foresight, Pembroke, Garland* and 16 Dutch warships. The gathering fleet must have made a tremendous sight.[38] To help navigate past the treacherous sand banks, Trinity House set well-placed buoys and sent pilots aboard most of the ships. The *Anne* was mustered on 28 May and found to have 459 men, only one short of her full complement of 460. Not all of them were aboard, 12 were sick ashore and 39 were either in one of her tenders or on leave. Of the 18 ships mustered at around the same time, she was almost the closest to having a full complement. Only the *Breda* had more; her captain reckoned he had 13 over the establishment with a further 15 sick ashore.[39]

Arthur Herbert, Lord Torrington, arrived in the *Fubbs* yacht and hoisted his flag at the main topmast head of the *Sovereign*. Salutes were fired at this and every other opportunity. It was of great benefit in getting the hastily assembled crews some experience using their guns. Most ships still had their tenders out pressing men. Many managed to get away, some deserted the ship but many more were discharged, probably because they were not

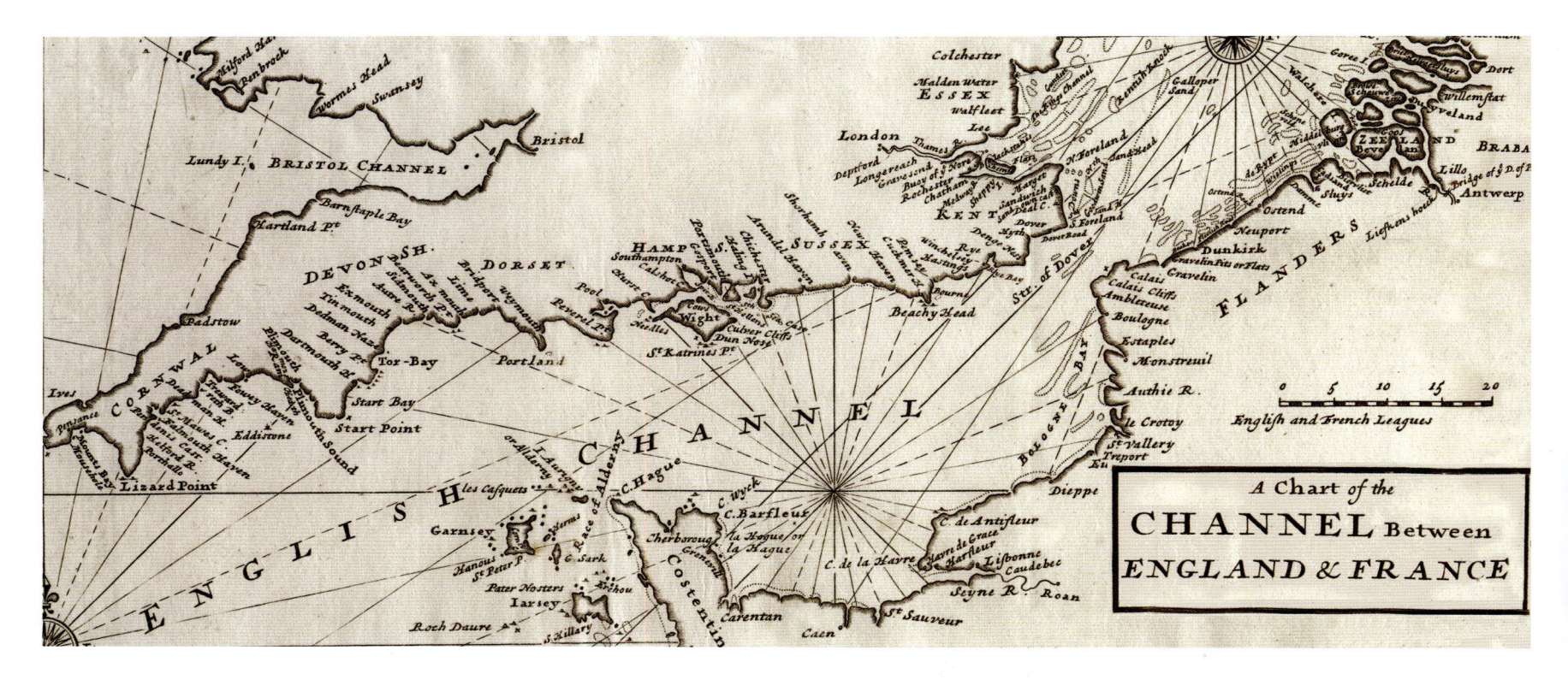

A contemporary map by H. Moll showing the area of operations during 1690.
Author's collection

seamen by trade. On 12 June, the Admiral hauled home his foretopsail sheets, then loosed his main topsail and fired a gun as the signal for the fleet to weigh anchors. At four the next morning they were off Beachy Head, but held up by gales they didn't anchor at St Hellens until 15 June.

On the same day, as the men intensively prepared for battle, Cale Taylor was killed aboard the *Anne*. It was dangerous work; during the previous four days two others, William Ellis and William Ayres, also died. From her paybook it seems her final number of seamen she went to battle with was 403. Their numbers were made up on 17 June by the addition of 169 soldiers of the Second Marine Regiment of Captain Mitchell's Company. The men were still in the process of getting used to their ships when late in the evening of 22 June, a Dutch privateer came into the fleet. It brought the startling news that the French fleet, under the command of the Comte de Tourville, was near Portland on the other side of the Isle of Wight.[40]

Strength of the fleets

It had been hoped the fleet would be joined by the Mediterranean squadron under Vice Admiral Henry Killigrew. He was returning home after failing to prevent the Toulon squadron joining up with the French fleet at Brest. His big ships not only included the second-rate, three-deck, *Duke*, but four third-rates and about seven Dutch warships under van Almond. The smaller fourth-rates in the squadron were left behind doing their intended task of escorting merchant convoys. Held up by all sorts of delays, Killigrew did not arrive at Plymouth until two weeks after the battle. His ships had very foul hulls making them slow, unwieldly, and in urgent need of cleaning and graving. The ships also had their reduced, abroad complement of men and guns, and were short of supplies. In no condition to fight a major action, they had little option but to enter the Hamoaze for their own safety. They were, in fact, lucky not to have been caught by the main French fleet returning home after the battle.

Another group consisting of four fourth-rates had sailed from the Nore and were only a day away before the battle was fought. Although the presence of the fourth-rates would only have made a minor impact, other ships, still fitting out at Portsmouth and Chatham, certainly would have made a difference. They included the second-rates *St Michael*, *Neptune* and *Ossory*, as well as the third-rates *Harwich*, *Kent*, *Northumberland* and *Monmouth*.

The fleet could also have been strengthened by the many ships supporting William III in his campaign against James II in Ireland. They were ordered to join the main fleet, but thwarted by the French arriving earlier than expected in the English Channel; they were cut off to the west. Two of these ships were in Plymouth on 1 July and were joined by three others a couple of days later. The largest was Cloudesley Shovel's flagship, the third-rate *Monck*, while three of the others were fourth-rates. Ten other ships from the west arrived off the Isle of Wight just after the battle. They included the third-rates *Swiftsure* and *Essex*, and five or six fourth-rates. The two third-rates carried 32lb demi-cannon guns on their gun decks. Of the fourth-rates, only the *Advice* is known to have carried guns as big as 18lb culverins while the rest only had 12-pounder guns.[41]

The huge difference in gun size between third- and fourth-rate-sized English ships, also applied to the Dutch and French. The guns were not only smaller, but also a third fewer in number. Added to that, fourth-rates were typically little more than half the size of a third-rate. Their timbers were proportionally smaller, making them very vulnerable if pitted against modern third-rate ships in the line of battle. Third-rates were manned by crews of well over 300 men, and new ones, such as the *Anne*, had 460. The dozen or so English fourth-rates that missed joining the fleet were manned by about 200 men each. During a battle, anyone aboard a fourth-rate would be very nervous or very brave at the approach of third-rate-sized warship, much bigger and harder-hitting than themselves. Other smaller ships, fifth or sixth-rates, fire ships and countless tenders were also involved, but they were too small to use in the line of battle.

The Anglo-Dutch fleet was in serious trouble: trouble caused by delays in getting the main fleet to sea and the failure to bring the scattered detachments together. They were outnumbered by 75 warships to 57[42] or, as another way of putting it, for every three Anglo-Dutch ships, the French had four. The Dutch forming the Van, or leading squadron of the allied fleet, consisted of 22 ships, eight of which were manned by less than 300 men.[43] The English ships forming the Red centre, and Blue rear divisions, consisted of 35 ships, and only four of them were manned by fewer than 300 men. The *Anne* was the lead ship of the Blue squadron. Of the French fleet of 75 ships 16 were manned by fewer than 300 men. Although the English ships were generally bigger than those possessed by the Dutch or French, the men aboard them had only recently been enlisted and were in need of familiarisation with their ships, guns, officers and each other.

Queen Mary II. Joint monarch with her husband William III.
Author's Collection

The French in sight

During the morning of 23 June the whole fleet stood out to sea before anchoring as the wind fell away. Knowing the French were so close, the ships were cleared for action, with cabins taken down and the yards slung so that cut rigging would not let them fall.[44] The wind picked up next morning as the fleet weighed anchor. Being outnumbered, they chose not to close with the French, and stood to the south-east shadowing them. They anchored that evening in 14 fathoms of water observing Culver Cliffs, at the east end of the Isle of Wight, four leagues away. Two English and two Dutch ships strengthened the fleet as scouts brought news the French were within six leagues to the west. The following day started out with rain and murky weather, but as it cleared the French fleet was seen three leagues away to the south-west.

Torrington saw an opportunity of weathering two thirds of them, with the Blue squadron leading. Noticing this, and acting with caution, the French tacked away, avoiding battle. Writing about the incident the next day, Torrington acknowledged he was rash in trying to attack them and '*not think myself very unhappy if I can get rid of them without fighting*'. He held a council of war and all of those attending, both Dutch and English agreed, they should shun the French, even as far as the Gunfleet, reasoning, as he later said, '*that whilst we had a fleet in being, they would not dare to make an attempt*'.[45] By refusing battle, time was given for Killigrew's squadron from Plymouth, other ships to the westward and the big ships still fitting out at Chatham and Portsmouth to join them. The conclusions of the council of war were sent to the Earl of Nottingham, but as William was away in Ireland, they were placed before Queen Mary. The final note in the council of war conclusions added that if the Queen had other considerations to command, they would be punctually obeyed.

Meanwhile, the fleet kept its distance from the French, anchoring at midday and getting under way again in the evening at slack tide. Torrington followed the council of war's decision for the next two days. He kept the French in sight, anchoring as the tide ebbed and tacking to maintain his position to the east of them. During these manoeuvres Beachy Head bore between the east-by-north and north, four or five leagues away. On 29 June, Torrington received orders from Mary, prepared with the advice of the Committee of Council. In response to Torrington's council of war conclusions, the orders judged a retirement to the Gunfleet '*fatal*' and, '*We chose rather you should upon any advantage of the wind give battle to the enemy.*' Confusingly they added he might find it necessary to get to the westward of the French to join up with the ships there and at Plymouth, but by no means ever to lose sight of the French in order to prevent them landing. Nottingham added a letter saying the ships from Plymouth had sailed to join him. The minute Torrington received the orders, he replied saying he would gather his flag officers together and was certain they would cheerfully obey Queen Mary's commands.[46] As Mary's orders were in contradiction to the earlier decision of the council of war, the debate was very lively, although the decision to fight was inevitable.

The *Anne* so much shattered

At four in the morning of 30 June the tide began to ebb to the west. At the same time, a fresh wind blew from the north-north-east. For the last few days the fleet had anchored as the tide turned to prevent it being taken closer to the French to the south-west. Instead, on this morning, the fleet bore down toward them, three or four leagues away. Torrington signalled to form into a line of battle. At the time, the French were scattered into two separate groups, but as soon as they realised the Anglo-Dutch fleet was heading toward them, they made signals to form a line themselves. After some manoeuvring under light sail, the French organised themselves into line of battle running from the south-east toward the north-west with their starboard tacks on board. That is, the sails and yards were pivoted so they were further forward of their masts on the right-hand side of the ship, the starboard side. Many used their head sails, the sails belonging to the foremast.

The Anglo-Dutch line closed with the French in a line almost parallel to theirs. At eight o'clock, as the fleets edged nearer, Torrington put up the red flag of defiance at the fore topmast head of his flagship, the *Sovereign* as the signal to engage the enemy. Half an hour later the Dutch in the Van, with their starboard tacks on board, and in excellent order, engaged the French. They met them several ships down from the head of their line. By nine o'clock the rear, Blue squadron, with the *Anne* leading, brought to at a distance of about twice gun shot. They and the French gradually edged nearer till they came within musket shot and opened fire. They became so close that shot was passing right through both sides of the ships. In the first broadside the *Anne*'s Boatswain, Samuel Thomas, was killed.[47] Torrington, with the centre, Red squadron was not so closely engaged, possibly, as he later alleged, because the French line bent away from him. The French

The morning of 30 June 1690 showing the leading ships of the Blue squadron heading toward the French fleet. The ships are from left to right, *Bredah, Exeter, Edgar, Bonaventure* and *Anne*. The *Anne* is viewed directly from the east at a distance of about 300ft. *Pencil sketch. Author*

noticed that the Red squadron, immediately ahead of the *Anne*, remained at long range and that it sometimes moved ahead toward the Dutch in the Van. This left the *Anne* engaged with a number of opponents opposite her. She was in the thick of the fighting between the English Blue squadron and the French rear squadron, the *Arrière-garde*. The battle raged for three hours when the stern of the French 74-gun ship, *Le Terrible*, was hit by a bomb that blew up everything from the lower deck to the poop and set the whole stern on fire.[48] The bomb was probably fired from a mortar piece known to have been given to some English ships just before the battle.[49] *Le Terrible* managed to come before the wind and turn out of the line. Once in comparative safety she managed to put out the fire. The *Le Fleuron* and *Le Modéré* were also forced out of the line for repairs after being holed below the water line. They both managed to make temporary repairs and pump the water out before re-joining the action. The absence of these ships left the *L'Illustre* exposed but she fought on with tenacity. Many of the damaged French fighting the Blue squadron set up their top gallant and main sails to get away.[50]

The *Anne* at about 1 o'clock in the afternoon at the time she lost her foremast. *Le Terrible* with her stern on fire can be seen in the background. The ship astern of the *Anne* is the fourth rate *Bonaventure*. The *Anne* is again viewed directly from the east at a distance of about 300 feet. *Pencil sketch, Author*

As time wore on, the outnumbered Blue squadron began to suffer badly as well. The *Anne* was at the front of her squadron with the next ship two miles ahead. This was the *Restoration*, the last ship of the Red squadron. Many of the French ships opposite the gap would only have the *Anne* as an opponent. The fourth-rate *Bonaventure*, the next in line immediately aft the *Anne*, noticed that they were fighting two flagships and three or four other Frenchmen. The good-rate of gunfire maintained by the French was also beginning to tell. The *Bonaventure* was holed many times and narrowly avoided sinking after having 5½ft of water in the hold.[51] The *Anne*, being even more exposed, suffered badly, especially forward on. At about one o'clock the whole of the foremast, some 28in thick, gave way and came crashing down, taking the sail and rigging with it. There was no respite; half an hour later the main topmast was also shot away.[52] Over the course of the next hour or two the *Anne* was slowly shot to pieces by the many opponents near her. The main mast, bowsprit and mizzen were all shattered to pieces.

The carnage amongst her men was equally appalling; Captain Tyrrell estimated that there were 100 men killed or wounded caused by over 60 shot that had smashed into her sides between wind and water.[53] It was not just the horrifying impact of iron cannon balls on men that killed so many. As the shot tore through the ship's sides, flying splinters of shattered oak caused more grievous wounds. Two 80-gun ships in the French rear squadron, *Le Grand* and

The Battle of Beachy Head

An engraving made to Admiral Torrington's orders showing the disposition of the Anglo-Dutch and French fleets at the Battle of Beachy Head. It is generally accurate although controversially he shows the French centre bowing away from him when it is most likely he bowed away from them. The *Anne*, number 22 and highlighted in red, is accurately shown at the head of the Blue squadron with a gap between her and the *Restoration* at the rear of the Red squadron. From Torrington's speech to the House of Commons, 1710. *Author's collection*

L'Intrépide, reported they had made two opponents mast-less hulks with their concentrated fire. In fact, only one English ship was reduced to that state, and that was the *Anne*.[54] Captain Mees in the *Exeter*, stationed three ships astern, noticed the *Anne* was disabled and bravely managed to get his ship between her and the enemy.[55] At about 3 o'clock the wind died away, it became calm and gave a chance of some respite for the *Anne*. Although she had six feet of water in the hold, the boats managed to tow her away with some difficulty so that she was able to stop the worst of her leaks.[56] Many ships in the French rear had also had enough, got their boats out and towed to safety as well.[57]

The casualties

Shortly after, the tide began to ebb. Taking advantage of this, the Anglo-Dutch fleet anchored, while the French allowed it to take them clear. As the fleets separated, the guns fell silent. The survivors aboard the *Anne* must have been immensely relieved but tired as never before. They were in desperate need of rest and time to recover. Instead, they had to clear up the horrific shambles on the decks and to attend the shattered remains of the masts, yards and rigging, for they were still in mortal danger. Below decks on the orlop, 29 men lay dead or dying. Among them was Thomas Mitchell, the Captain of the Marine regiment of the Earl of Pembroke. One of his two Lieutenants, Nicholas Bennett of St James's, Westminster, was badly wounded. He survived long enough to be taken to hospital ashore, where he died of his wounds. His widow, Debora, was very poor and was left with their children to support. Another who gave his life was Paul Clarke, a mariner from the Norfolk coastal village of Mundesley. He joined the *Anne* as an Able Seaman at the same time as many others on 31 March, just after she left Chatham for the Thames. He left a grieving widow, Anne. Another Able Seaman who died was Thomas Cunningham from Jarrow in County Durham. His wife Barbra had just become pregnant when he left to join the *Anne*. She safely gave birth to a baby daughter delivered by her midwife, Amey Cooke. Barbra named her daughter Thomasin after her father.[58] Such misery and sadness was repeated many times. Many badly wounded men were now undergoing the horrors of seventeenth-century surgery down in the dim light below water level on the orlop. Among them was a marine, Edward Matchett, whose left leg was amputated. He was not the only one. The same fate befell another Marine, Charles Liddle, and Able Seaman, Robert Hardcastle. John Kirby lost half his left foot. There were scores of other injuries, including fractured arms, burnt legs, head wounds, dislocated wrists and contusions to all parts of their bodies.

The families of those who were slain were entitled to their wages and a bounty payment to help cope with their loss. To make their claim, they needed to prove of who they were by certificate, often made out by their

The Anne *at about 3 o'clock in the afternoon. Dismasted and with six feet of water in the hold the* Anne *is being towed to safety by boats. Behind her and offering protection is the* Exeter. *Although the wind has died away, the fleets were separated by the ebb tide. The* Anne *is viewed directly from the east. Pencil sketch, Author*

local churchwardens. The men who survived with permanent life-changing injuries, such as Edward Matchett, who had lost a leg, were given an annual pension of £6 13s 4d, the standard amount for the loss of a limb. This was a little less than the earnings of a farm labourer and a lot less than a skilled and qualified shipwright who earned about £25 a year. Those with less serious injuries, such as Midshipman Thomas Grey, who had both legs burnt, received £8 from the Chatham Chest pension fund. The least seriously injured received payments of one or two pounds.[59] Such an injury was sustained by Able Seaman Gabriell Powell, who lost the little finger on his right hand, for which he received a payment of two pounds. The 41 men from the *Anne* who received payment from the fund must have had injuries at least as bad as his. They would be in no position to carry out any further duties on the *Anne* that day. Captain Tyrrell had estimated that 100 men were killed or wounded. The 41 injured men, together with the 29 men killed, left 30 others to make up the number. These 30 wounded men could not have been hurt badly enough to receive payment. Tyrrell really does not seem to have exaggerated.

To Pett Levell

Although the *Anne* had suffered badly, the Dutch at the head of the Anglo-Dutch line suffered even worse. Outnumbered and exposed by the lack of support from the Red squadron, they became surrounded and were severely beaten. One of the Dutch ships, *Friesland*, was unable to anchor and, after falling into the French fleet, was captured and later burnt. The *Anne* was in a perilous condition and in need of help. A topmast was raised as a jury, or makeshift, foremast. They managed to set a foresail but it proved too small for the ship to work with.[60] The fourth-rate *Swallow*, another ship in the Blue squadron, which had only two men killed outright, was ordered to take the *Anne* in tow.[61] That night the fleet continued to anchor with the ebb tide, keeping themselves as far away as possible from the French. The next day Torrington resolved to make his best way eastward using the tides and towing the disabled ships. If the French came too close he reasoned it better to abandon the disabled ships and burn them rather than risk further battle.[62] The *Swallow* was having difficulty towing the *Anne* and the *Edgar*; the second ship behind the *Anne* in the line of battle was ordered to help. At that time, the *Anne* was two leagues to the south-east of her and as there was so little wind, the *Edgar* never got near. Late in the day the *York*, a third-rate from Rook's rear division of the Red squadron, took her in tow just south of Hastings.

That night, the badly damaged Dutch ship, *Noord Holland*, was scuttled to avoid capture and *Gekroonde Burg* burned.

At six in the morning on Wednesday 2 July, the *York* and the *Anne* anchored in Rye Bay. The *York*'s main mast was damaged by shot and repaired with a strengthening fish.[63] Other damaged ships were in difficulty keeping to the east of the French. Unable to keep up, the Dutch ship *Wapen van Utrecht* was destroyed and sunk off Pevensey during the night of 2–3 July. Over the next two days, three more disabled Dutch ships were run aground, *Maagd van Enkhuizen* and *Elswout* at Hastings and *Tholen* at White Rock, a mile west of the town. All three were burnt to avoid capture. The following day, the French came closer as a wind began to blow hard from the east-north-east. The *York* and *the Anne* weighed anchor at about noon but couldn't get into Rye Harbour for safety as the *Anne* drew 19ft of water when the entrance was only 14ft deep.[64] At the same time, the strong wind stopped them getting out of the bay. Captain Tyrrell wrote '*Our ship being so much battered, God Almighty send us clear of our enemys*'.[65] With little alternative and with the advice of many people in the fleet, he was advised to anchor as near as he could go to the shore. They took all the marines out of her and stood into the bay, finally running ashore at Pett Level about four that afternoon.[66] It became her final resting place, where she would remain for hundreds of years, if not forever.

The *Swallow* was still in attendance and came close in to take back her boats that had been used in helping the *Anne*.[67] Tyrrell wrote that the *Anne* was within pistol shot, about 100ft, of the shore at high water and when the tide went out it was possible to walk right round her. She was in a sorry state and had so many holes near the waterline that water came in and out as the tide ebbed and flowed. In spite of this, Captain Tyrrell was still hopeful of saving her if French fireships did not come in and burn her.[68] About noon the following day, the French did come into the bay and as two of their ships came close in to burn her, Captain Tyrrell set fire to her himself.[69]

Some of the *Anne*'s men left her as soon as she beached, leaving their clothes behind to be burnt in the ship. They later claimed an allowance for them from the Navy. The Navy Board officers were not at all impressed with their petition for they heard the men had deserted the ship as soon as she came ashore and could have stayed to save their clothes, if not the ship. They found no precedent for compensating men who left a ship that was not being

The Dutch squadron suffered the greatest casualties in both men and ships. They were eventually relieved by ships of the Red squadron. In the centre is the *Stirling Castle*, the *Lenox* is the nearest ship and the *Sovereign* is to the right. A view looking from the north. Collection of Mr R.B.Mafit. *Oil on canvas, Author*

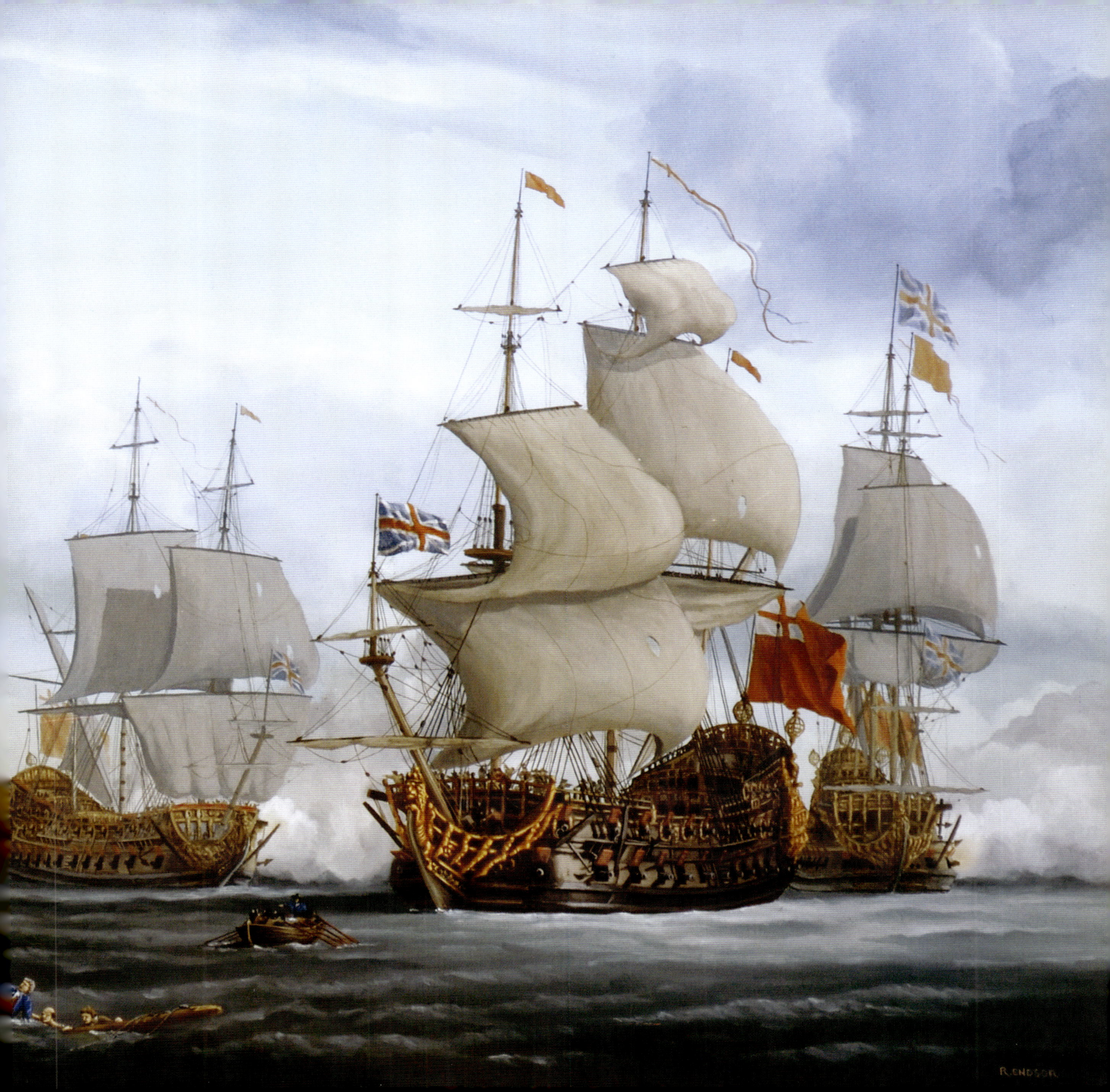
R.ENDSOR

destroyed or taken. The officers and several of the men who did stay, not only saved their own clothes but some of the ship's stores as well.[70] Being accused of desertion could have meant the men would get no compensation for their clothes and have an 'R', for run put against their names in the ship's pay book. They would then have forfeited their wages, at the very least. No blame was placed on Tyrrell for the loss of the *Anne* for within a day he was promised another ship.[71] He wrote of the battle '*my men were very cheerful and behaved themselves with a great deal of gallantry.*'[72]

At 10 o'clock at night, only two days after the *Anne* was burnt, many of the men who had deserted her unexpectedly turned up at Chatham. They must have walked about 45 miles cross-country and were immediately seen by Edward Gregory, the Commissioner. Showing remarkable resilience after their recent shocking experience, they still wished to do their duty and fight for their country. They agreed to be entered on board the second-rate *Neptune*, but with a condition. Should Captain Tyrrell be appointed another ship, then they would be returned '*to their own commander*'. Their loyalty and wish to join Tyrrell was agreed to by both Gregory and Captain Wright of the *Neptune*.[73] A month later, Tyrrell was promoted and appointed Commander of the second-rate *Ossory*. The men from the *Anne* went to join him but were still in dispute about their clothes and wages. They understandably swore that they would not come aboard the ship till they received their pay especially, as they claimed, Queen Mary had promised to pay for their lost clothes. Forty of them were together and Tyrrell said '*so saucy that I have been forced to put the ring leaders in the bilboes*' or leg irons.[74] Happily, the dispute was rapidly and sensibly resolved for just a few days later Tyrrell was writing to the Navy Board giving them his most heartfelt thanks for their care in procuring the *Anne*'s men's wages and bedding.[75]

At sea, the danger of an invasion passed as the French fleet failed to press home their advantage. Many of their ships were also damaged and with men falling sick, they returned home. Two years after Beachy Head, the Anglo-Dutch allies gained ample revenge at the Battle of Barfleur-La Hogue. It established the English fleet as the world's supreme maritime power until the end of the days of sail.

The medal struck by Louis XIV in celebration of the victory. The *Anne* would be one of the trophies under the winged victory.

Captain John Tyrrell Memorial

Captain Tyrrell died only two years later in November 1692 and was buried in his family chapel at St Mary's, Oakley, a charming Buckinghamshire village. The inscription on his ledger reads:

'Here lieth Captain John Tyrrel (Son of Sr Timothy Tyrrel of Oakley and Dame Elizabeth his wife) who was made by K: Charles the 2^d Admiral in the East Indies and in the sea fight 1690 did withstand ye violence of the whole French Navy Always shewing himself a true lover of his Country a Valiant and Skilfull Commander He was born Anno 1646 and died December 6th 1692'.

Interestingly, a brass bell hangs next to Captain John Tyrrell's ledger. It is too small for a church bell and intriguingly may possibly be a ship's bell. For the moment its provenance is unknown.

The ledger of Captain John Tyrrell. It is in excellent condition in a protected position against the southern wall of St Mary's Church, Oakley. *Author*

A list of the men who gave their lives defending their country from invasion while serving aboard the *Anne* at the Battle of Beachy Head on 30 June 1690.

Samuel Thomas	Boatswain	Thomas Ile	Midshipman
William Creswell	Qtr Master	George Hoblin	Able Seaman
Thomas Sampson	Qtr Master	Henry Sprye	Yeo Nippers
Richard Bones	Qtr Master	William Baker	Able Seaman
John Young	Able Seaman	Henry Taylor	Able Seaman
Johnathon Taylor	Able Seaman	Thomas Vickers	Able Seaman
Jacob Jenouay	Qtr Master	John Gregor	Able Seaman
Richard Evans Snr	Able Seaman	John Granger	Volunteer
Robert Jolley	Able Seaman	James Castle	Able Seaman
John Johnson	Able Seaman	Thomas Mitchell	Captain Marines
Elias Barnes	Qtr Gunner	Nicholas Bennett	Lieutenant Marines
Simon Dexter	Able Seaman	John Bowley	Marine
Paul Clarke	Able Seaman	Richard Heath	Marine
George Walker	Able Seaman	Edward Philkin	Marine
Thomas Cunningham	Able Seaman		

The *Anne* burning. Her position in relation to the background was taken with the accuracy of photography. Collection of the Nautical Museums Trust. *Oil on canvas, Author*

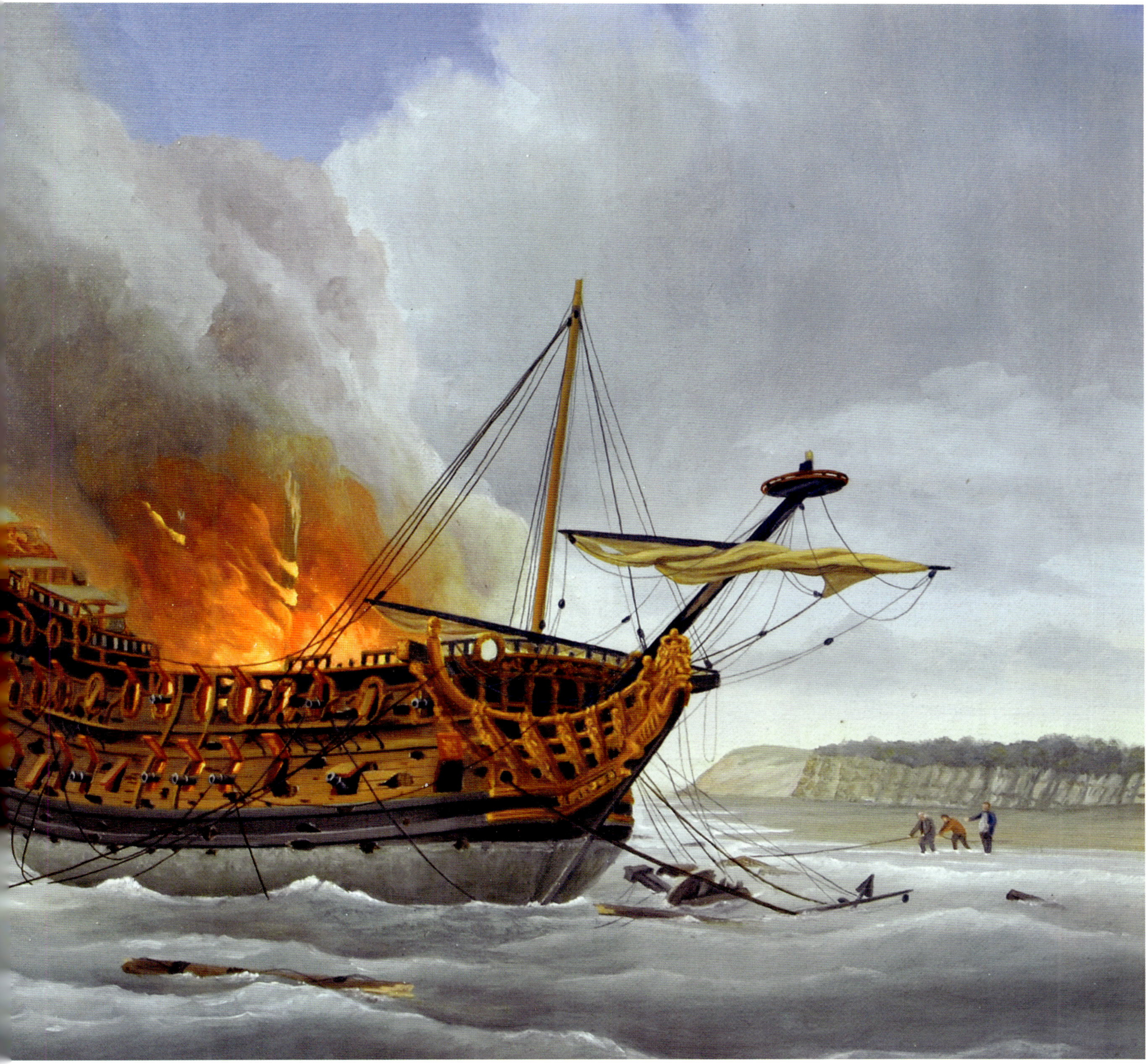

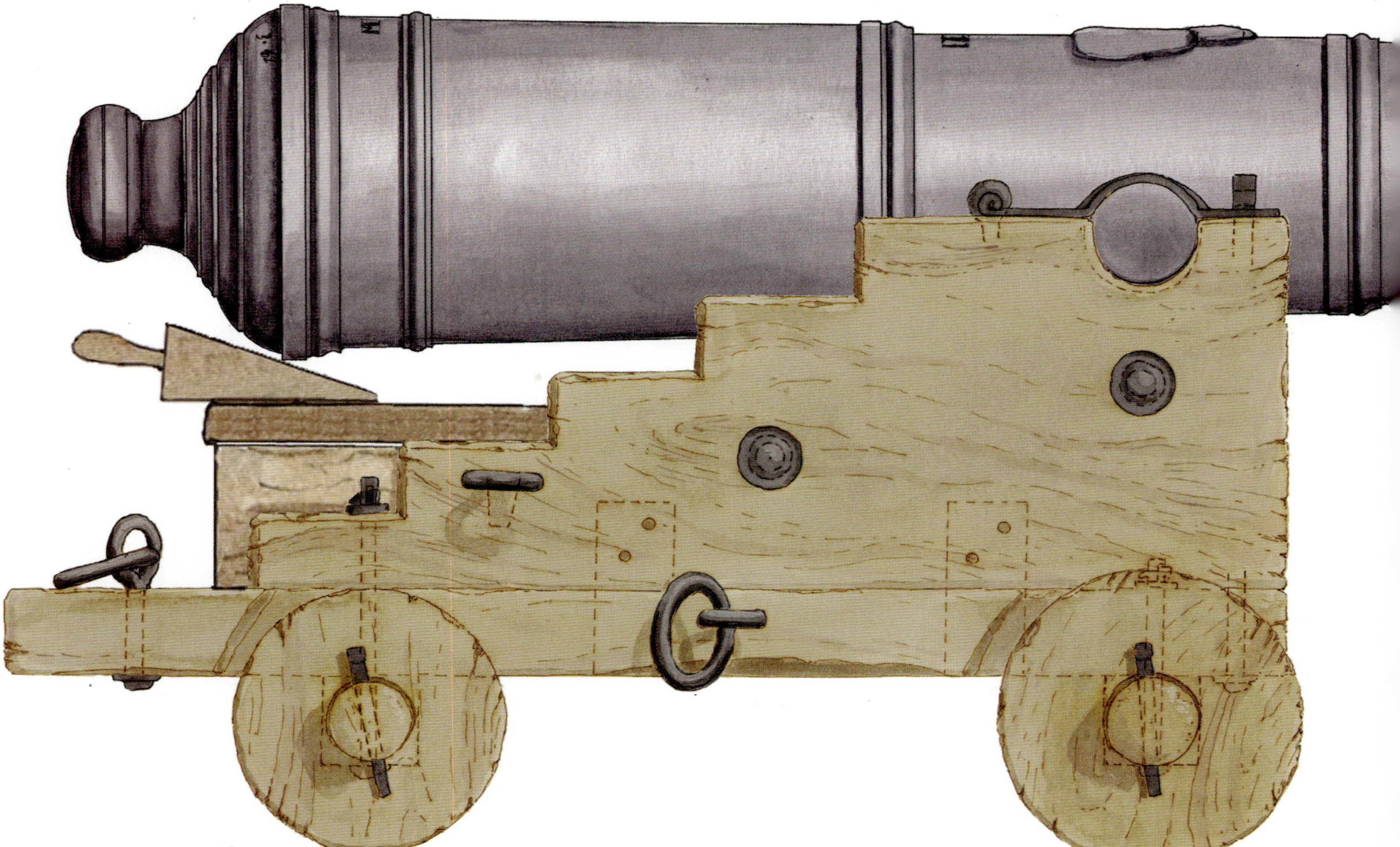

Chapter 6: The Guns of the *Anne*

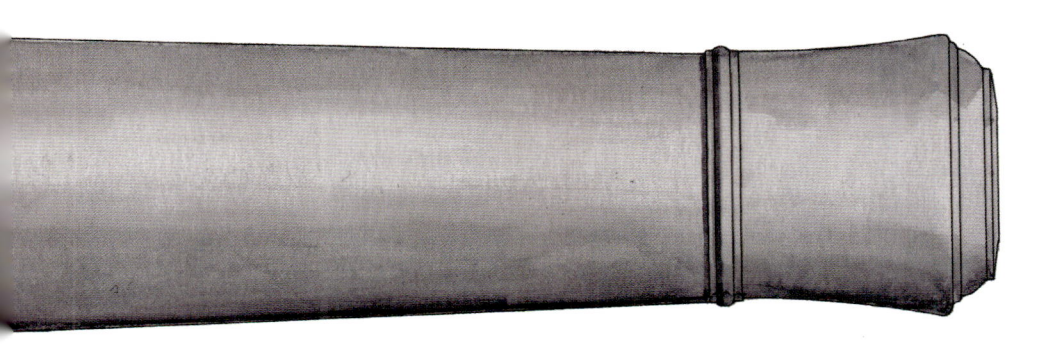

Establishment of guns for the New Ships

The guns used by the Army and Navy were very similar. So similar, that land guns were sometimes used on ships and naval guns in forts. It made sense therefore that a single body, the Board of Ordnance, looked after both services. When new ships were built, their allocation of guns required careful consideration. Naturally enough, the Admiralty and sea officers wanted to have as many big guns they thought their ships could carry depending on where they would be sent. If it was in the North Sea against the Dutch, then more of the carrying capacity could be given over to guns than if it was going to the Caribbean. It also depended upon whether it was a time of peace or war. Another consideration was the type and number of guns available in store. The desirable 12-pounder gun had been recently introduced and was in short supply. New guns were not necessarily made for new ships as guns outlived ships by a considerable margin.

Before the *Anne* was built, Brown's 'fine metal' guns of earlier years were better than new 'rough iron' guns. The technology of casting large iron guns had improved considerably by 1677, but expensive brass guns continued to be used in prestigious ships. The *London*, blown up by accident in 1665, carried a set of brass guns on the gun deck, including one made during the Commonwealth and at least one other dating from Tudor times. She also carried a number of brass land guns, once owned by the City of Amsterdam and captured from a Dutch warship[1]. Sometimes, in fact quite often, the over-optimistic estimates of the weight of guns a new ship would carry were exposed when it was found that the gun ports were only three feet from the water. But rather than take the obvious solution and reduce the load, they always preferred to alter the ship. This involved attaching extra-thick plank on the outside to make the ship wider, a practice known as girdling.

All the many considerations were deliberated on by members of the Navy Board and Ordnance Office before an establishment for war, peace and abroad could be approved by the Admiralty. Needless to say the debates had the potential for dispute. The problem was discussed at a Privy Council meeting at Hampton Court in July 1679, at which an order was made that the General of the Ordnance must comply with all directions issued by the Admiralty. The loss of status was softened by the letters having to be signed by a quorum of members and, to maintain civility, they must be in the style of '*pray and desire*'.[2]

An establishment list of guns for the whole fleet was started in March 1674, although little progress was made.[3] The matter needed urgent resolution after Parliament approved the Act for building the 30 new ships on 22 March 1677. The Navy Board officers attended the following Admiralty Board meeting to discuss the matter and were ordered to think about the number and weight of guns for the new ships.[4] The Ordnance Board prepared a paper on 26 April which proposed the third-rate ships have 24-pounders on the gun deck, 12-pounders on the upper and demi-culverin, which fired a 9-pound shot, in the upper works.[5] The total weight of guns was estimated to be 120 tons. By 10 May the debate had moved forward with suggestions to replace the 24-pounders with heavier, 32-pound demi-cannon on the gun deck but retaining the 12-pounders on the upper and lighter, 7¼-pound sakers and 3-pounders in the upper works. The weight of gunshot increased considerably at a modest increase of four tons in the total weight of guns.[6] The Ordnance Board estimated that the 70 ordinary iron guns would cost £2,232 at £18 a ton. With powder, shot, blocks, tackle, carriages, small arms and accessories, the whole cost of a third-rate's armament amounted to £4,754 0s 9d.[7]

On 16 May, the establishment was further advanced with an addition of an estimate for the manning of the ships[8] which was discussed the next day at an Admiralty Board meeting.[9] Various versions were signed for approval on 1 and 3 November and among the signatories were the Earls of Danby and Arlington.[10] The final version was issued on 15 December 1677.[11] In early 1678, contracts were made with Mary Browne, a principal gun founder, to supply guns for some of the new ships. Surprisingly, it included 11-foot long culverins, a gun not mentioned in the 1677 Establishment.[12] It seems that after four years of deliberations they had forgotten to include long chase guns. They were mounted at the ends of the ships and could be moved from the broadside position to fire in the fore or aft direction depending upon whether you were chasing, or being chased.

The guns of the *Anne*

The Act for building the 30 new ships of 1677 included money to provide new guns for every ship. Fortunately, many good old guns were already in store and the money saved by using them helped pay for Charles's insistence on building bigger ships than that allowed for by Parliament. No one would notice as the guns were not put aboard a ship until they were made ready to go to sea. Once this had happened the guns belonged to a ship and

The forward chase guns. The foremost two long 12-pounders on the upper deck and the two long sakers on the forecastle have been moved from their usual broadside positions to fire directly forward in the chase position. The port 12-pounder is shown being loaded from the outside, making the operation quicker to perform. Author

were not normally reissued to another, even when they were laid up out of service. Most of the new ships did not receive their guns until at least 1688, at the time of the Glorious Revolution. Many of the last ships to have their guns issued had to make do with old demi-culverins, which fired a nine-pound shot, as the recently introduced 12-pounders were in particularly short supply. This could be an advantage. Some of the later armed ships, such as the *Lenox*, were equipped with practically no guns according to the establishment, and ended up with older, nealed and turned high-quality guns instead of the establishment rough iron.[17]

As part of their gunner's stores, 60 rounds of iron round shot, and six rounds of double headed hammered shot, was allowed for each gun. For close-range fighting, three rounds of tin cases filled with musket shot was supplied for each saker, 4cwt of bace and bur, and 350 iron bars. To propel all of this ammunition, 285 barrels of corn gunpowder, worth £890 12s 6d, and 10cwt of match powder, worth £12 10s, was provided. Canvas and paper royal was also supplied for cartridges to be made aboard.[18] This was done in the protected area of the powder room near the step of the fore mast. An accident could cause a disaster such as happened to the *London* in 1665. It nearly happened to the *Eagle*, a third-rate of 1677 being made ready for war at Chatham in January 1691. As recorded by Commissioner Edward Gregory, an apprentice, Thomas Marsh, was working there when: *'the accidental fall of his candle put all into flame and disorder about him, the poor fellow is singed to some purpose. I have the gunner of the ship under examination who confesses that in the powder room there were two chests at considerable distance from each other, one containing sundry canvas cartridges, the other of paper and parchment. The former had never been filled, the latter had indeed been filled but carefully emptied … the powder room was swept with all possible care and afterward duly swabbed'*. This account was confirmed by his mate, the yeoman of the powder room, and the boatswain's yeoman.[19]

Details of the *Anne*'s ordnance and gunner's stores for six months and dated 1687.[20] It is broadly in accord with other sources.

Barrels of powder 300 Price of powder £900
Weight of shot 58 tons Price of shot, cast and hammered £1044
Weight of guns 127 tons Price of iron guns, new £2413
Price of Gunner's stores £440

106 The Warship Anne

This rare survivor is an example of an 11-ft-long culverin chase gun. It is the same weight as a demi-cannon, but only fires an 18lb instead of a 32lb shot. Its extra length made it more accurate and it took a longer cartridge. They would be mounted in the four aft broadside ports on the gun deck so they could be moved to fire directly aft through the four stern gun ports. This particular gun was cast by George Brown in 1668 and the survey number 4632 cut into it shows it was at Tilbury Fort at the end of the seventeenth century. It is now conserved at the Canadian War Museum, Ottawa, Ontario. *Author*

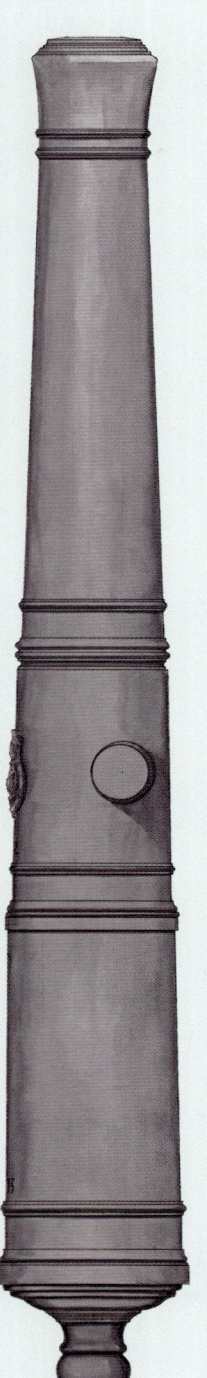

A 9ft 6in Rose and Crown demi-cannon cast by Thomas Westerne between 1693 and 1695, it is the same weight and length as those used on the *Anne*. It fired the same size 32lb shot as the heaviest guns on Nelson's *Victory*. The weight of 54cwt. 1qtr. 01lb. is cut into the first reinforce. Forward is the 1698 survey number 12844, which confirms it was aboard the *Lancaster* at the time. Next to the number is the broad arrow made when it passed proof firing. The cross was made years later when it was de-commissioned. In the second reinforce is the Rose and Crown cypher and the number 5 is probably a battery number. Today it is on display at the entrance of the Barbados Museum. *Author; measurements and research by Charles Trollope*

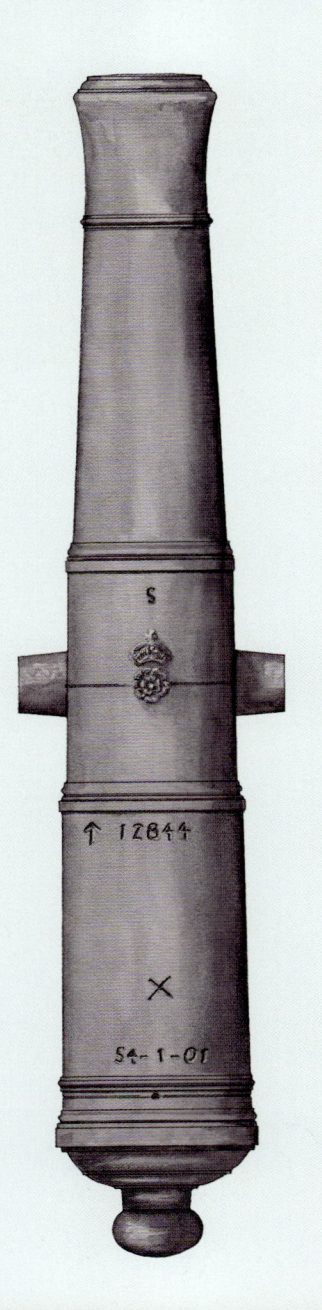

The Guns of the *Anne*   107

A 9ft 6in-long 12-pounder in excellent condition preserved at Mullins Bay, Barbados. It was the type of gun that formed the upper deck armament of the *Anne*. It served aboard the third rate *Southampton* according to its 1698 gun survey number 307. *Author; measurements and research by Charles Trollope*

Note: The scale shown applied to all guns and carriage drawings.

A long 9ft 3in saker of the type that would have been at the forward position on the forecastle of the *Anne*, from where it could fire in the broadside, or point directly forward in the chase. This gun is mounted on a ship's carriage at the top of the Curfew, or Bell Tower, at Windsor Castle. It has been there since at least January 1670, at the time Edward Wise the Storekeeper made a survey of guns. He recorded the weight as being 24cwt 0qtr 2lb but unfortunately no markings can be seen on the gun today. *Author*

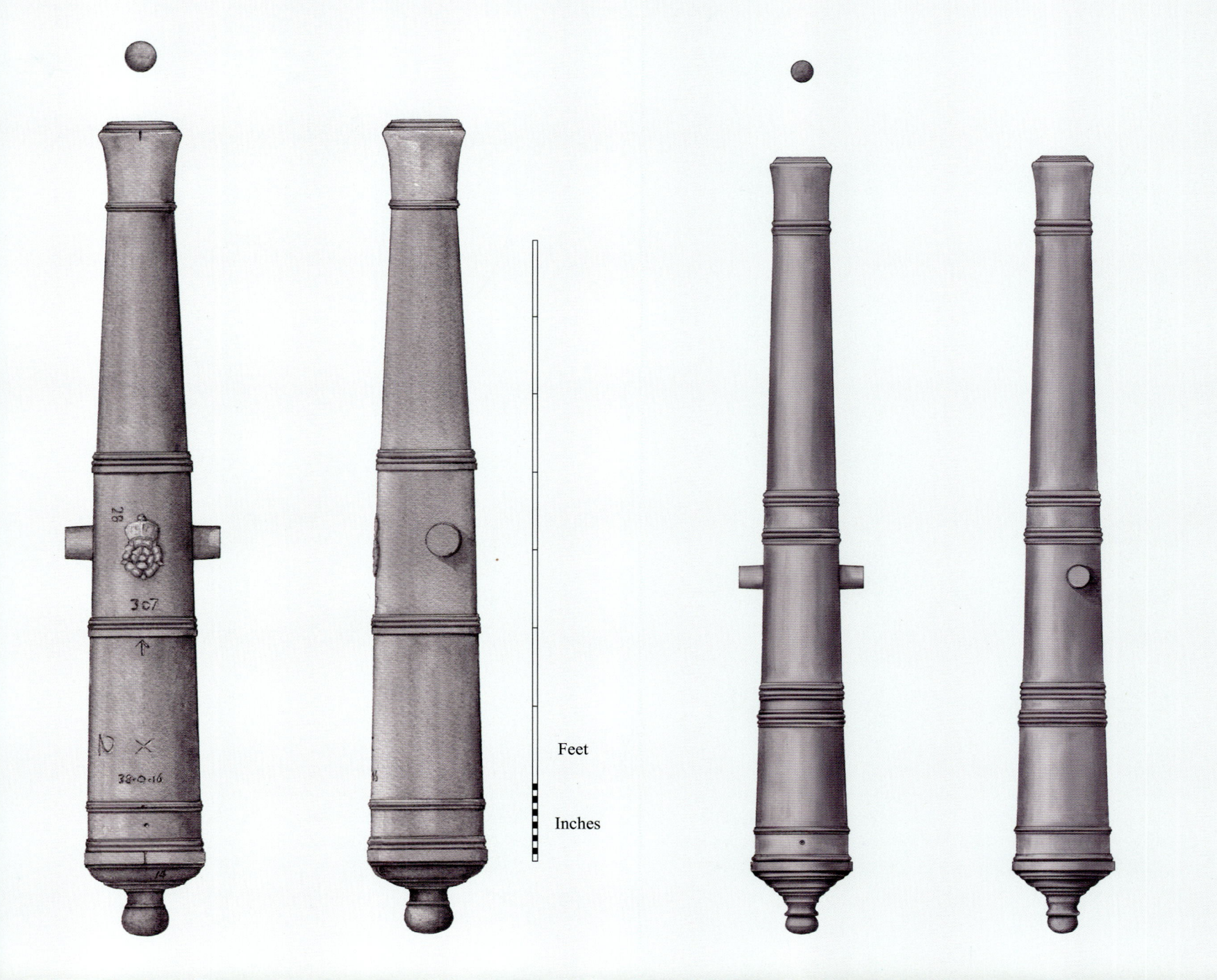

Feet

Inches

108 The Warship Anne

A 7ft 3in saker dating from about the middle of the seventeenth century of the type used on the quarter deck and forecastle of the *Anne* in 1690. This example was found recently on waste ground in Potters Field near Tower Bridge and had been used in the past as a bollard. It was found with trunnions and button missing but has now been expertly restored. *Author; Private possession of Julian Kingston, Director of Build the Lenox project*

This 3-pounder gun dating from 1691 is a foot longer than the 5ft specified in the establishment for the *Anne*. In practice there was a considerable variation in gun lengths in ships' batteries. This gun served aboard the *Cornwall* in 1698. It is conserved and on display at Fort Nelson Museum, Portsmouth. *Author*

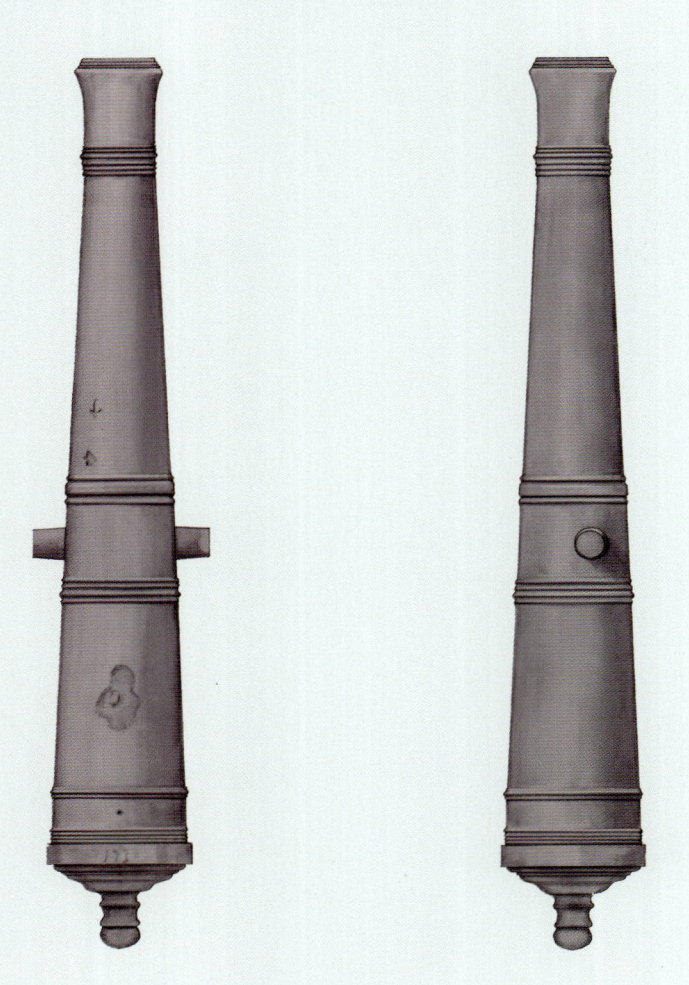

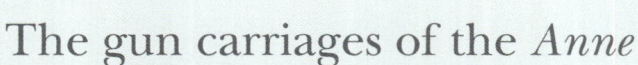

The gun carriages of the *Anne*

On 1 March 1678, some months before the *Anne* was launched, a contract was made between the Ordnance Office and William Sheepey, their Master Carpenter, for the supply of the gun carriages for the first of the new ships. Another contract was made with Edward Silvester, the Master Smith, for the carriages ironwork, their bindings. Deliveries began soon afterward and six months after her launch on 11 March 1679, the *Anne* received her carriages.

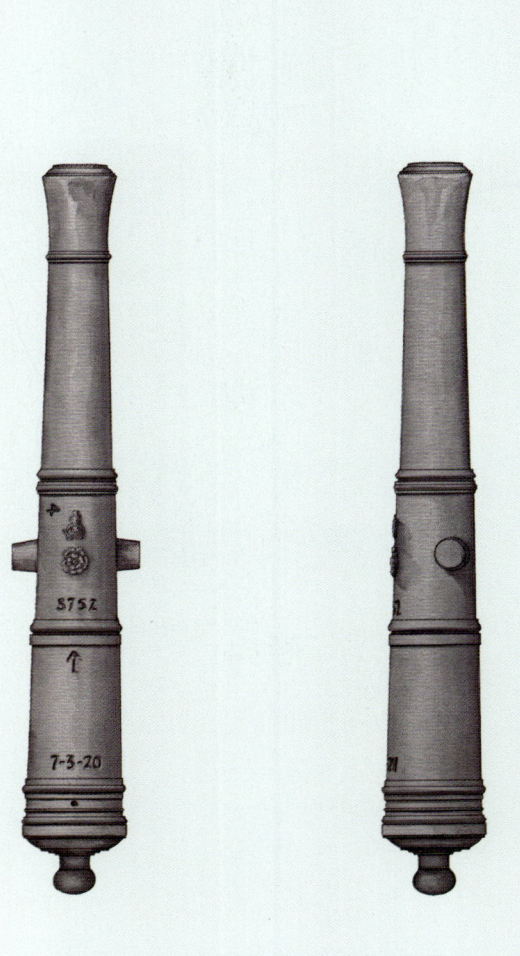

Anne's guns for the Mediterranean voyage

Not counting the small voyages made by some of the 20 new third-rate ships from their building place to the fleet anchorages at Chatham or Portsmouth, the *Anne* was one of only three of the ships that went to sea before 1688. Being one of the first ships to actually have a set of guns on her decks, it would seem reasonable to suppose they would be in accordance with the

Type	Number	Length of gun (ft)	Weight of shot (lb)	Weight of each gun (cwt)	Total weight (tons cwt)	Position	Men each gun	Total number of men
Demi-cannon	22	9½	32	54	59.8	A	6	132
Culverin	4	11	18	54	5.8	B	6	24
12-pounder	2	10½	12		3.4	C	4	8
12-pounder	24	9	12	32	38.8	D	4	96
Saker	2	9½	5¼		1.12	E	3	6
Saker	12	7	5¼	16	9.12	F	3	36
3-pounder	4	5	3	5	1	G	2	8
To carry powder								20
To fill and hand powder								10
To carry wounded men								8
Surgeon and his crew								5
Carpenter and his crew								4
Purser and his crew								5
To man the boats								16
For the tops if no flag								5
For the helm								2
To conn* the ship								2
Small shot								35
To trim and tend sails								36
Total	70				124			458

*The helmsman had a restricted view of the sails from his position at the whipstaff. During severe weather or in action when he could not rely on the compass in the binnacle, he was 'conned' by having directions shouted down to him from above.

Details of the numbers of guns and men for 'home at war' carried by the Anne compiled from the 1677 Gun Establishment[13], Establishment of 16 May 1677, Dimensions of Old Ships and State of Ordnance 1688.[15] In time of war abroad, and peace at home or abroad, the complement of guns was reduced to 62 by the removal of two demi-cannon, two 12-pounders, two sakers and two 3-pounders. The number of men for war abroad was reduced to 380, and for peace abroad or at home to 300. Extra men were allowed to flagships. An admiral of the White or Blue was allowed 30 extra, and vice admirals of the Red, White or Blue, 20 extra.[16] The position of the guns is shown on page 112.

establishment. She would, however, be on a very unusual mission taking the future Queen of Portugal to Lisbon under the command of King Charles's son, the Duke of Grafton. After that she was ordered on to the Mediterranean to visit Algiers, Tunis, Tripoli and Malta. In accordance with the peace and abroad establishment, her armament should only be 62 iron guns and 300 men.[22] Her unusual assignment with royalty aboard made a considerable difference; brass guns were placed in the cabins and an extra 60 seamen, 52 soldiers and 30 men for the Flagg Officer, allocated to her crew. This resulted in an allocation of 442 men[23] although in fact she seems to have gone to sea with 410 men.[24]

The first activity to make good the Anne's gun carriages for sea came in January 1687 when Thomas Moore, a carpenter working for the Ordnance Office, went down to Chatham. He repaired 20 of Anne's carriages as well as those on 19 other ships.[25] Then Valentine Bayley, the Master Painter, set to work on many of the Anne's, including four demi-cannon (probably a mistake for the four culverins located in the gunroom) on the lower deck, all the upper deck 12-pounders and the

An upper deck gun ready to fire. It is rigged with a thick breaching rope to stop it recoiling too far. After reloading it was hauled back to firing position with the train tackles. *Author*

Right: The ship's carriage belonging to the long saker in the Curfew Tower at Windsor Castle. It was made to wide manufacturing tolerances with trucks of different thickness. The 'dead' rear trucks were a common feature in ships of the period. *Author*

Bottom left: A 24-pounder gun carriage from the wreck of the *London*, lost in 1665. The carriage appears to have been heavily modified to suit a gun for which it was not originally built. It includes an extension at the rear and spacers on the inside of the cheeks. Many of the *Anne*'s original carriages, dating from 1687, may have been similarly modified to suit the different guns given her in 1690. *Author*

Bottom right: A demi-cannon carriage from the 1703 wreck of the third rate *Stirling Castle*. Much of the ironwork was concealed by concretion at the time of recording. It is now under conservation. *Author*

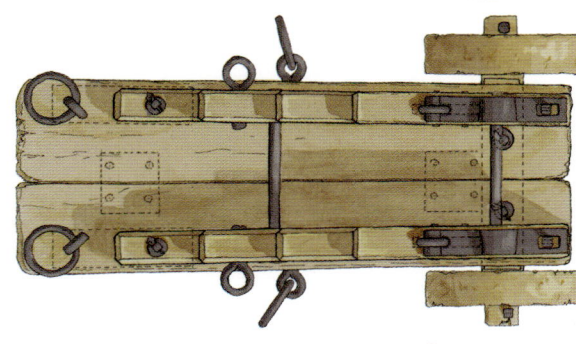

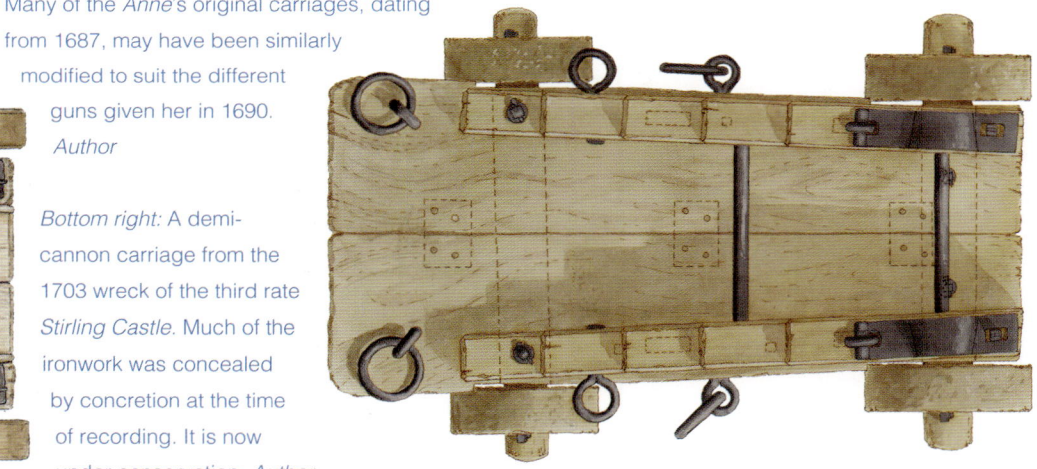

Details of the carriages supplied to the *Anne*. The cost of the iron bindings for each carriage was not given in the contract although a price of 3¾d per pound weight was. It also gave the number and type of carriage and the total cost. Using the cost proportion for the types of carriage given in the Master Carpenter's contract, the cost of the iron bindings was calculated with reasonable certainty. It includes two pence each for a pair of forelocks.[21] Once delivered, the carriages were stored on the *Anne*.

Type of carriage	Thickness cheeks elm	Thickness bed elm	Cost of carriage	Cost small bed	Cost coyne	Cost iron binding	Total cost of carriage
Demi-cannon	6'	5'	40s 0d	1s 8d	0s 9d	46s 3d	88s 8d
Culverin	5'	4½'	30s 6d	1s 8d	0s 9d	35s 1d	68s 0d
12-pounder	4½'	4'	30s 6d	1s 8d	0s 9d	35s 1d	68s 0d
Saker	3½'	3½'	22s 9d	1s 8d	0s 9d	26s 0d	51s 2d
3-pounder	3'	3'	19s 0d	1s 8d	0s 9d	22s 1d	43s 6d

Right: A brass 6-pounder gun cast in Amsterdam in 1642 and later captured from the Dutch. This is a very small gun to fire a 6lb shot and would normally have a violent recoil. To reduce the danger it was fired with a reduced charge in a taper bored barrel. Its weight of 682 Amsterdam pounds is inscribed on the base ring and the English 1698 Ordnance Board survey number 6269 is inscribed in the first reinforce. At the time of the survey it was aboard the third rate *Stirling Castle* of 1677. When the fleet was fitted out for war in 1690, the *Stirling Castle* was the last third rate at Chatham to be given guns. As a result, many of them did not conform to the establishment, including this brass 6-pounder. The survey also shows that the *Stirling Castle* was the only third rate of 1677 with some small brass guns, and it is quite possible this gun served aboard the *Anne* before being given to the *Stirling Castle*. Conserved at Ramsgate Maritime Museaum. *Author. After Nico Brinck*

Far right: A brass 8ft 6in saker cast by Thomas and Richard Pitt dating from 1627. It is the type of gun issued to the *Anne* for her voyage to Lisbon and the Mediterranean. *Author. After Nico Brinck*

Below: A ship's carriage from the model of a 1677 third rate in Vienna, it is of exactly the same design as the carriage in Windsor Castle. This type is seen on the upper decks of other models from the period. The dead rear trucks reduced recoil but must have caused a great deal of wear to the dead truck and deck. *Author*

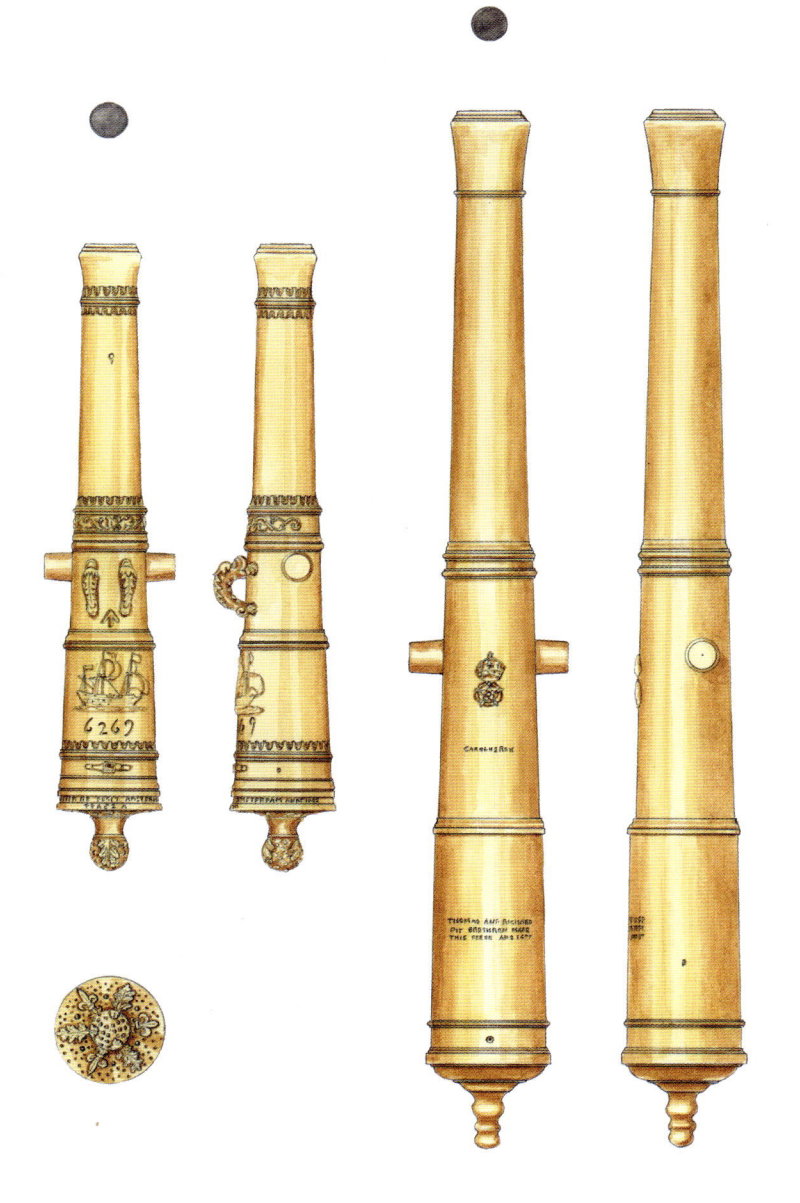

saker carriages on the quarter deck and forecastle. In the most prestigious areas they were white and veined, and the rest wainscot coloured.[26] During the evening of 23 May, 18 prestigious brass guns were brought aboard[27] and mounted on the painted carriages in the areas that would be seen by Royalty in the coach, steerage, and quarter deck. The guns came from the gun stores at Chatham where the *Anne* was still moored. As a final touch of elegance, the ordinary rope gun tackles of the brass guns were replaced with white rope. The reduced number of guns left the gun ports in the great cabin, aft on the upper deck, redundant. To improve the homeliness, glass windows were fitted.[28] At the beginning of June, the *Anne* set sail up the Medway and moored in the *Hope*, where she received 44 iron guns brought down from Woolwich Arsenal. Every one of them was greater than 30cwt indicating they must have been her demi-cannon and 12-pounders.[29] These 44 iron guns, together with the 18 brass guns, made up her establishment quota of 62 guns. Also received were 19 tons 10cwt of round shot and 310 barrels of gunpowder.[30]

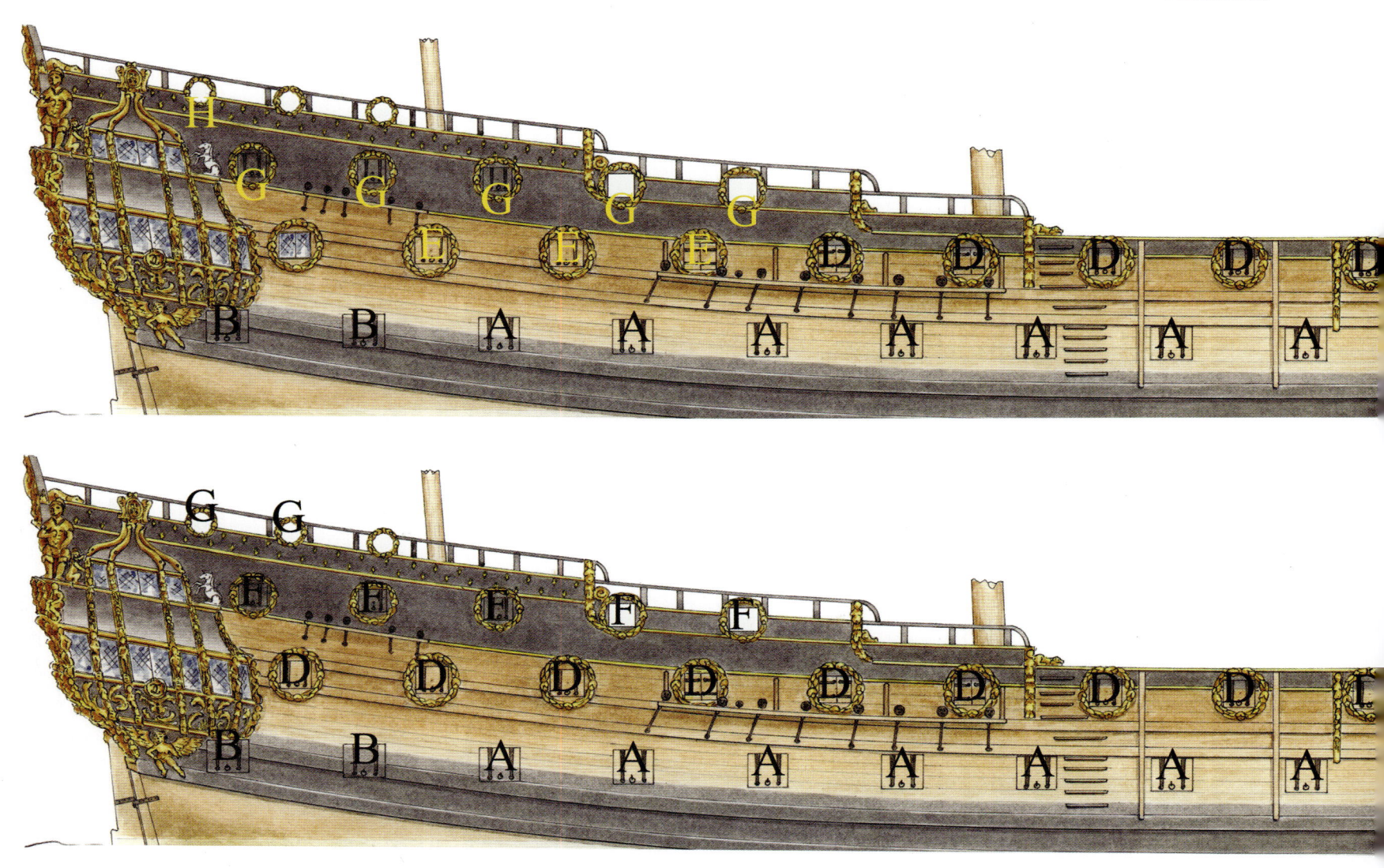

On 7 June, while the *Anne* was riding to her anchor at Blackstakes, Edward Silvester, the Master Smith, arranged for one man to work three days on some of the carriages, providing new bolts, rings, forelocks,

The Guns of the *Anne*   113

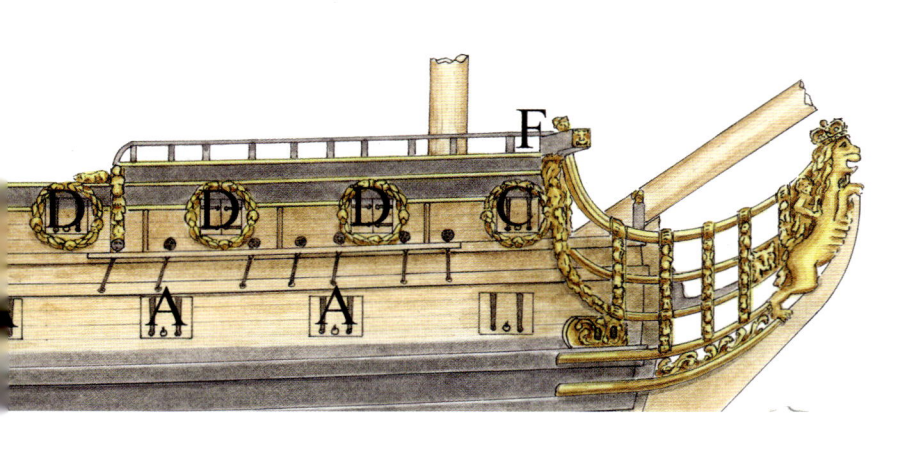

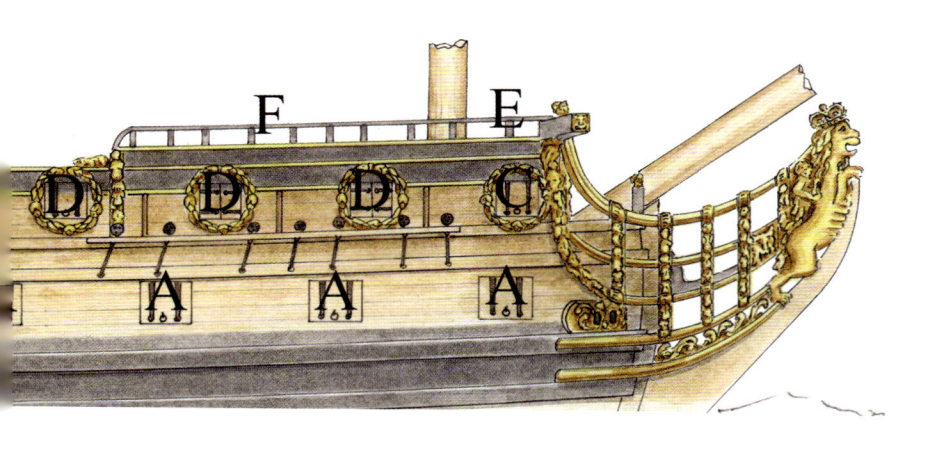

Type of gun	Guns mounted for Mediterranean cruise 1687–1688 Location	Guns mounted for Mediterranean cruise 1687–1688 Number	Guns mounted for war 1690 Location	Guns mounted for war 1690 Number
Iron demi-cannon 9½ft	A	20	A	22
Iron culverin 11ft	B	4	B	4
Iron 12-pounder 10½ft	C	2	C	2
Iron 12-pounder 9ft	D	16	D	24
Brass 12-pounder 9ft	E	6		
Iron saker 9½ft	F	2	E	2
Iron saker 7ft			F	12
Brass saker	G	10		
Iron 3-pounder 5ft			G	4
Brass 3- or 6-pounder 5ft	H	2		
Total		**62**		**70**

Top left: The location of the *Anne*'s guns at the time of her Mediterranean cruise in 1687. The black letters represent the 44 iron, and the yellow, the 18 brass guns. The yellow brass guns are all located in the cabins of the quarter deck, the round house above, and two on the poop. Two of the 11ft long chase Culverins 'B' in the gunroom aft were put down in the hold during the long voyage to the Mediterranean.

Left: The location of the *Anne*'s guns at the Battle of Beachy Head in 1690. They are according to her establishment for war and at home. The only positioning that is not absolutely certain is that of the two 7ft sakers 'F' shown on the forecastle. They may have been put at the empty ports on the poop deck to join the 3-pounders, but this is unlikely as the deck was not designed to take guns of their weight.

repairing 16 pairs of capsquares and a side bolt.[31] With a long voyage ahead, two of the chase guns, almost certainly culverins from the gunroom, were put down in the hold. This would improve sailing performance and create more space. After her ten-month cruise, the *Anne* returned to Chatham where the last guns taken off were the brass guns abaft.[32] On 5 April 1688, Nicholas Cheltenham, the Ordnance Office Storekeeper, went aboard and took an account of her stores, her remains. Then labourers were employed to lay new skids for rolling and to store the guns on after they were taken ashore. Then all the other Gunner's stores, shot and cordage was taken out, stacked and stowed ashore.[33]

Anne's guns at the Battle of Beachy Head

On 15 March 1688, as the *Anne* was sailing up the Channel on her return home, an account of all the ships in the fleets' guns and their carriages was made out by the Ordnance Board.[34] It showed that a full complement of 70 iron guns was allocated to the *Anne*, although at the time she only had her abroad complement of 62 guns, 18 of which were brass. The only ships listed as having brass guns were some of the significant first-rates. In February 1690, an account of ordnance was made for several ships at Chatham, including the *Anne*, which had been ordered to be in readiness for war. It confirmed her guns were now in accordance with the establishment, with no mention that any of them were brass. The ship worst off in the list was the *Stirling Castle*, which had no guns belonging to her at all. It was suggested that she would have to wait for some newly cast demi-cannon to be proofed as no establishment rough iron guns were available. It was even proposed she carry 24-pounders on her gun deck[35] but not willing to reduce her fire power, she was given the last demi-cannon remaining in store. These happened to be Prince Rupert's fabled and expensively produced Rupertino high-quality demi-cannon. She was also given taper bored brass 6-pounders for her poop, presumably as they must also have been the only suitable guns left in store. The rarity of such brass guns lying at Chatham make it a good possibly that her brass 6-pounders had previously served aboard the *Anne*.[36]

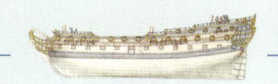

At Chatham in March 1690, as the *Anne* was being armed, Stephen Bassett of the smack *Stephen & Anne* brought her gunpowder and some hammered shot down to her from the Tower of London.[37] During the same period, a workman, John Berry, was employed drilling and clearing some of the vents of her guns which were clogged up with stones.[38] The carriages also had some minor repairs carried out to their ironwork under the instructions of Edward Silvester.[39] The *Anne* unmoored and left Chatham for the second and last time. On 19 March, she was near Gillingham when Robert Harrison, Master of the *Hopewell Hoy*, came alongside with some of her guns. More Gunner's stores were brought to her by John Kirkham, Master of the *John and James* smack[40]. The *Anne* was fully armed with 70 iron guns for war at home.

Recovery of guns

At the Battle of Beachy Head, the *Anne* was dismasted and run ashore at Pett Level between Hastings and Rye. With the French closing in she was burnt, destroying all her structure above the water. The temperature of the wood fire would not be expected to damage the guns lying in the wreckage, and efforts were soon made to recover them. Five days later, Robert Bennett, the Purveyor for the Board of Ordnance, made his way to Rye and made arrangements to save as much as possible from the *Anne*. He made two visits during 1690, the first staying until the end of July and returning again for two weeks in September.[41] During his time there he employed Robert Robinson and Robert Jefferson with nine men to save what shot they could from the wreck at low water. He also hired a boat from Jacob Hall, with two men to

A Rupertino demi-cannon salvaged from the wreck of the *Stirling Castle*. These high-quality guns were machine turned on the outside. *Author*

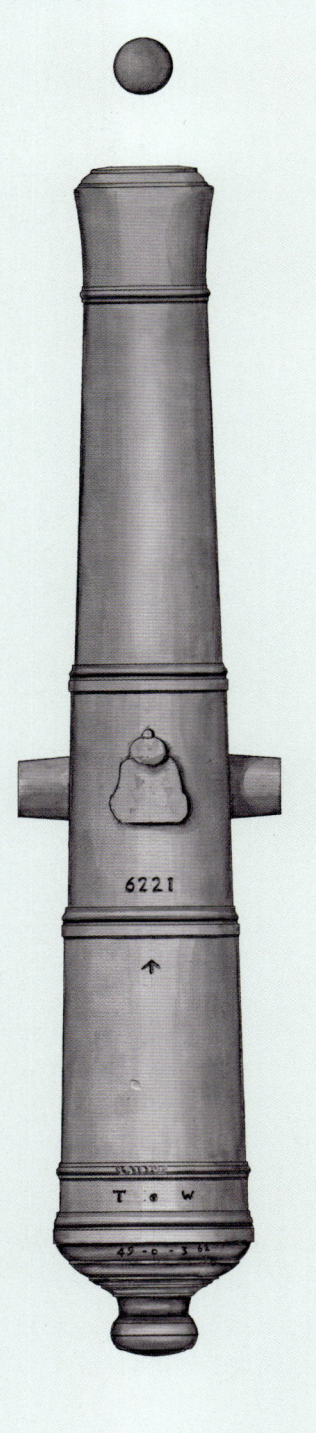

A hoy. A small one-masted fore-and aft-igged vessel with a spritsail. Often used to take stores to and from naval ships. From Thomas Blanckley, Naval Expositor 1750. Author's collection

A smack. Another transport vessel often employed by the Navy and Ordnance Board. From Thomas Blanckley, Naval Expositor 1750. Author's collection

bring the shot and other stores from the *Anne*, while the wet and dirty job of putting the shot into the boat was done by John Kirby. Once ashore, William Yeames carried some of the smaller guns and shot in wagons to Winchelsea and Rye, while John Hall's '*great boat*' was used to take stores to Winchelsea, nearly three miles away to the east in the direction of Rye. For safekeeping, Robert Browne and three men carried the recovered small arms, in the form of muskets, pistols, swords, pikes and the like, from several places into the Church Hall. Two warrant officers from the *Anne* were also involved; the first, Thomas Adams the Gunner and his men spent three days helping the Purveyor sort out the stores.[42] It must have been a particularly sad time for Adams as he had served aboard the *Anne* for many years and was responsible and knowledgeable enough to persuade the Navy to move her foremast in order to improve her sailing performance. The second, Richard Penny, the Carpenter, stayed at Rye until the end of July, helping William Yeames make a list of the goods he was holding on behalf of the Navy.

Account of goods from the *Anne* in the possession of William Yeames 30 July 1690:[43]

Anchors, 2 at Rye & 3 at the hull of the ship
One mainsail and one main topsail, one spritsail topsail
One main topsail staysail & some pieces of new sails
The main shrouds, some whole and some in pieces
A piece of the mainstay & a piece cable about 6 fathoms
A parcel of rigging in pieces
A parcel of blocks great and small
Two pieces of the main mast, ½ the main yard & two pieces of (other) yards
One barge
Iron, about twelve ton and a half
Shot lead, eighty six pound
Two copper furnaces and two copper kettles & a copper funnel weighing six hundredweight & two quarters
Iron bound dead eyes, three
Futtock plates, eight and ¼ of a back of leather
Boats pintles & gudgeons, six pair
Chain plates five, nails as small and great one cwt, one qtr, fifteen Lbs

The relatively small sums of money involved in these early recovery operations make it unlikely that any of the 2½-ton demi-cannon or 1½-ton 12-pounders were removed from the wreck. All the same, what ordnance that had been brought ashore now needed bringing back to London. To do this, William Reed of the *Charity Hoy* was paid seven pounds, at a-rate of ten shillings a ton for bringing guns, round shot and small arms from Rye Harbour to Woolwich and the Tower.[44] At London on 1 August, a John Packman was paid for moving four of the *Anne*'s guns from the '*crane*'. These guns were all under 1½ tons, suggesting they were probably *Anne*'s sakers or 3-pounders.[45] The official recovery operation would seem to have ended during October, as the cold weather closed in.

This did not seem to affect the local '*country people*' who, it was reported, '*do take all opportunity of pulling her to pieces and carrying away what may be of any use or value to them*'. Rather than employ people themselves to break up the *Anne* to recover worthwhile timbers, the Navy Board wrote to the Admiralty saying they thought it better to sell the wreck to someone else. They could save the heavy timbers: '*such as futtocks, floor timbers, floor riders, keel and keelson pieces, thick stuff and four inch plank not cleft or defaced by fire and to deliver the same into their Majesties stores at Chatham and Portsmouth as we shall direct at 40 pence per load*'.

They treated with a shipwright, Joseph Bingham, who employed himself in such affairs and offered to let him have her for £20[46]. The transaction does not seem to have happened, as most of the timbers mentioned in the proposal remain in the ship to this day and no record has been found to show an agreement was completed. Later Ordnance Office bills show he would be paid for saving guns still '*belonging to their Majesties*'.[47] Bingham's will of 1709 also makes no mention of the *Anne*.[48] He continued his business and records do show that he was the supplier of a good quantity of timber to Plymouth Dockyard in 1698[49] and that in later life he lived in Plymouth with his wife, Ann, and four children.[50] After 1690, the Navy seems to have had no further interest in the wreck, although she remained the property of the Crown.

The sale of the *Anne* to Bingham for £20 may well have collapsed because most of her guns were still within her remains and must have been worth about £2,000.[51] They belonged to the Ordnance Board and although the Navy lost interest, the Ordnance Board certainly did not. They soon made arrangements with the handy Joseph Bingham to recover the guns during the following summer. He mounted a serious and professional operation, first laying skids to roll the guns up the beach, then hiring teams of horses to pull them. A log resting alongside the port bow today may be part of Bingham's skid. He also bought new cordage and built a shed necessary to store his equipment and provide for the men.[52] A contract for the work was signed by him on 9 June 1691, in which it was agreed he would receive 50 shillings for every ton of guns recovered, once certified by the Mayor of Winchelsea. On one occasion he recovered nine guns weighing in total 23 tons 6 cwt, this makes the average weight of each gun 51¾ cwt. That is about the weight of each 9½ft long demi-cannon.[53]

Although the heat of the fire could not reach the melting point of iron, it may have caused some distortion, especially if the guns had fallen some distance and perhaps hit each other as the *Anne* collapsed. With the recovery operation successfully underway, it was decided to proof test the guns at Winchelsea. The ways for land carriage were mended in five days by eight men allowing an initial 15 guns to be transported. They were followed ,by a further 27 tons of ordnance, which was moved from the wreck site to Winchelsea by Richard Thomas and John Chrenlow.[54] George Potter, Master of the *Bachelors Hoy*, brought the necessary gunner's stores for proof testing down from the Tower of London to Rye.[55] The shot and powder was brought the final two miles from Rye to Winchelsea by William Beats in his boat, while a wagon was hired to move stores and hay for wadding from the quay at Winchelsea. The proof loading and firing was carried out by Captain Tokey's men under the direction of Ordnance Officers, Silvester and Hooper, helped by Thomas Punnett, a blacksmith.[56] Tents for the men to stay in, along with their equipment, were brought to the site from Tunbridge by John Slade, the Board's Labourer, who stayed on site to help prove the guns.[57] On its return to the Thames, the *Bachelors Hoy* took the gunner's stores and small arms to the Tower and the *Anne*'s proved ordnance to Woolwich.[58] The re-proved guns would have entered the lists of spare guns waiting to be issued to other ships. There seems to be no surviving record of any guns failing the proof testing at Winchelsea, but if any large guns were condemned, they would probably have been sent back to gun founders for re-casting.

In April 2009, a gun was seen at the Winchelsea Museum by Jacqui Stanford, Winchelsea Beach resident, Director of the Shipwreck Museum, Hastings, and appointed Licensee of the *Anne*. The Shipwreck Museum has a particular interest as it is now the owner of the ship. As the gun was clearly very old and reportedly found locally, she brought it to the attention of historians interested in the ship. In March 2010 it was examined by the independent gun expert, Charles Trollope, who identified the gun as an iron saker dating from about the middle of the seventeenth century. It is 77in long with the remains of an 'F' cast on the end of the right trunnion identifying it as being cast by the Finspong Foundry in Sweden and given the generic name *Finbankers*. They were suppliers of guns to the Dutch fleet. He found no other visible markings and added that guns of the type were of good quality. When they were captured from the Dutch they were reamed out to English bore sizes, proof tested and issued to English ships. The button is missing at the rear and the outside surface shows evidence that it had been buried upright at a depth of about five feet. Some groves are visible in the bore, suggesting an iron spike had been inserted so that it would act as a fulcrum for a pivot gun. This suggests it was part of a traversing platform in a battery and may have been part of the canal defence system introduced in the 1790s. Charles also observed that a possible site for the gun would have been the battery constructed in the 1790s at Winchelsea Beach where Rye New Harbour used to reach the sea. When the battery was constructed, it was the local engineer's responsibility to find a solid pivot for the guns. In all likelihood he used an old gun that had failed proof testing at Winchelsea 100 years before. With the completion of the Royal Military Canal and Martello Towers, it would have been redundant and removed by the landowners in about 1840.

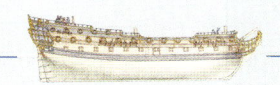

Although the gun is not exactly the length given in the *Anne*'s 1690 gun list, it is certainly near enough to qualify as one of her 12 seven-foot long Sakers. The button may have been lost in 1690 and was the reason for its rejection or may possibly have been removed at the time the battery was constructed. Although it is not possible to say with certainty, there is no reason why it should not have come from the *Anne*.

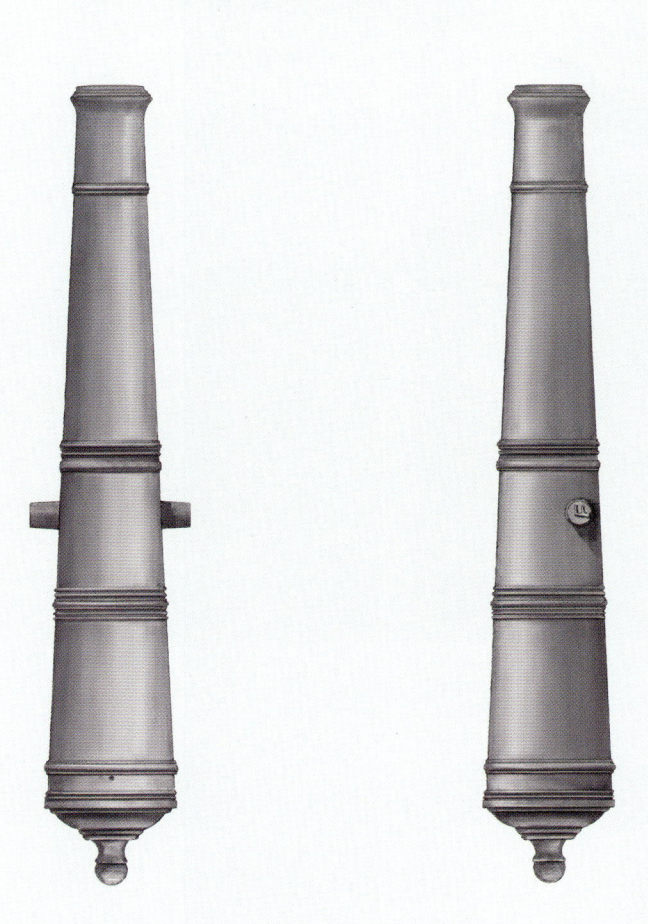

The saker that probably served on the *Anne* in 1690 at the Battle of Beachy Head. It is shown in the condition it would have been when in operational service. The gun is conserved today at Winchelsea Museum. *Author*

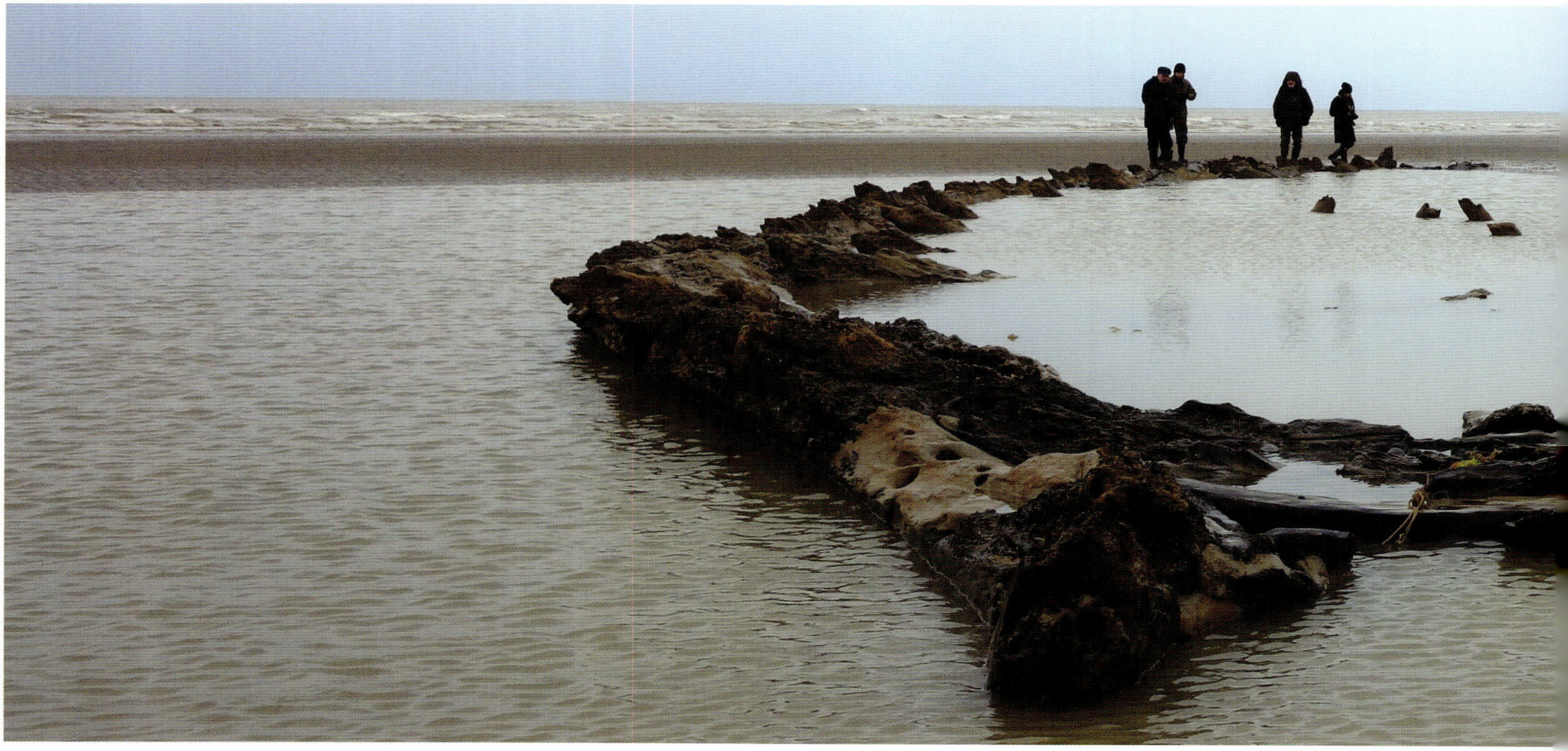

Chapter: 7 The *Anne* today

The extent of the remains of the *Anne*. Author

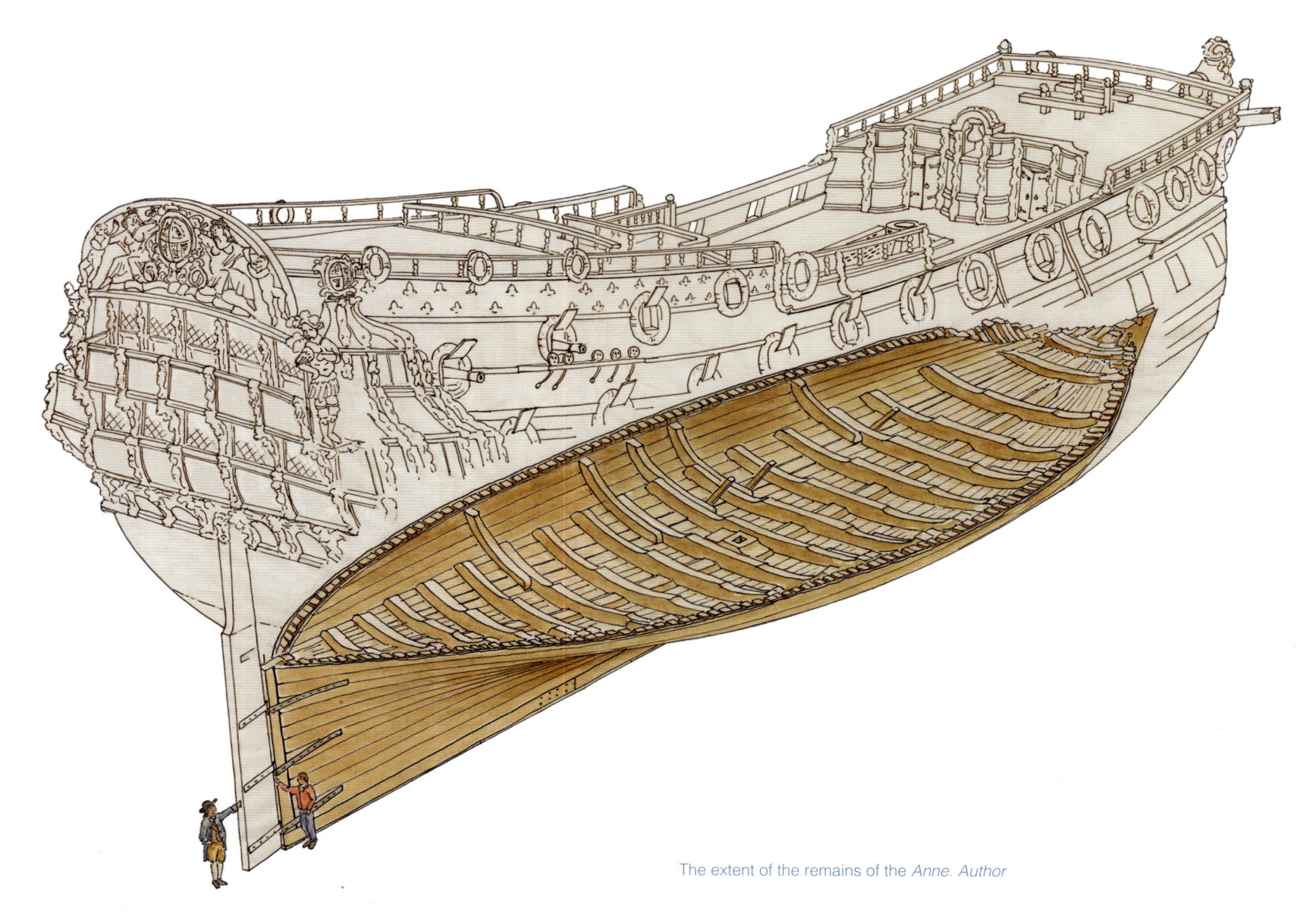

The environment since 1690

The nearest landmark when looking for the *Anne* today is the Smuggler's Inn Pub, a few miles to the east of Hastings at Pett Level. The name 'Pett' is familiar to those interested in the *Anne*, but it is just a coincidence that the ship built by Phineas Pett should end up at Pett Level. From the Smuggler's Inn Pub car park, travel 600 yards eastward along the road in the direction of Rye. Walk up the steps to the top of the modern sea wall where an information board about the ship will be found. From there the *Anne* lies directly out to sea, about 250 yards out from the normal high tide mark. The exact position was recorded in 2008 by Louise Martin of Historic England, who gave the GPS position to the centre of her survey as 589709.046, 113636.344 on the OS grid.[1] The *Anne* site is only exposed a few times a year at very low tides. The uppermost timbers lie about 1ft 7in (0.5m) above the Admiralty tide tables datum. Low water springs reach as low as 4in (0.1m) above the datum, leaving her above water for about three hours, depending a great deal on the strength and direction of the wind. There is always a minimum of 16ft (5m) of water above the *Anne* at high tide. Typically, there are about 20 days each year when the site is above water, but about half of these occur during winter when the exposed beach is very cold indeed. Of those remaining days, when it is comfortable enough for a visit, the low tides often occur when it is too dark to see. Roughly speaking that leaves only six or seven days each year when a casual visit to the *Anne* is worthwhile. Usually two low tides follow one another at dawn and dusk.

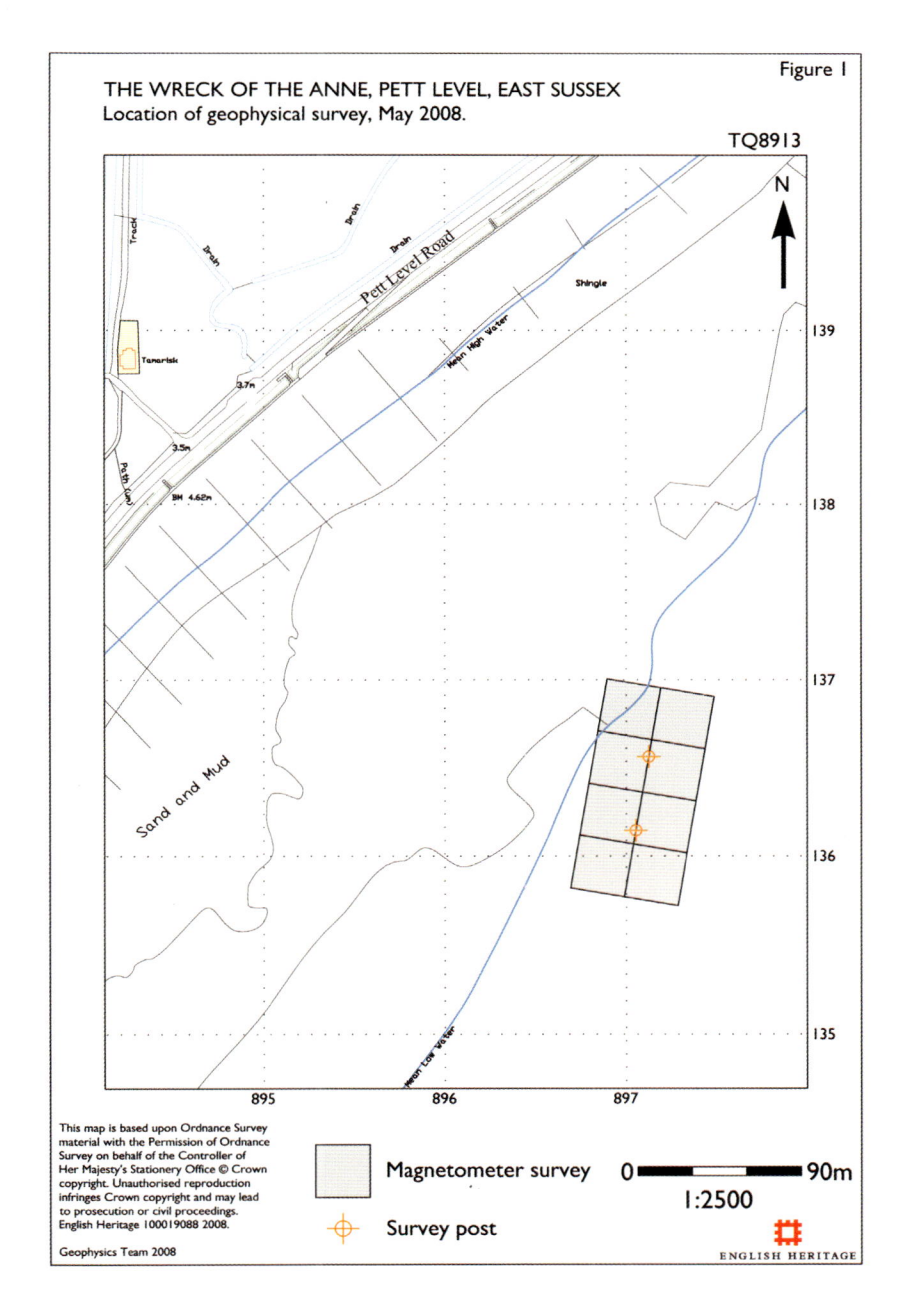

The plan made by Louise Martin of English Heritage, now Historic England, showing the precise position of the *Anne*. The yellow survey posts are those set at each end of the ship as an aid to recording her profile. *Many thanks to Historic England Geophysics Team*

The beach at Pett Level in December 2005 looking toward the wreck site from the top of the sea wall at a very low tide. In the foreground is the gravel sea wall, followed by the prehistoric remains of a forest, and furthest away is the unstable beach. The archaeologist Robert Peacock of the Seadive Organisation is seen in the distance, standing next to the *Anne*. Author

The Anne looking from the bow toward the stern. After a number of years of being completely covered by sand, she was exposed on 29 March 2013 down to the clay level. The sand bank just past the ship on the seaward side is holding back the tide and stopping the site completely draining. Author

The *Anne* is embedded in stable grey estuarine clay of unknown depth with her uppermost timbers projecting about 2ft (0.7m) above. The clay is usually covered by over 3ft (1m) of mobile sand, leaving the *Anne* under beach level and protected from wave and marine organism damage most of the time. Sometimes the sand is partially replaced by very soft mud that is extremely dangerous to enter. Just inshore of the site, the clays are overlaid by ancient freshwater peat and numerous birch and alder tree stumps, trunks and branches that were long ago drowned by rising sea levels. They have been dated by carbon-14 to 3,200–3,300 BC. The remains of the trees that once grew in a swampy wooded landscape at the start of the Bronze Age are interesting in themselves and well worth seeing. Further up, the beach becomes gravel and very steep to form part of the modern sea wall that protects the low-lying marshland beyond.[2]

The sand covering the clay substrate is mobile and affected by the weather. Moderate wind and wave direction from the south and west gradually moves the sand along the beach at low tide. Winter gales seem to form sand banks and depressions which lie parallel to the beach. These sand banks gradually move up the beach and sometimes cover the wreck site by about 2ft (0.7m) and sometimes form a trough leaving the timbers exposed. The *Navy* issue for December 1930 reported the wreck was exposed in 1902 as well as 1930.[3] Once in a while, winter gales strip the site down to the clay levels. It is probable these gales come from the opposite or easterly direction. In 1913 and again in 2013, the sand was completely stripped away, but just how many times this occurred in the intervening 100 years is unknown. In 2013, a sandbank on the seaward side held back the tide so that the timbers remained under water for most of their height.

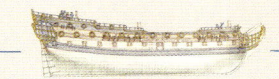

Archaeology

The *Anne* lies where she ran aground in 1690 with her bow facing almost directly due north. As far as anyone living in the area can remember and without any historical research, the wreck has always been known as the *Anne*. It is very likely that local knowledge has been passed down through the ages by word of mouth. In 1847, W. Holloway wrote in the *History and Antiquities of the Town of Rye*, '*Anne, a small ship of war carrying brass guns … was afterwards sunk on the shore near Pett Horse Race where, at low water, it is said part of her wreck is still visible.*'[4] Another notable recording of the ship occurred in 1913, when

A photograph of the *Anne* taken in 1913. It has been enhanced and colour added by the author. Inset is a photograph made during the 1997 archaeological survey. A large transverse internal timber, a rider, can be seen in both images. They show a slightly lighter area of concretion around the in and out iron bolt that secures it to the ship's frame. This is indicated by a white arrow in both views. Erosion can be seen to have taken place to the top of some of the frame timbers, causing a certain amount of smoothing to the upper edges. *Anonymous photographer. Copy with the Warship Anne Trust*

the weather had exposed the site at a fortunate time when no significant sand bank to seaward stopped the water draining away. Taking advantage of the conditions, an unknown photographer took a beautiful picture of her.

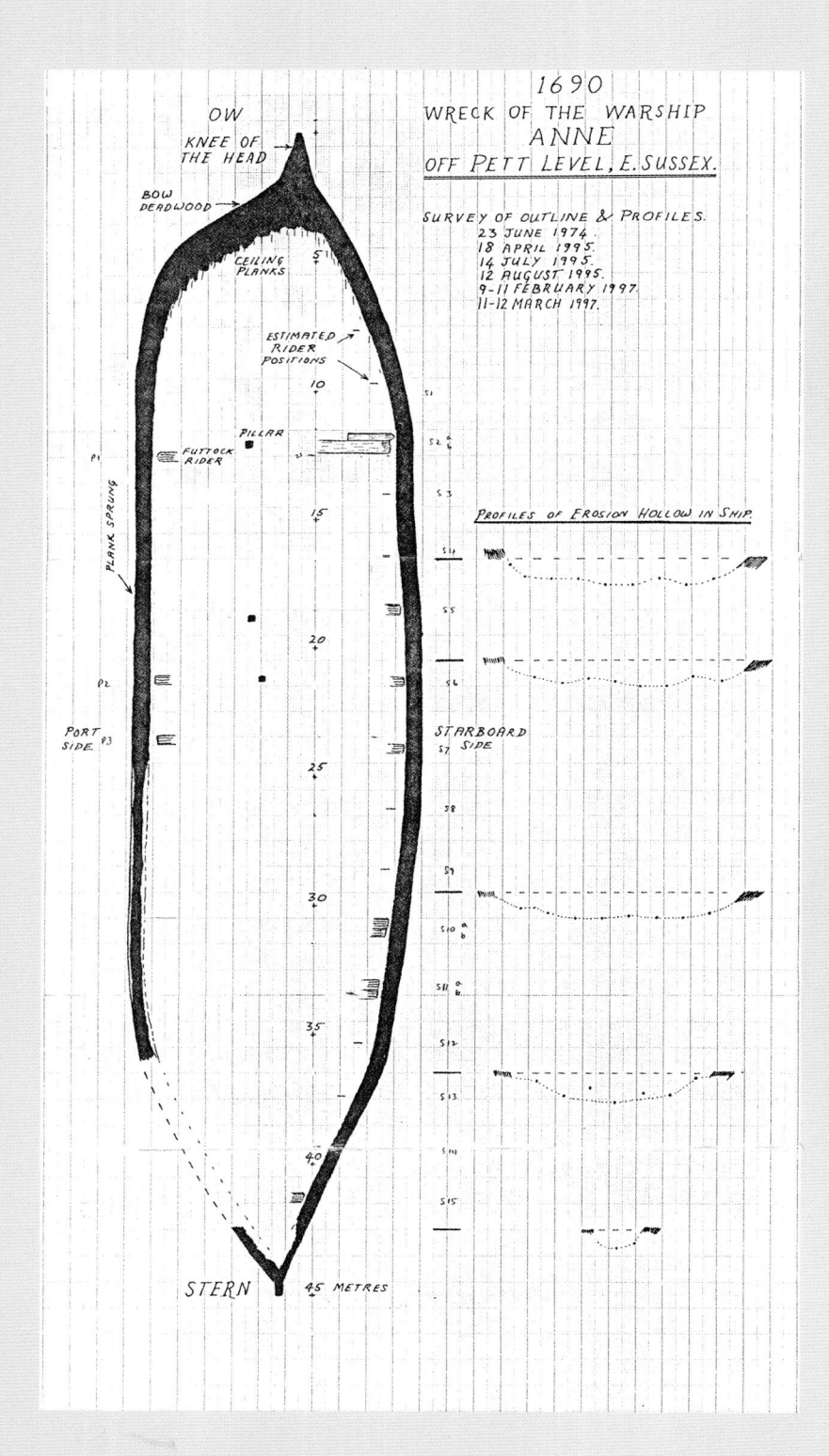

The next significant event in the ship's history occurred in April 1974 when some locals, taking a cue from their ancestors, the '*country people*' of 1690, took a mechanical digger down to the beach at low tide and excavated inside the hull. An unknown amount of damage was done, it was even reported that the bottoms of three masts were pulled out. This cannot be reconciled with the photograph taken earlier in 1913, which shows no evidence of masts. It was also claimed that many artefacts were found and taken away. Concerned local residents reported the activity to their local archaeologist, Dr Peter Marsden. Aware of Parliament passing the Protection of Wrecks Act a year earlier, he applied for a temporary protection order from the Department of Trade and Industry. The designation order was permanently confirmed on 20 June 1974. The artefacts reportedly taken away by local people include iron cannon balls, grenades, lead musket balls, fragments of wooden barrels, clay pipes, a spoon and a pewter plate. They allowed their finds to be retrieved, and handed over the cannon balls, grenades, one musket ball and fragments of wooden barrels. These went to Portsmouth Museum for conservation on behalf of the Receiver of Wrecks. Once in the possession of archaeologists, the finds were examined and recorded. The cannon balls included two of 6in diameter from the 32-pounder demi-cannon, two of 5in diameter from the 18-pounder culverins, seven of up to 4.4in diameter from the 12-pounders, including one with a broad arrow, and three of about 2in diameter, which must be bace and bur, (later known as grape shot) for the 12-pounders. In spite of the admirable work done by Peter Marsden, the artefacts have now gone missing. He wrote that they were deposited in Hastings Museum[5] but they are not acknowledged by anyone there today. Artefacts handed over by members of the public for the benefit of history and safekeeping must be able to rest assured their finds do not get mislaid, lost or stolen. They must be taken care of in safe storage even if they are not on display in a museum.

The site plan of the *Anne* made by Peter Marsden. The asymmetric appearance of the hull between port and starboard is caused by the ship heeling over to port. *Warship Anne Trust*

The *Anne* today   125

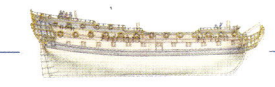

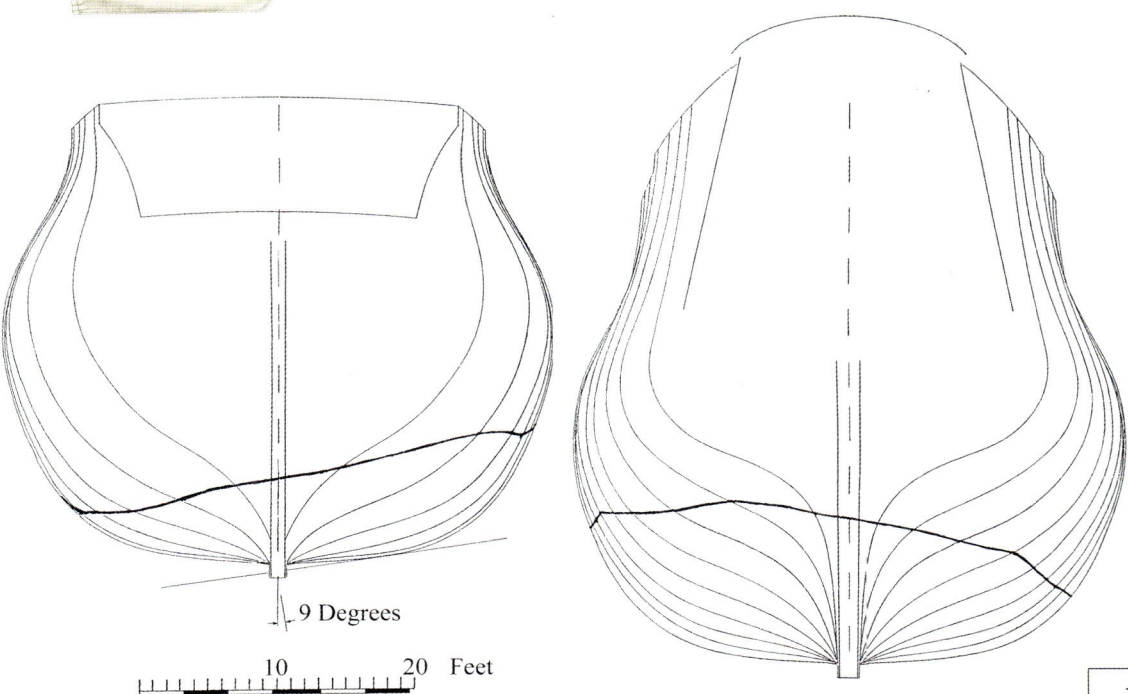

The estimated surviving remains of the *Anne*'s hull. A great deal is known about the missing, lighter structure above, both how it was built and its size. All the heavy and important timbers that are only partly understood by historians and archaeologists today have yet to be excavated. *Author*

Apart from the amateur attempt with a digger, only limited archaeological work has been done on the ship. Dr Marsden made a preliminary site plan in June 1974 even though he was hampered by a sandbank covering the seaward end of the wreck, which not only covered much of the structure, but kept the site under water. Over the next 23 years, as site conditions permitted, further surveys of the *Anne*'s profile were made, enabling the site plan to be gradually refined. This was principally carried out using an artificial axis as a baseline fixed between two survey posts, one at each end of the wreck. Perpendicular offsets were then taken from the axis at known distances along its length. Early on it was thought the asymmetric profile in the sand was caused by the port side collapsing outward. Following research into the hull shape of the *Anne*, the site plan was reconciled with it. A comparison was made with the reconstructed hull profile and a horizontal flat plane taken at the top of the wreck. A near-perfect fit was made with the ship heeling over to port by nine degrees and intersecting the stern at 13ft (4m) up from the bottom of the keel and 8ft (2.4m) at the bow. Knowing that such a significant and articulated part of the ship survives, a regular watch has been maintained over the years, including a limited excavation on the port inner side in 1997. It is interesting as the area revealed is also shown in the 1913 photograph.

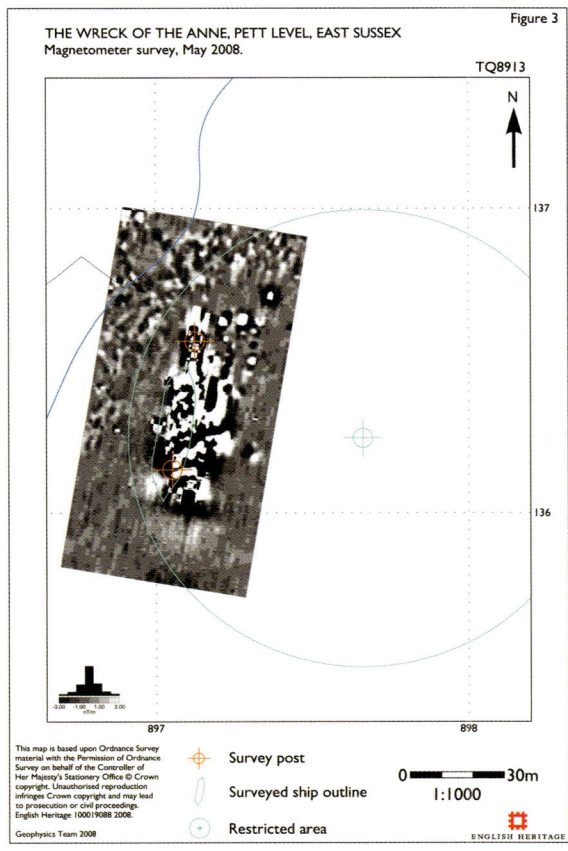

The results of the magnetometer survey carried out by Louise Martin. *Many thanks to Historic England Geophysics Team*

On 6 May 2008, a magnetometer survey was carried out by Louise Martin of English Heritage[6] which revealed a distinct area of strong ferrous response defining the extent of the remains of the ship. This response is more than would be expected for a wooden ship. It may have been caused by the burning process, but more likely it indicates there is still a considerable amount of iron in and around the wreck.

The status of the *Anne* today

Concerned by the vulnerability of shipwrecks and in particular a fifteenth-century sailing barge found at Blackfriars, Peter Marsden founded a charitable trust with the intention to preserve her and other wrecks. This was the Nautical Museums Trust incorporated by the Registrar of Companies on 19 April 1982 and subsequently registered with the Charity Commission. The first Chairman was Cranley Onslow MP, a descendent of '*Stiff Dick*' Sir Richard Onslow, a Lord of the Admiralty at the time the *Anne* was lost. A major objective in the memorandum of association was to advance the education of the public in nautical history and archaeology by the provision of a museum. With considerable awareness, Peter Marsden observed that there was little use for the *Anne* in the modern Navy to which she still belonged. He therefore negotiated a deed of transfer between the Ministry of State for Defence and the Nautical Museums' Trust. This was completed on 10 June 1983, when the ship was transferred to a subsidiary trust, the Warship Anne Trust.

A museum was required and the Trust was fortunate that Hastings Borough Council offered the Victorian stables in Rock-a-Nore Road, in the historic Old Town of Hastings alongside the shoreline. The building was originally used to house the horses that powered the winches used to haul fishing boats up the beach. They gave the Trust a 60-year lease and some money for its conversion into a museum. As part of the agreement it remains open every day from Easter to October and at weekends in November and December. The Shipwreck Museum, at that time called the Shipwreck Heritage Centre, was opened by Lord Montagu of Beaulieu on 29 July 1986. Being a charity, it pays no rent or business rate. As of 2016 the museum is able to offer free access to the public, maintained by the income of the museum's nautical gift shop. Artefacts and images of the *Anne* are on display at the museum.

In 1993, a project was started by the Trust with the intention of recovering the *Anne* and placing her in a dedicated new museum where her story could be told. To avoid the enormous cost and many years it took to conserve and dry out the *Mary Rose*, it was proposed to keep the *Anne* in a pool of water that would also act as a training centre for amateur divers. The proposed new museum complex was to be located at the West St Leonards bathing pool site and would also have areas dedicated to related subjects, such as life aboard the *Anne*, how she was built and the Navy of Charles II and Samuel Pepys. A meeting was convened in 1995 at the National Maritime Museum, attended by maritime and heritage consultants who agreed the *Anne* was of such historic importance, and in such good condition, that she should be preserved if technically and financially feasible. The plan put forward by the Trust would have been of benefit to tourism in Hastings as well as preserving

The *Anne* during filming of the television series *Empire of the Seas*. The presenter, Dan Snow, is shown at the site, which remained completely covered by sand. *Author*

the ship. In spite of the advantages, the project depended on funding from the Heritage Lottery Fund, who in 1998 decided not to support it. Without the necessary funds the project had to be cancelled.

The Trust continues to support and promote the *Anne*. Her Majesty the Queen visited the museum on 6 June 1997 and expressed her interest in the ship. The presenter, Dan Snow, filmed at the site in 2009 for his television series, *Empire of the Seas*. Events are occasionally held including a day-long programme of talks in 2015 given by seventeenth-century naval historians. The current licensee appointed to look after the ship by Historic England is the Museum Director, Jacqui Stanford, and her appointed archaeologist is Robert Peacock. The information board located at the top of the sea defences near the *Anne*, was erected by the Trust, Historic England and the Environment Agency. In 2014, a virtual model of the ship was produced at Birmingham University by two French students, Emilien Bonhomme and Cécile Thevenin, under the tutelage of Professor Robert Stone. A solid model of the *Anne* is also under construction by Phil Reed, the well-known model maker. It still remains the long-term ambition to raise the ship for the benefit of the nation. In the meantime the Warship Anne Trust retains close association with other bodies who have close ties with *Anne*'s sister ships, the *Stirling Castle* wrecked on the Goodwin Sands and a project to build a replica *Lenox* at Deptford.

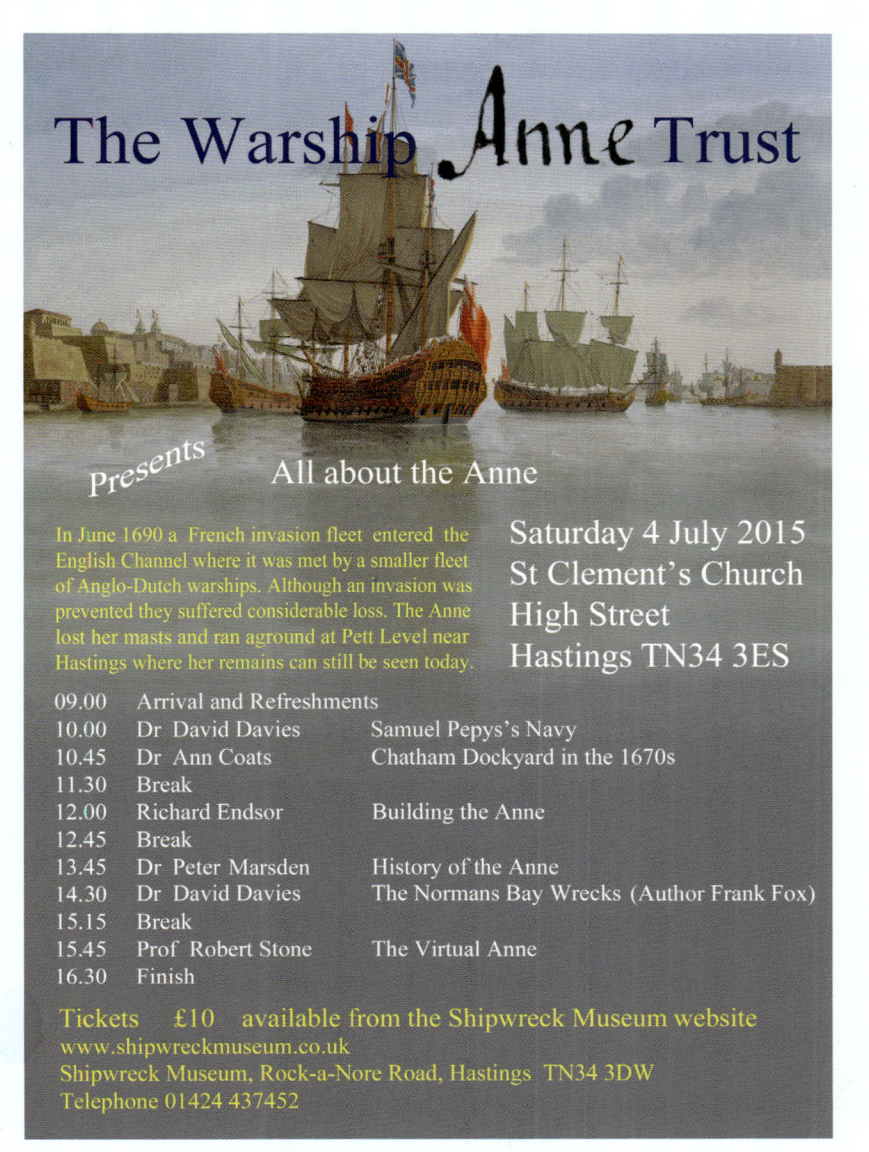

Examination of the wreck

The whole of the lower hull of the *Anne*, where all the heavy timbers are situated, appears to have survived intact. They are the only known substantial and unaltered remains of a warship from the Restoration period. The complex construction in the surviving hull is that part least understood and could answer many questions about how ships of the period were built. The missing structure above, the upper frames, planking and decks are much less complex and very well described in literature and models. All the other ships of the period that have been discovered are far less complete, with their structures largely disarticulated.

Keel

One of the interesting features of the *Anne*, much talked about by Phineas Pett when he built her, is the question of whether he really used five pieces of elm rather than four, as all the other shipwrights had when they built their ships. He told the Navy Board it was '*in so many pieces, being five in number which I could most heartily have wished might have been in four*', but did he? Earlier he had also suggested using oak, then beech, and it may be that on reading his letter the Navy Board found a way of getting four longer pieces of elm for him to make the keel. We will not know until the keel is seen again for the first time in hundreds of years.

The programme for a series of talks about the Anne held in 2015. Author

Frame timbers

The average spacing of the frame timbers, the space and room, was measured at a little over 27in in line with the official scantling list and in agreement with the Vienna model. It is also in accord with Pett saying the *Anne* had 61 frames. The master frames, the frame bends, which were made up before being placed in the ship, can also be seen. They are identified as two timbers placed tightly together and are the only timbers joined together with fore and aft treenails. The *Anne* is particularly important as she had not been rebuilt or undergone extensive repairs that would affect the arrangement of her frames.

A section of the frame of the *Anne* viewed from the inside looking out. The nearest horizontal timber is the footwaling. The two vertical timbers fitting closely together are part of a frame bend consisting of a first and second futtock. They were joined together by fore and aft treenails before being placed in the ship. One of them is exposed at the top of the surviving timbers. The in-and-out treenails can be seen in all the futtocks to secure the planking to the frames. Notice the greater gaps between the other fill-in futtocks. *Author*

Footwaling

The internal fore and aft planking, treenailed against the frames to strengthen the structure, appears to be in accordance with contemporary scantling lists for the 30 new ships. What little that has been recorded

A section of the internal footwaling showing the rough scarph joint partially exposed during the 1997 excavation. To the right is the foremost rider on the port side and is the same one seen in the 1913 photograph. The light brown patch is the concretion over the head of an iron bolt that secured the rider to the frames and is also just visible on the early photograph. *Author*

during the limited archaeological work in 1997 shows that a 2ft long scarph was used in places.

A number of timbers are on display in the yard of Winchelsea Museum, reputedly from the warship *Anne* wreck. The smaller pieces are difficult to interpret although one sharply curved piece is probably part of a knee. The largest piece, measuring 5ft 9in long and 14in by 5in in section, is more easily identified. It is almost certainly a timber known as a clamp. Clamps ran in the fore and aft direction and were recessed to secure the beams that rested on them. The position of a recess is clearly visible in the clamp fragment. Many treenail holes of about 1¼in diameter show how it was once fastened to the ship's frames and the outside planking. The piece of clamp is of a size suggesting it may have come from the forward end of the orlop, where the nominal size of 16in by 7in in midships had been reduced through the tapering of the ship to 14in by 5in. The profile of the piece is a neat match, although the angle of the beam slot may not be great enough for the shape of the ship at this point. It was also situated at a level in the ship just above the existing structure and may have become detached sometime in the past. The size of the timber also matches the size of clamps and the beams for the upper deck, and it may possibly have belonged there.

Timbers at Winchelsea Museum which reputedly come from the *Anne*. One appears to be part of a small knee but the largest piece has all the attributes for being part of a clamp on which the beams laid. *Author*

It would be helpful to accurately record the timber and enquiries made to establish its provenance. It would also be beneficial to establish the age of the timber by either dendrochronology or carbon-14 dating. If it can be established that the timber came from the *Anne*, it would be of great importance, as the area in the ship it came from no longer exists. In view of the timber's potential importance, it should be moved from its present position of exposure to the weather and preserved indoors.

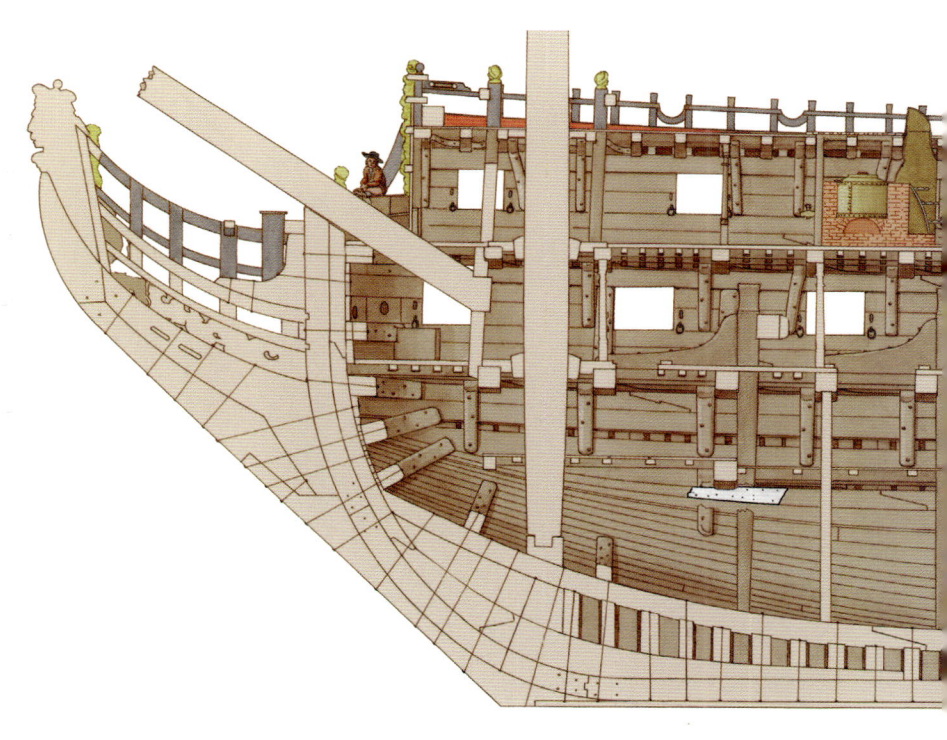

Although speculative, this timber would fit perfectly as part of the orlop clamp or middlebands as they were generally known. Shown here in light grey. *Author*

Riders

The floor riders, large transverse internal strengthening timbers that cross the centre of the ship, were measured by Peter Marsden as 18in the fore and aft direction, precisely in agreement with the official scantling list for the 30 new ships. Above them, the futtock riders seem more numerous and smaller than anticipated. Large timber was much more difficult for Pett to find than smaller pieces. He appears to have come up with an innovative solution in using smaller but more numerous pieces to make up the strength. The *Berwick*, sister ship of the *Anne*, is known to have had three smaller main wales each side rather than the almost universal two large wales.[7] Some of the riders now appear a little detached from the footwaling.

Cross pillars

The tops of a number of cross pillars can be seen standing up inside the wreck. They are intended to brace the hull against distortion when the ship was beached so the outside of the hull could be cleaned of weed. Three of them are visible, but probably the remains of more are buried. They are of tremendous importance in reconstructing the *Anne* as they establish the position of the gun deck beams above to which they were bolted. Knowing there was always one beam under each gun port and one between, it is possible to determine the position of the gun ports, both on the gun deck and the upper deck. The position of the riders is also associated with the cross pillars, and gun deck beams. With very precise recording of these features it is possible to accurately reconstruct the *Anne* from her surviving structure.

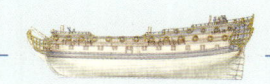

A view on the port bow from the outside looking inward. The horizontal outside planking lying beneath the eroded oak frame timbers appears to be beech, or possibly elm. It is in much better condition than the oak frame.

Planking

Most of the outside planking of the *Anne* is four-inch thick oak, as expected, and appears in very good condition. Near the bow some of the lower strakes of planking are visible and they are beech or elm. This is encouraging, as these third-rate ships were allowed to be planked with elm, oak or beech for 10ft up from the keel.[8] It confirms that the substantial amount of the ship remains.

Stern post

The stern post was visible for a short space of time in 1997 and again in 2013. At first appearance, it seems the largest wide piece of timber to the fore is the sternpost, with the two elements of the rudder extending aft from it. This is not the case as the wide timber is too small fore and aft. It is in fact the sternpost within while the next, considerably eroded element aft of it is the main sternpost and the third element aft of that is the false sternpost without. There is evidence of material between the last two elements that may be lead sheet. Mention of the false sternpost without is almost non-existent in contemporary records but appears in a building report for the *Lenox*, a sister built at the same time as the *Anne*, in which it mentions '*false sternpost fayed*' when the ship was almost completed. It is also mentioned by William Sutherland in his *Ship Building Unveiled 1717 Part 1*, p.76. The sternpost appears to be leaning over a little more to port than the nine degrees estimated for the main part of the hull.

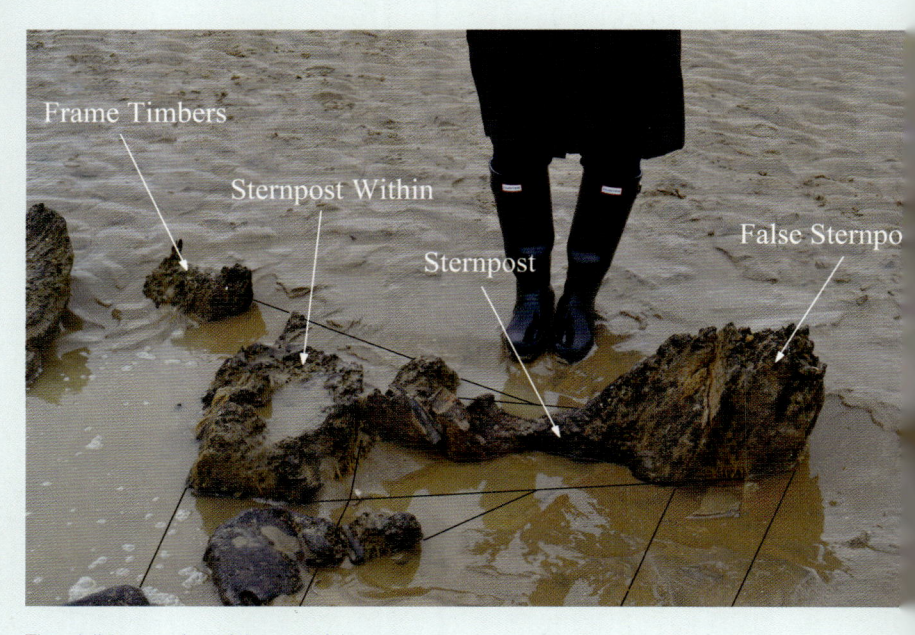

The visible remains of the top of the stern post.

Stem

The stem itself is difficult to identify amongst the complex of timbers at the bow. The knee of the head projecting forward would be in agreement with estimates for the depth of surviving structure.

These observations of the wreck are based on the extremely limited recording so far made of the *Anne*. At the moment, seventeenth-century shipbuilding practice, midway between the *Mary Rose* and the *Victory*, is not fully understood. The method of building the frames during this period has been interpreted in many ways. When the *Anne* has been fully examined, much valuable understanding of how ships were designed and the practical skills needed to build them, will be revealed to history. As an artefact, the *Anne* would be an incredible sight, revealing the immense size of the timbers in her lower regions. The uniqueness and historical importance of the ship would surely make her a major attraction should she ever be excavated and conserved. In the meantime she should be 3D-scanned at the earliest opportunity so that the missing structure can be recreated.

The *Anne* and Historic England (formerly English Heritage)

Historic England is the Government's advisor on all aspects of the historic environment in England. One of their statutory functions is to advise on the protection and management of shipwrecks in English territorial waters designated under the Protection of Wrecks Act 1973. The Act allows the Secretary of State to designate a restricted area around a wreck to prevent uncontrolled interference. These protected areas are likely to contain the remains of a vessel, or its contents, which are of historical, artistic or archaeological importance. To date (October 2015) 49 shipwrecks in England have legal status under the Protection of Wrecks Act 1973. Their policy regarding the *Anne* is:

Policy 1
Historic England will continue to support and develop authorised access to the site as a mechanism to develop the instrumental value of the *Anne*.

Policy 2
Through liaison with the Nautical Museums Trust, Historic England will support and develop authorised access for surface recovery of vulnerable artefacts as part of an agreed project plan.

Policy 3
Through web-based initiatives and publication, Historic England will continue to improve the accessibility of related material and support appropriate links so as to develop public understanding.

Policy 4
Historic England will work with the Nautical Museums Trust to publish previous investigations on the site.

Policy 5
Historic England will seek to develop a programme of environmental monitoring of the *Anne*.

Policy 6
Through liaison with the appropriate authorities, Historic England will seek to stabilise and afford preservation in situ where necessary.

Policy 7
Unless a clear and agreed research framework has been devised, unnecessary disturbance of the seabed within the restricted area should be avoided wherever possible in order to minimise the risk of damage to buried archaeological remains.

To access the site a licence is required under the Protection of Wrecks Act 1973. You can find out more about this at:
https://historicengland.org.uk/listing/what-is-designation/protected-wreck-sites/

Find out more about the *Anne* designation at:
http://www.historicengland.org.uk/listing/the-list/list-entry/1000060

Many thanks to Alison James of Historic England

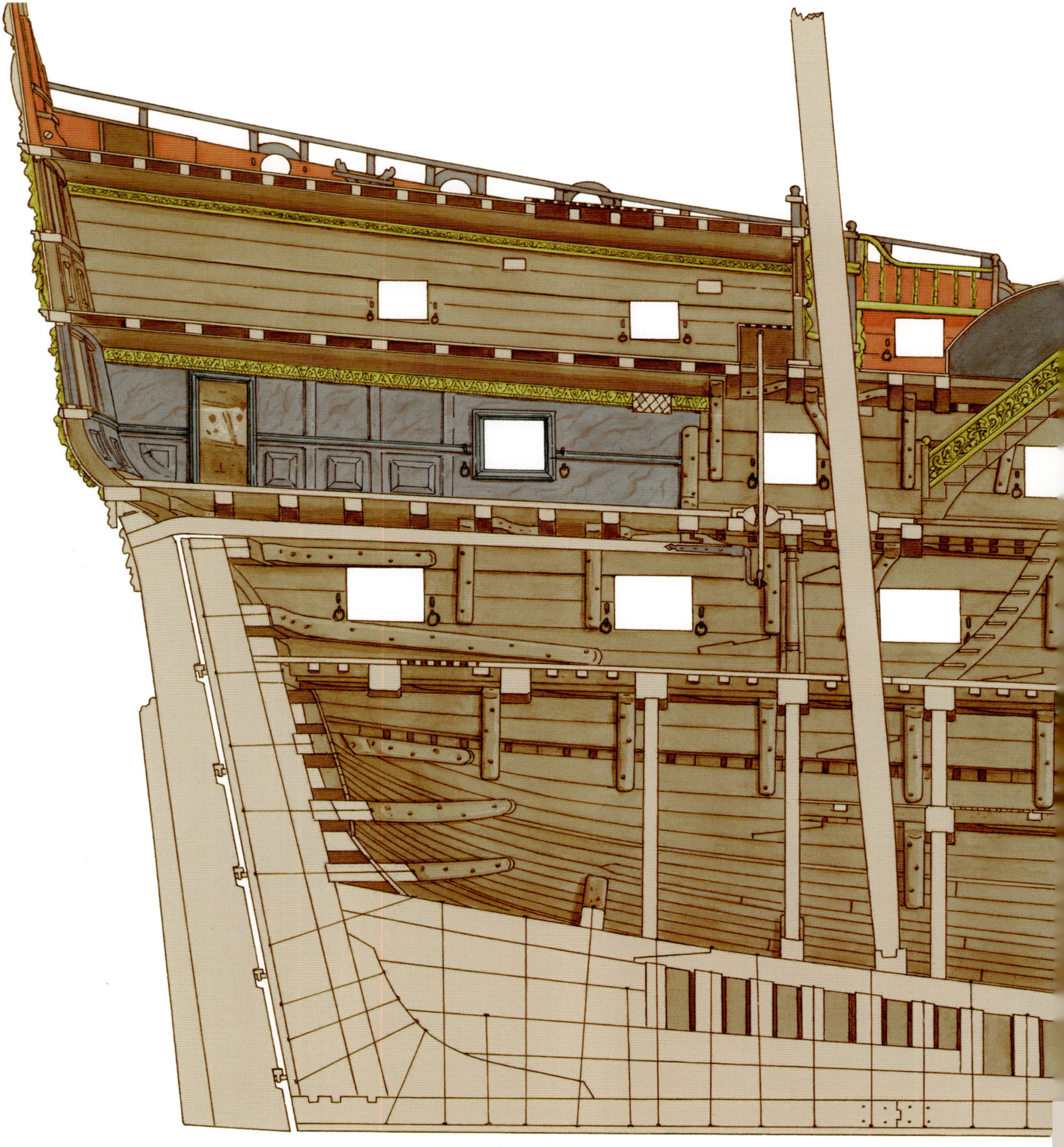

Appendices 1-5

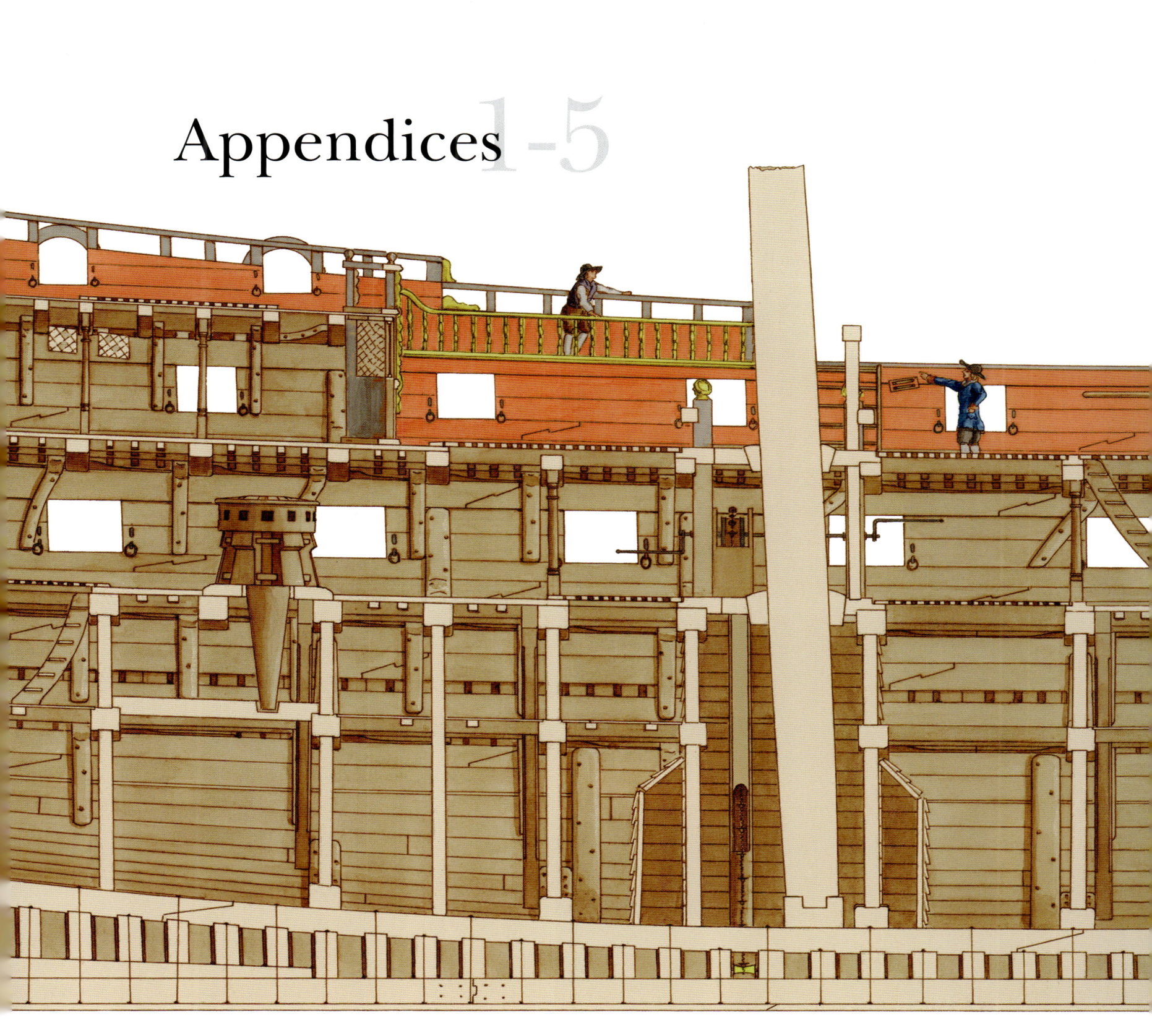

APPENDIX 1

The approved principal dimensions for the third-rate ships of 1677 (TNA, ADM 106/36).

Length of the keel	–
Length of the gundeck from the rabbet of the main stem to the rabbet of the stern post	150ft
Greatest breadth from the outside to the outside of the plank	39ft 8in
Breadth at the main transom within the plank	25ft 6in
Breadth at the top the stern at the gunwale	17ft
Breadth of the ship at the top of the side in the waist from outside to outside of the timber	30ft 4in
Breadth at the beakhead at the top of the gunwale being the foremost toptimber	26ft
Depth in the hold from plank to plank	17ft
Height between the gundeck and second deck from plank to plank at the side	7ft 3in
Number of ports on the lower deck on each side	13ft
Bigness of the ports on the lower deck fore and aft	3ft 6in
Depth of the same	2ft 9in
Number of ports on the upper deck on each side	13ft
Bigness of the ports on the upper deck fore and aft	2ft 8in
Depth up and down	2ft 5in
Number of ports on the quarter deck in all	12ft
Bigness of the same fore and aft	2ft 4in
Depth up and down where the work is not cut	2ft
Ports on the forecastle cut through the beakhead or over the gunwale	4ft
Memorandum: not to exceed in draught of water when all provisions are on board for the allowance of men according to the establishment	18ft

APPENDIX 2
Scantling lists

A poor copy of the official 'Scantlings of the 30 Saile of Ships of 1677' survives in the National Archives (ref: ADM 7/827 f151 f152). The section relating to third rates, of which the *Anne* was one, is reproduced with additions where known from ADM 106/327 f215 and ADM 106/ 329 f70. The following scantling list is compiled using the clearest or fullest description provided by the originals. Where numbers of items are given, for instance two tier of carlines, they relate to one side of the ship only.

FRAMES		
	Length of the gun deck	150ft
	Breadth at the transom	25ft 6in
	Breadth from outside of the plank	39ft 8in
	Depth in hold from ceiling to underside of the gun deck	17ft
Keel	Length of the keel	125ft
	Square in the midships	1ft 6½in
	Scarph tabled in ye keel	4ft 6in
Stem	Rake of the stem	22ft
	Breadth of the same at the head	1ft 4in
	Fore and aft of the same	1ft 6in
False Stem	Thickness of ye false stem	10½in
	Breadth of the same	2ft 4in
	Scarph long	1ft
Sternpost	Rake of the Sternpost	5ft
	Breadth at the head	1ft 10in
	Fore and aft at the head	1ft 10in
	Fore and aft at the foot	2ft 4in
	The post within it fastened to the mainpost fore and aft and as broad as the mainpost	1ft 8in
	Each arm of the knee at the post long	8ft
Transoms Sided	1st Main	1ft 2in
	2nd	1ft
	3rd	11½in
	4th	11½in
	5th	10½in

Fashion Pieces	sided	10½in
Floor Timbers	Space of the floor timbers or Timber and Room	2ft 3in
	Floor timbers fore and aft	1ft 1¼in
	Depth of the same on ye keel	1ft 1¼in
	In and out at ye wronghead	1ft ¼in
Naval Timbers or first futtocks	Naval timbers fore and aft	1ft 1¼in
	Scarphs of the same	6 ft 8in
Middle or Second Futtocks	Timbers in and out at ye gundeck	10¼in
Futtocks Upper or Third Futtocks	Fore and aft of ye same	1ft ¼in
	Length of the scarph	6ft 6in
Top Timbers	Top timbers sided at ye head	8in
	Sided at ye foot	11½in
	In and out at ye gunwale	4 ¼in
Keelson not more than 5 pieces	Depth in the middle	1ft 4in
	Breadth in the Midships	1ft 6in
	Hause pieces broad at least	2ft 4in
WALES		
	Depth of ye Lower Wale	1ft 2in
	Thickness of ye same	10in
	Depth of ye Upper Wale	1ft 2in
	Thickness of ye same	10in
	Six Strakes of thick stuff without board, two above, two between & two below ye Wales	6in
	Chain Wales depth	10in
	Thickness of ye same	6in

HOLD

Footwaling	One strake of plank next to ye limber board	4in
	7 strakes of sleepers in ye hold whereof 5 are thick	7½in
	Thickness of ye other two	5in
	To be broad	1ft 4in
	Thickness of ye middle bands or Orlop Clamps	8½in
	Broad, tabled under the beams	1ft 6in
	The rest of the footwaling in hold broad	1ft 6in
	The rest of the footwaling thickness	4 in
Orlop Beams	Orlop beams Fore and Aft	1ft 4in
	Up and down of ye same	1ft 3in
Floor Riders	Floor riders Fore and Aft	1ft 6in
	Depth on the keelson	1ft
	Depth at the wrongheads	1ft 1in
	Scarph of the same	7ft
Futtock Riders	Length of the futtock riders	14ft
	Depth at the beam	2ft
	And sided at the end of the beam	1ft 3in
Knees Orlop	Knees Sided to the Beam	10in
	Fore & Aft	5ft
	Square of the pillars in hold	8¼in
Steps	Steps for the Main mast deep	1ft 6in
	Thickness of ye same Fore Aft	2ft 5in
	Step for the Fore mast deep	1ft 6in
	Breadth of the same	2ft 2in
Brest Hooks	Four brest hooks in hold	
	Deep	1ft 2in
	Long	14ft 6in

GUNDECK

Brest Hooks	Two brest hooks between decks	
	Deep	1ft 2in
	Long	14ft
Knees under Ports	2 Knees to each Beam under the Ports Sided	10in
	Shortest length of each Arm	3ft 6in
	Depth of the same in the throat	1ft 8in
Riders between Ports	1 rider and 1 Knee between the Ports at end of every other Beam	
	Length of Rider	13ft 6in
	Breadth of the same by the beam	2ft
	Broad	1ft 1½in
Carrick Bitts	Square of the Fore bitts	1ft 6in
	Square of the After bitts	1ft 6in
	With cross pieces of equal bigness as the bitts and knees of equal goodness	
Clamps	Two strakes of clamps thick	8½in
	Broad	1ft 6in
Partners	Thickness of partners for ye main mast	10in
	Thickness of partners for ye fore mast	9in
Beams	Gundeck beams sided	1ft 4½in
	Depth of the same	1ft 3¼in
	Hatchway beams asunder	8ft
Carlines	Two tier of oak carlines each side between beams	
	Broad	10in
	Deep	10in
	Long carlines sided (Hatchway)	7½in
	Depth of the same	1ft 2in
	Short carlines sided (Hatchway)	7½in
	Depth of the same	6in
	Spirket Wales 2 strakes	6in
	The ledges between the ledges to lie asunder	9in
Ledges	Ledges sided	5in
	Depth of the same	4in

Water Ways	Thickness in the chine	6½in
	Breadth of the same	1ft 2in
Plank	The rest of the gundeck plank to the hatchway	4in
	Upon the gundeck between bitts and main partners	3in
	Hatchway plank	2in
	Memorandum: every plank and waterway hath two spikes in each beam and in each ledge 2 treenails	

UPPER GUNDECK

Beams	Depth of the upper deck beams	9in
	Breadth of the same	1ft
	Distance between the Beams except near the hatchways	5ft
	Rounding of the deck	10in
Knees	Double kneed arms length	4ft
	Sided	7in
Clamps	Thickness of the clamps	5in
	Breadth of the same	1ft 5in
Carlines	Two tire of carlines	
	Squaring of the long carlines	1ft
	Depth of the short carlines	6in
	Breadth of the same	8in
Ledges	Sided	4in
	Depth	4in
Spirket Plank	Thickness of the spirketting	4in
	Plank on the deck thick	2 ¾in
Water Ways	Thickness of the waterways	5in
	Breadth of the same	1ft 2in
Standards	Three pair of standards sided	8½in
	Arms long at least	5ft 6in
String	Depth of the string prickt home to the side	8in
	Thickness of the string	10in
Partners	Main Partners	9in
	Fore Partners	7in
	Mizzen Partners	5in

Plank between ports		3in
Turned Pillars	Square	7in
Capstans	Main Drum fashioned diameter in the barrel	2ft 9in
	Jeer Drum fashioned	1ft 10in

QUARTERDECK

Beams	Quarter deck beams sided	8in
	Depth of the same	6in
Rising	Rising under the beams in the wake of the cabins	
	Thick	8in
	Depth	11in
Knees	Knees in the wake of the forecastle and steerage sided	5½in

FORECASTLE

Beams	Beams sided	8in
	Depth of the same	6in
Clamps	Thickness of the clamps	8in

BOLTS

	Bigness of the iron Floor bolts	1¼in
	Bigness of bolts for the Orlop	1⅛in
	Ditto Gun Deck ports	1 1/16 in
	Ditto Upper deck ports	1in
	Ditto Quarter Deck Forecastle ports	¾in

APPENDIX 3

Building contract for the *Yarmouth*

Although some of the third-rate ships of 1677 were built according to a contract, no copies have survived. Following the loss of the *Anne* and two other ships of the same programme, replacement ships were ordered. The design was so successful the specification was not altered, apart from a minor reduction of three inches in the depth of the hold. A copy of the contract to build the *Yarmouth* survives in The National Archives, ref: ADM 106/3071. The contract is reproduced in its entirety with the inclusion of headings to the margin where missing for easier reference.

23rd January 1691
Yarmouth (In a later hand)
Contract with Mr Nicholas Barrett for the building another 3rd rate ship at Harwich
To be launched last (of) December 1691
11:0:0 pounds per ton

This indenture made the three and twentieth day of January in the year of our lord one thousand six hundred and ninety (old style) between the Principal Officers and Commissioners of their Majestie's Navy (for and on the behalf of their Majesties) of the one part and Mr Nicholas Barrett of Wapping in the county of Middlesex of the other part. Witnesseth that the said Nicholas Barrett for the considerations hereafter expressed doth covenant, promise and grant to and with the said Principal Officers and Commissioners (for and on the behalf of their Majesties) that he, the said Nicholas Barrett, his executors, administrators, servants or assignees shall and will at their own proper cost and charges well and workmanlike erect and build off the stocks, for the use of their Majesties at their yard at Harwich one good and substantial new ship or frigate of good and well seasoned timber and plank of English oak and elm.

Overall Dimensions

And that the said ship or frigate shall contain in length upon the gun deck from the rabbet of the post to the rabbet of the stem, one hundred and fifty feet. Breadth from outside to outside of the plank thirty nine feet eight inches. Depth in hold from the top of the ceiling to the upper edge of the gun deck beam sixteen feet nine inches. Breadth at transom twenty five feet six inches. The rake forward at the harpin to be reckoned at three fifths part of the main breadth. The rake aft five feet nine inches to the main transom.

Keel

The keel not to be made of more than four pieces, to be sixteen inches and a half broad in the midships and fifteen inches and a half up and down. To be sheathed with a four inch plank well fastened for a false keel. To have four feet six inches scarph tabled in the keel and to be well bolted with eight bolts of inch and half quarter inch auger.

Stem

To have a firm substantial stem of sixteen inches thwartships and seventeen inches fore and aft with a sufficient false stem of nine inches thick and two feet six inches broad with scarphs one feet long to the false stem and not less than four feet to the main stem.

Sternpost

To have a substantial sternpost of two feet two inches broad at the head and one feet ten inches fore and aft at the head and two feet six inches below on the keel fore and aft and another post within it to be fastened to the main post of sixteen inches fore and aft and as broad as the main post.

Rising Wood

Unto which shall be joined the rising wood sufficient for the run of the said ship and also a long armed knee of six feet long at the least. Each arm to be well bolted with an inch quarter and half quarter auger fastening the same to the keel and to the sternpost at every twenty two inches length at furthest.

Timber and Room

The space of timber and room to be no more than two feet three inches.

Floor Timbers

The floor timbers of the said ship to be thirteen inches and one quarter of an inch fore and aft and sixteen inches and one half inch up and down upon the keel and twelve inches and one quarter of an inch in and out at the wrongheads or twelve inches full when wrought and to be twenty three feet long in the midships.

Naval Timbers

(Sometimes known as the first or lower tier of futtocks) The naval timbers to fill the rooms being at least thirteen inches and one half inch fore and aft and to have at least six feet nine inches scarph.

Middle Futtocks

(Sometimes known as the second tier of futtocks) *The middle futtocks to have six feet six inches scarph.*

Gun Deck Timbers

(Sometimes known as the third or upper tier of futtocks) *The timbers at the gun deck to be ten inches in and out and twelve inches fore and aft and to have at least six feet scarph.*

Keelson

To have a substantial keelson of not more than five pieces to be sixteen inches up and down and eighteen inches broad in the midships and to end at the stem and sternpost in proportion to run fore and aft. Each scarph to be three feet long at the least and to be well bolted with inch, quarter and half quarter auger through every other timber and to bolt every other floor timber through the keel and one bolt through the stem.

Toptimbers

The toptimbers to be sided allow twelve inches, at the head eight inches, and to be in and out at the gunwale or top of the ship's side four inches and a half inch.

Ceiling

To put in one strake of four inch plank next the limber board and seven strakes of sleepers in hold on each side the wrongheads, three of them eight inches, two of seven inches and a half inch and the other two of five inches thick and fifteen inches broad and to run fore and aft. To have two strakes of middlebands on each side of seven inches thick and fifteen inches broad and to run fore and aft. To have two strakes of clamps on each side fore and aft under the beams of the gun deck of eight inches and one quarter of an inch thick and seventeen inches broad each and to be hooked one into the other to prevent reaching. To have an opening of six inches under the clamps for air. All the rest of the footwaling or ceiling in the hold to be good four inch English oak plank.

Orlop Beams

To put in ten beams for the orlop, to be sixteen inches fore and aft and fifteen inches up and down, five of them to be placed before the mast and the other abaft.

Riders

To have five bends of floor and futtock riders. The futtock riders to be of fifteen inches the floor riders to be eighteen inches fore and aft and twelve inches deep upon the keelson, fifteen inches deep at the wrongheads. The floor riders to be bolted with nine bolts of inch, quarter and half quarter of an inch auger. The futtock riders to have seven bolts of inch quarter and half quarter of an inch auger. Each rider and to have seven feet scarph upwards and downwards.

Orlop Platform

And to make platforms upon the orlop beams for stowing cables and other stores and to lie five feet nine inches from the gun deck between plank and plank. To have one knee and one rider at each end of the beams or double kneed, but if riders then the riders to be each thirteen feet long, twelve inches sided and sixteen inches deep at the beam, fayed into the beam and to be well bolted with eight bolts of inch quarter and half quarter of an inch auger in and out, and two into the beams with one knee fore and aft at each end of every beam. The shortest arm to be three feet in length and to be ten inches sided bolted with six bolts to each knee of inch and three eights auger.

Mainmast Step

To have a saddle for the step of the mainmast of two feet seven inches fore and aft and depth sufficient for the same.

Gun Deck Beams

To have a pillar in hold under every beam of the gun deck and orlop eight inches square. The gun deck beams to be sixteen inches and one quarter of an inch broad and fifteen inches up and down and to be placed one beam under each port of the gun deck and one beam between each port of the gun deck, excepting in the main hatchway, which must be eight feet asunder and to be kneed with two knees at each end of the beams, one lodging the other hanging, where the beams fall under the ports of not less than three feet long each arm and ten inches sided to be bolted with six bolts of inch and one quarter of an inch auger. The beams that fall between the ports to be in like manner double kneed at each end, if knees can be procured, but if so many knees cannot be had then to have one knee at each end of the beams and of the bigness of the other knees before mentioned and one rider at each end of the said beams, to be thirteen feet long, thirteen inches broad, and twenty inches depth at the beams, to be bolted with eight bolts of inch and three eights auger.

Cross Pillars

To have five pairs of cross pillars in hold of ten inches square and to be well bolted to the beams and riders and to be kneed at the upper ends well bolted.

Gun deck

And to have a double tire of carlines on each side fore and aft of oak to be nine inches thick and ten inches broad and the ledges to lie within nine inches one of another and six inches broad five inches deep. The waterways to be six inches in the chine in thickness and fourteen inches broad. All the rest of the gun deck as far as the hatchways from the side to be good four inch English oak plank well seasoned and of good lengths the said plank and waterways to be treenailed, spiked with two good spikes in each beam and two treenails in each ledge. To put out nine leaden scuppers on each side of the gun deck.

Storerooms

To make as many hatches in the hatchways as shall be convenient of two inch plank with the hatchway abaft the mast for the stowing of provisions and the hatchway to the steward room and for boatswain's and gunner's store rooms and powder rooms which said store rooms and powder rooms are to be built of ordinary deals of such bigness and continuance as equals any of their Majestie's ships of the like burthen.

Hawse Pieces

To make a manger on the lower deck to have four scuppers in it of lead, two whereof to be four inches diameter and to put in four hawse pieces not less than two feet three inches broad each and to cut out four hawse holes in them.

Bitts

To place two pair of conic bitts eighteen inches square the aftermost, and sixteen inches square the foremost pair with cross pieces to the same of equal bigness and two pair of knees suitable to the said bitts and to bolt them with five bolts in each knee of inch and half quarter auger.

Breasthooks in Hold

To have four breasthooks in hold fourteen inches deep and fourteen feet long each and seven bolts in each breasthook of inch and three eights auger.

Foremast Step

To have a step for the foremast two feet four inches broad and of sufficient depth and length bolted with eight bolts of inch and quarter auger.

Gun Deck Spirket

To have two strakes of spirket wales on the lower deck of six inches thick from the waterway unto the lower edge of the ports fore and aft.

Gun Deck Gun Ports

To cut out thirteen ports on each side the same deck three feet six inches broad and two feet nine inches deep with four ports abaft between the transoms and to make and hang portlids with hooks and hinges and to fit and drive two ringbolts and two eyebolts to each port of inch and quarter auger for the guns.

Gun Deck Fittings

To place partners for the main and fore mast of ten inches thick and a pillar for the main capstan to be iron bound for the end of the spindle to stand on in the hold. A step for the mizzen mast on the keelson. To have three inch plank upon the gun deck between the bitts and the main partners in the wake of the hatchways and to raise the hatches above the deck and to have turned pillars under the beams on the upper deck as shall be found convenient and placed upon a four inch plank for the pillar to rest upon the gun deck. To make a staircase up into the quarterdeck and the stairs and ladders to all the conveniences. To bring on two breasthooks between decks fourteen feet long fourteen inches deep and to fasten them with seven bolts in each hook of inch and three eights auger.

Transoms

To have as many transoms abaft below the ports as may lie within eighteen inches one of another. The wing transom to be fourteen inches thick and the rest not less than twelve inches thick and one transom at the upper edge of the ports under the helm port to take hold of the sternpost. All the said transoms to be well kneed with long armed knees as is usual, fastened with six bolts in each knee by inch and three eights auger.

Upper Deck Gun Ports

To make twenty four ports on the upper deck (that is to say) twelve on each side, two chase ports forward and four right aft to be two feet eight inches broad and two feet five inches deep each port and to garnish them with carved work fore and aft.

Upper Deck Clamps

To bring on clamps fore and aft of six inches thick and fifteen inches broad under the beams of the upper deck and to shut up between decks with four inch oak plank fore and aft.

Upper Deck Beams

The beams of the said deck to be eleven inches up and down and thirteen inches broad fore and aft to lie between and under each port and not to exceed five feet asunder excepting in the wake of the hatchways and the beams over the main capstan and under the bulkheads to lie as near as conveniently they may. To be in height between the said decks between plank and plank seven feet three inches in the midships. The beams to round ten inches to go flush fore and aft all the said beams to be double kneed with four knees to each beam of seven inches and half an inch sided, the shortest arm three feet long, the hanging arm to come down to the spirketting under the port and to be well bolted with three bolts in each arm with bolts of inch and half quarter auger.

Upper Deck

To have two tier of carlines on each side fore and aft, to be twelve inches square, the long carlines and the other short carlines eight inches broad and six inches up and down with sufficient ledges of four inches square to lie not more than nine inches asunder. To lay the said deck with good three inch oak plank in the wake of the guns, the rest with the like plank or with good dry Prutia deals, to answer the said plank in thickness. To have a waterway five inches thick fourteen inches broad.

Upper Deck Fittings

The Spirketting to be of four inch plank fore and aft. To have a string of English oak of six inches deep and ten inches thick, to be pricked home to the outside plank and to make the lower sill of the upper ports to be well spiked and treenailed through and between the timbers. To have coamings, head ledges with grating hatches before and abaft the mast to vent the smoke of the ordnance. To fit topsail sheet bitts, jeer bitts or knightheads cats and supporters, a davit and clasp of iron. To fit partners for the main and jeer capstans and partners for all the masts, and to put out nine scuppers on each side of the upper deck.

Capstans

To make a main capstan (drum fashion) thirty inches diameter in the barrel and a jeer capstan (drum fashion) of twenty two inches diameter in the barrel with capstan bars and iron pauls sufficient for the said capstan.

Quarter Deck and Forecastle Beams

To make a large quarterdeck and a large forecastle. The beams of the same to be eight inches fore and aft and six inches and a half up and down and to lie within two feet one of another and each other beam to be kneed with one up and down knee at each end of good length and six inches sided and bolted with five bolts in each knee by a three quarter of an inch auger.

Quarter Deck and Forecastle Fittings

To have round bulkheads in the bulkheads of the said forecastle and quarterdeck for four cabins next the side and in the midships of the bulkhead of the forecastle. To place the cookroom for roasting and boiling and to set all the bulkheads upon oaken plank fayed on the deck for the foot of the stanchions of ten inches broad and four inches thick, laid with tar and hair and the seams leaded. To have two ports in the bulkhead of the forecastle and two in the bulkhead of the steerage and twelve ports on the quarterdeck, six ports on each side of two feet four inches wide and two feet deep. The beams in the wake of the bulkheads to be double kneed at each end. To have three pair of standards on the upper deck in each bulkhead one pair, to be nine inches sided and not less than three feet and a half feet long each arm and to have one pair in the bulkhead of the coach to be bolted with six bolts with inch and half quarter auger. The quarter deck to be laid with two inch oak plank well seasoned next the side, and the rest with Prutia deal of like thickness. To have a rising of elm under the beam of the great cabin of eight inches thick and ten inches deep the beams to be dovetailed and bolted into the same. To make and hang with port lids about the whole ship with substantial hooks and hinges. To have a transom abaft under the windows in the cabin and one under the ports and the same to be kneed and bolted with six bolts in each knee and to have an open balcony abaft out of the great cabin with rails and bannisters, and to have as large a rounhouse and coach as the works with conveniency will bear. To be completely fitted with bulkheads joiner's work and doors to the same.

Rooms in Hold

To make all platforms in hold with bulkheads and partitions viz for the powder room and gunner's store rooms, sailroom, boatswain's carpenter's and steward's store room and steward room, a fish room and a store room for the captain's provisions and as many cabins for lodgings as shall be convenient. To make a large bread room and sheath the same with lead or tin plate, the lead or plate thereof to be at their Majestie's charge.

Without Board Planking

Without board the ship is to be planked up from the keel ten feet in height with elm, oak or beech plank of four inches thick and from thence up to the chainwales with four inch oak plank excepting six strakes which is to be six inches thick and fourteen inches broad in the midships and to lessen in thickness in proportion toward the stem and stern as is usual, ending at the stem and stern in four inch plank viz: two strakes below the wale, two between the wales and two above the wales. To have two formed wales of fourteen inches up and down and nine inches and a half of an inch thick and to have two chainwales for the conveniency of the chain plates and bolts and to go fore and aft both to be six inches thick and ten inches broad to be chocked between the timbers with oak in the wake of the chain bolt. To have one strake of three inch oak plank between the chainwales ten inches broad and the work upwards so high as the waist from the upper chainwale to be wrought up with three inch English oak plank and the quarter with well seasoned Prutia deals of two inches thick.

Head
To have a fair head with a firm and substantial knee and cheeks treble rails, trail board, beast, brackets, keelson, cross pieces and standard. To have catheads and supporters under them.

Stern
To have a fair lower counter with rails and brackets and open galleries garnished with carved works. To have a house of office in the gallery windows and casements into the cabin. To have a fair upright and to put in it a complete pair of King's arms or other ornament of like value maskheads, pilasters and forms.

Rigging Attachments
To have a pair of chesstrees fore, main and mizzen chainwales well bolted, chain bolts and chain plates sufficient for the shrouds and backstays of all the masts.

Gripe
To have a sufficient gripe well bolted, stirruped and dovetailed and a stirrup on the skeg well bolted.

Rudder
To make and hang on a complete rudder with six pair of braces, gudgeons and pintles a muzzle for the head and a tiller thereto.

Decoration
To gunwale and planksheer the said ship fore and aft and to put on brackets, hancing pieces and to garnish them complete. They are likewise to do and perform all the carved work, painting and guilding answerable to their Majestie's ships of the like bigness in the Navy. The guilding work being intended to be only the lion in the head and the King's arms in the stern. The head stern and galleries in carved work not inferior to those of the thirty ships formerly built and to find and provide all materials for the same.

Details
Likewise to do and perform all the joiner's works finding deals, locks, iron bars, hinges for store rooms, steward rooms, doors, settlebeds and cabins. The cabins to be as many and as well adorned in all respects as any of their Majestie's ships of the like burthen and to equal them in all respects both withinboard and without. They are to find all plumber's work, lead and leaden scuppers and all glazier's work of stone ground glass with sash lights, scuttles for the cabin windows and all painter's work for painting and gilding as aforesaid within and without board and to do and perform whatsoever belongs to the carpenters to do for the finishing and completing the hull (without masts and yards) in like manner as is usually done and performed to the like ships built in their Majestie's own yards and to set the masts at his or their own charge with the help of the boatswain (that is to say) heel the masts wedge them and shut them in.

Materials and Delivery
And the said Nicholas Barret, for himself his executors and assignees doth covenant and grant to and with the Principal Officers and Commissioners of the Navy that he will at his or their own cost and charges find and provide all manner of iron work of the best Spanish iron or what shall be equal to the same in goodness and all spikes, nails, brads, likewise all timber planks, boards and treenails of Sussex well seasoned which are to be all mooted from Prutia deals above the chainwale down to the keel. To find white and black oakum, pitch, tar, rozin, hair, oil, brimstone and all other materials that shall be needful to be used or spent in or about the work and premises aforesaid for the complete finishing the said ship and in like manner to discharge and pay all manner of workmanship touching all and every part of the work herein expressed and hereafter expressed or to be done and performed and to finish complete and launch the said ship or frigate, and to deliver her safe on float in the river of Harwich unto such person or persons as shall be duly and sufficiently authorised by the said Principal Officers and Commissioners to receive her for the use of their Majesties by the last day of December next coming after the date hereof.

Quality
And it is further agreed that the said Principal Officers and Commissioners shall have liberty to appoint such person or persons as they shall see fit to inspect and oversee the building of the said ship which person or persons shall

have free liberty at all times to discharge his or their duty therein without any lett or molestation and if at any time during the building the said ship or frigate herein contracted for, according to the dimensions proportions and scantlings herein expressed and set forth or intended to be expressed and set forth there shall be found and discoursed of the said person or persons any unsound, insufficient timber, plank or other materials used in the building of the said ship or which shall be of different scantling from what the same ought to be by this present contract, or that any insufficient workmanship or such as is not answerable to this contract shall be performed on the same that then after due notice thereof given in writing by the said surveyor or surveyors unto the said Nicholas Barrett or to his chief master workman under him on the said ship there shall be an effectual and speedy amendment reforming of all and every such default in stuff and workmanship whereby the same may be made agreeable to this contract in dimensions goodness and workmanship and the said amending or reformation shall be certified in writing by the said surveyor or surveyors to the said Principal Officers and Commissioners of the Navy for the service of their Majesties in this behalf. And the said Nicholas Barrett do further oblige hiself his heirs, executors and administrators and every one of them to comply with the said Principal Officers and Commissioners.

Supply of Stores

To transport from the river of Thames to Harwich free of charge to their Majesties the masts, yards, rigging, sails and sea stores for Boatswain and carpenter necessary to be provided by the office of the navy for the said ship the same to be got ready to be embarked in the River of Thames by the said Principal Officers or their substitutes by the first of October next or thereabout after the date of this contract.

Draught

And also the said Nicholas Barrett for the well building and finishing the said ship in all respects shall produce unto the Navy Board his master workman together with a fair draught or design of a ship according to the dimensions herein set forth for the approval of the one and for the correction and approval of the other which afterwards is and shall be the design and draught which he shall cause his master workman to follow in the framing and building the said ship intended and agreed as aforesaid to be built.

Payment

And the said Principal Officers and Commissioners of the Navy for and behalf of their Majesties shall according to the custom of the office of the Navy sign and mark out bills to the Treasurer of the Navy to be paid to the said Nicholas Barrett his executors, administrators or assignees after the rate of eleven pounds per ton for each ton the said ship shall measure with the dimensions and limitations before expressed and the main breadth to be reckoned as is hereby mutually condescended and agreed unto. To be four inches on each side without the timber and tonnage to be cast according to the accustomed rule of Shipwrights Hall. The said money to be paid in manner form and payments following (that is to say) sixteen hundred pounds at and upon the sealing this contract. The like sum of seventeen hundred pounds more when the floor of the said ship shall be laid across and bolted. The sum of two thousand five hundred pounds more when the second futtocks to the said ship shall be all fast. The sum of eleven hundred pounds more when the orlop beams shall be fast and footwaling in. The sum of eleven hundred pounds more when the gun deck beams are all kneed and fastened. The sum of one thousand pounds more when the upper deck beams are kneed and fastened and both her upper and lower decks shall be laid. The sum of one thousand pounds more when her quarter deck and forecastle beams shall be all kneed and fastened and the remainder when the said ship shall be launched and delivered on float as aforesaid. It is further agreed that if the said ship shall be exceeded in dimensions and scantlings contrary to what is herein before agreed that no satisfaction or allowance shall be made for such overwork or increase in scantling unless the said increase of works or scantling have been made by order first given therein in writing by the said Principal Officers and Commissioners. In witness whereof to and part of these put to indentures the said Nicholas Barrett hath set his hands and seal and to the other part thereof the said Principal Officers and Commissioners of the navy have accordingly to the custom of their Majestie's Navy set their hands and caused the common seal of the office of the Navy to be affixed the day and year first above written.

Witness
Edmund Dummer
Nicholas Barrett   N. Dalkes

APPENDIX 4

Contract for the carvings of the third rate ships of 1677 built at Deptford and Woolwich

(National Archive ADM 49/24, f57)

21st January 1677/8

Contracted the day and & year above said W:th Ye Principal Officers & Commissioners of His Ma:ts Navy by me Jos: Helby Carver & I do hereby oblige myself at my own proper cost & charges His ma:ts finding timber well and workmanlike to perform upon all His Ma:ts new Ships of the Third rates now in building in His Ma:ts yards at Deptford and Woolw:ch in part of the 30 Ships appointed to be built by Act of Parliam:t in such manner & with such time as the Ma:r Shipwrights of ye said yards shall direct The severall Carved works hereafter particularly expressed Viz:

The Stern	Lower Counter Brackets	6
	Side Brackets	2
	Mask Heads	8
	Second counter Brackets	8
	Badges	7
	Gallery Badges	2
	Lower Cabin Lights Brackets	8
	Gallery Badges	2
	Second Counter Brackets	8
	Badges	7
	Round House lights	8
	Vazines (Terms)	2
	Large Taffrail	1
	Rother Face	1
Gallery	Gallery bottom pts	2
	Lower Brackets	18
	Badges	14
	Light Brackerts	18
	Brackerts above the Lights	14
	Turritt Brackets	14
	Pieces a top the Stool	2
Side	Upper Tier of Ring Ports	24
	Quarter Deck Ring Ports	14
	Poop Halfe Rings	4
	Fore Castle 1/2 Rings	4
	Lights	2
	Hancing pieces	8
	Main Chestrees	2
Head	Supporters to the Catts	2
	Catt faces	2
	Catt sides	None
	End of the upper Rails	2½
	Head Brackets	12
	Half Brackets	2
	Lyon of ye Head	1
	Stem top	1
	Trayle board	1
	Tack faces	2
ForeCastle bulkhead forward	Brackets	6
	Half Brackets	2
	Ports Round	4
ForeCastle bulkhead abaft	Belfry Cheeks	2
	Cap	1
	Brackets	10
Steerige of ye bulkhead	Brackets	10
Roundhouse bulkhead	Brackets	6
Gangways in the waist	Before	2
	Abaft	2
	Top sail sheet Bitts	4
	Jeer Bitts	4
	Halliard Blocks	3
	Winding stair String	2
Great Cabin large cornice the whole depth round Roundhouse ye same		1

I do further oblige myself that all the aforesaid carved works shall be equal in goodness to the carved works performed on His ma:ts ship the Defiance. For and in consideration of £160. To be paid one third part in hand by was of imprest at the beginning of each ship, One third part thereof when halfe of the afore mentioned works are performed & the remainder when Certificate shall be produced from the Master Shipwright that the whole work is in every respect duly and completely finished according to the true intent & meaning of this Contract.

Jo: Helby

APPENDIX 5

Duke of Grafton's instructions
Preserved in The National Archives (ref: ADM2/1727 122-124v).

James R

Instructions for our Right trusty & Right entirely beloved cousin Henry Duke of Grafton, our Vice Admiral & Lieutenant of ye Admiralty of England and Lieutenant of the Navy and Seas of our said Kingdom.

To go to Holland with these ships.

Anne, Bristol, Hampshire, Sedgemoor, Pearl, Richmond,

Fubbs Yacht, Henrietta Yacht, Isabella Yacht. *He to repair in ye yachts to ye Brielle to return … [incomplete]*

Whereas by our commission bearing date ye 5th day of June last, you are appointed Admiral and chief Commander of our ships to be employed in the Narrow Seas for this summer's expedition; and forasmuch as by one other Commission of even date with these presents, we have committed to you the further charge and command of all and every of our ships and vessels you shall meet with during one other expedition wherein we have thought fit to employ you into ye Mediterranean in ye execution of both which you are directed to govern yourself by such orders and instructions as you have or shall receive from us. Our Royal will and pleasure is, that with the first opportunity of wind & weather after receipt hereof, you do proceed with our ship ye Anne *to ye Gunfleet where having taken into your company and under your command, our several ships and vessels named in ye margin (whose Commanders are all required to follow your orders) proceed to ye coast of Holland, as near to ye Brielle as (with ye advice of pilots you shall have with you, or can there procure) it shall be judged you with safety may.*

Where being come, you are yourself, taking with you the three yachts, immediately to repair to Rotterdam, there to attend upon our good sister the Queen of Portugal, in order to your receiving her with her retinue and equipage, first on board the said yachts, and by them on board our ship before mentioned, that is to say, the person of our said good sister, with such of her retinue as she shall direct upon the Anne, *disposing of the residue on such other of our said ships as may best suit with their accommodation, and the satisfaction of the Queen.*

Which having done, you are to leave the Fubbs & Henrietta *yachts at liberty to repair to Luckstadt for ye attending for, & bringing over our most dear son in law Prince George of Denmark according to instructions already by us given their Commanders on that behalf.*

After this, you are to improve the first opportunity of wind and weather for the proceeding with our fore mentioned ships, and Isabella Yacht *directly to Lisbon in ye Kingdom of Portugal, there (yourself attending) to put on shore our said good sister with her retinue and equipage, causing the same to be performed with all the dispatches, consistent with their convenience that may be.*

You are moreover to see that ye said Queen be both at her coming onboard in Holland, and landing in Portugal, saluted from our ships with such number of ordnance and in such manner & order as you in your direction shall judge most suitable to ye extraordinariness of the occasion. But you are not in any wise in your passing by any of the castles or forts upon ye river of Lisbon, to depart from ye ordinary known practice of salutes between foreign castles and forts on our ships bearing flags of equal quality with that bourn by yourself.

Moreover you are before your departure from Lisbon to leave your necessary orders with Sir Rodger Strickland, Commander of our ship ye Bristol *to continue there with our ship ye* Richmond *so long time as our said good sister shall desire in order to the receiving onboard our said two ships such persons as she shall direct to be brought from thence to England and the same having taken onboard together with ye several of our servants of our own household appointed to attend this service to make the best of their way back to Portsmouth or ye Downs, giving notice of their arrival at either to our Secretary of the Admiralty [Samuel Pepys] for our information and attending there for our further orders.*

Anne, Hampshire, Sedgemoor, Pearl

After you shall have thus dispatched at Lisbon ye several matters before directed, our further pleasure is, that you proceed with the residue of our ships named in the margin, & ye Isabella Yacht *(if you judge the same convenient or otherwise send her home with ye* Bristol & Richmond*) directly to Gibraltar, from whence you are without delay to dispatch away the* Pearl, *with instructions to her Commander to attend ye service of ye present war between us and that people, following therein such orders as (in your absence) he shall from time to time receive from Captain Henry Killegrew Commander of our ship ye* Dragon.

You are likewise upon your arrival at Gibraltar to issue your orders to ye Commander of our ship the Swan *now upon that service, for his returning home as soon as may be with directions to call in at Plymouth, and for want of orders there, to proceed to ye Downs, giving notice of his arrival at either, to ye Secretary of our Admiralty for our information.*

Dragon, Charles Galley, Mermaid, Sapphire, Garland, Swan

If upon your coming to Gibraltar you shall happen to find there, ye Charles Galley *and any two of the 5th rates (the* Swan *only excepted as before) of the Salley squadron, a list of which is given you in the margin, you are to join them with the ships that shall accompany you thither, and proceed with the one and the other directly to Argier. The like you are to do with the* Charles Galley *alone in case of your meeting with no 5th rate there, or with two 5th rates without ye* Galley *if you shall happen to miss of her; But in no case to proceed without one or the other, with this addition, that in case of your finding either the* Galley *alone, or only one of the 5th rates you are at liberty (not withstanding what is before said touching the* Pearl*) to take her along with you to Algier for supplying such effect, and the better enabling you to observe our aforementioned directions for sending home ye* Swan.

And if it shall so fall out that Captain Killigrew shall not come into Gibraltar before your departure thence for Argier, you are in that case to leave such an account of your proceedings therein & instructions for him as you shall think convenient, in relation to his most effectual prosecuting of the service he is now upon against Salley, with his own & such other of ye ships before mentioned as shall be by you left with him for that purpose.

And herein it is our especial will and pleasure, that you do in a particular manner recommend it to him to take care that for as much as ye ships of our subjects employed in the Newfoundland fishery may be expected from thence on their way to their markets in Spain & Italy about the month of November next, the ships so left with him may be appointed to cruise about that time off of ye southward Cape, the Rock of Lisbon & such other stations as he shall judge convenient there carefully to look out for & give protection to our said subjects ships, in case of him or their falling in with any number of the said ships, to give them convoy out of danger from the ships and vessels of Salley.

Which having done at Gibraltar, you are to make the best of your way (with your ships before directed) to Algier, there to use ye best means you can (both by our Consul residing at that place or otherwise) for informing yourself in the present state of affairs there, with relation to ye treaty now in being between us and that Government, causing the letter which you carry with you from us thereto, be safely delivered, and all manner used consistent with our honourable contents of ye treaty, and the purpose of this our letter, for the preservation of ye present peace & good understanding between us & them.

Wherein if (as we greatly desire) your negotiations shall succeed, you are without any unnecessary stay there, to proceed to ye ports of Tunis & Tripoly, making your like enquiries after ye state of affairs between us and the people of those places respectively, & finding the same well on their part, you are to give them a furtherance of ours, of ye sincerity of our intentions to maintain & preserve ye present good correspondence with them.

Dragon, Charles Galley, Sedgemoor, Sapphire, Pearl

After which having done, with as little expense of time as may be, you are to return with our ships under your command to Gibraltar, & from thence (leaving Captain Killigrew in his present command relating to Salley, with the ships named in ye margin) to make the best of your way for England with ye Anne, Hampshire, Garland *&* Mermaid, *calling in at Plymouth, and in want of orders there, proceeding to ye Downs, and giving notice of your arrival there to our Secretary of ye Admiralty for our information; you being nevertheless in ye execution of this article touching your return for England, to take notice, that in case ye* Mermaid *&* Garland *shall not happen to be at Gibraltar at your coming hither you are not to wait for them, but proceed for England leaving your necessary orders there for their following you.*

But if it shall fall out that your negotiations at Algier shall determine in a rupture with that people, you are in such case to use all the means you can to meet with, take, sink and destroy any of their ships & vessels, and otherwise so annoy that place & people, and to give the best countenance and protection you are able to ye ships of our subjects trading in those seas. And to this end, you are to give your earliest advice you can of the said rupture, not only to us here, but to all ye ports abroad on ye Christian shore, where the navigations of our people is most conversant. And this you are to see done, not only by some braceras to be to that purpose expressly hired by our consul, for ye giving notice thereof to ye neighbouring ports of Malaga, Gibraltar & Cadiz, the reasonable charge whereof shall be effectively made good to him by us; but by your dispatching away such two ships of your squadron as you shall judge most proper for that service, to alert Mascetti, Livorno, Calarry, Napoly, Messina, Gallipoly and Cant, in order to ye advising such ships of our subjects as they shall find in any of those ports, of the said rupture also, for preventing as much as maybe the hazard of their putting out to sea without convoy, by their remaining in port till the return of these our ships from the execution of the service they are thus by you sent upon; and to render this the more effectual, the Commanders of our said ships are to be directed (as far as they are able) to adjust with ye Masters & Commanders of the ships of our subjects at each place respectively, the times about which our ships may be looked for back and accordingly our said ships having run up as high as Cant, their Commanders are to return in ye same order back to Galipoly, Messina and the other aforenamed ports, with all diligence, bringing along with them there from all such ships of our subjects as shall be ready to come away, & touching at Malago and Gibraltar, proceed to Cadiz where our said two ships with what others (if any) you shall think fit to add thereto, shall take the whole number of ye ships of our subjects bound for England, and see them on their way northward out of danger, or continue their voyages through with them, as you shall see the same requisite for their safety, consistent with our service.

And this having done, you are to dispose of the rest of our ships, either before ye port of Algier, about ye Streights mouth, or in such other stations as you shall judge most likely to meet with and annoy our enemies both of Algiers & Salley. Toward purpose you are without distinction hereby, in case of ye fore mentioned rupture, to employ and dispose of our whole number of ships, as well those of the present Sally squadron as those which shall accompany you from hence, and with that joint force to continue in a vigorous prosecution of the war with both of these people until you shall receive our further orders giving a full and frequent account of your proceedings from time to time therein to us or to ye Secretary of our Admiralty for our information.

And whereas our ship ye Crown, *Captain Neville, Commander may within a little time after your arrival in the Streights be looked for from Turkey with our Ambassador returning thence; our pleasure is, that in case upon your meeting with her, you shall find our said Ambassador the Lord Chandon on board with purpose of coming home in her, you are to suffer her to pursue her said voyage according to ye present instructions given her on that behalf. But in case he shall happen not to be on board, or not designed to continue in passage quite through to England in her, and that a rupture shall (as before) happen to arise with Algier, you are in such case to take our said ship the* Crown *in like manner under your command disposing of her in prosecuting of the said war, as you shall judge best for our service. Causing it to be made known to her officers & company that in regard of ye long arrears of pay due to them, care shall be taken for ye effectual payment of part thereof to their relations, or other their lawful attorneys here as they shall desire. Given at our Court at Windsor this 3rd day of July 1687.*

By His Majesties Command

JR,   Samuel Pepys

References

Chapter 1

1. Richard Ollard, *Man of War*, London, 1974, p.157, Anne Doedens and Jan Souter, *1666 De Ramp Van Vlieland en Tesrschelling*, Zwolle, 2013, pp.223–224
2. Pepys' Diary, 22 June 1667
3. MSS Private Collection
4. Cat Pepysian MSS, NRS, Vol. IV p.406
5. Pepys Naval Minutes, NRS, p.394
6. R.A. Wardrobe 79916 Jusserand, Antonia Fraser, *King Charles II*, London, p.269
7. British Library ADD MSS9322 f.56v
8. Richard Endsor, *The Restoration Warship*, London, 2009, pp.11–16
9. A.W. Johns, *The Mariner's Mirror*, Vol. 12, 1926, No. 4
10. The National Archives ADM106/322 f.223
11. TNA ADM 106/326 f.154
12. TNA ADM106/332 pt II f.364
13. Cat Pepysian MSS, NRS, Vol. IV, p.468
14. Pepys Naval Minutes, p.14

Chapter 2

1. Act of Parliament, 15 Feb 1677, pp.145–146
2. TNA ADM106/322 f.134
3. TNA ADM106/321 f.194
4. TNA ADM106/322 f.260
5. TNA ADM106/322 f.237
6. TNA ADM106/321 f.213
7. TNA ADM106/321 f.237, f.239
8. TNA ADM106/322 f.239
9. TNA ADM106/3538
10. TNA ADM106/329 f.5
11. Hoppus's Measurer, 1790, intro XL
12. Pepys Library, Magdalene College, Cambridge, PL1339
13. TNA ADM106/322 f.274
14. TNA ADM106/322 f.158
15. TNA ADM106/322 f.160
16. TNA ADM106/322 f.244
17. TNA ADM106/321 f.303
18. TNA ADM106/322 f.246
19. TNA ADM106/322 f.266
20. TNA ADM7/827
21. TNA ADM106/332 f.161
22. Courtesy Robert Peacock of Seadive Organisation
23. TNA ADM106/329 f.11
24. TNA ADM106/329 f.13
25. TNA ADM106/329 f.17
26. TNA ADM106/329 f.19
27. TNA ADM106/329 f.21
28. Thomas Fagg, *The Bends of a Ship*, c.1680
29. TNA ADM106/322 f.264
30. TNA ADM106/3542 Part II
31. Bodleian Library, Oxford, Rawlinson A191 f.125
32. Richard Endsor, *The Restoration Warship*, London, 2009, pp.19-21
33. TNA ADM106/3538 Part II
34. TNA ADM106/3538 Part I
35. Thomas Fagge, *The Bends of a Ship*, c.1680
36. Pepys Library, PL1339
37. TNA ADM106/322 f.287
38. TNA ADM106/3538 Part 1
39. BM Stowe 144 f.12 and BM 534 k5
40. Bodleian Library, Oxford, Rawlinson A191 f.127

41. TNA ADM106/331 Part 1 f.217v
42. TNA ADM106/331 Part 2 f.295
43. TNA ADM106/331 Part 2 f.303
44. TNA ADM106/331 Part 2 f.331
45. TNA ADM106/330 f.231
46. TNA ADM106/332 f.165
47. Pepys Library PL1339
48. TNA ADM106/330 f.340
49. TNA ADM106/330 f.233
50. TNA ADM106/331/1 f.240
51. TNA ADM106/332 f.167
52. TNA ADM106/332 f.180
53. TNA ADM106/332 f.182
54. TNA ADM106/330 f.418
55. BM Stowe 144 f.12
56. TNA ADM106/330 f.467
57. TNA ADM106/330 f.465
58. TNA ADM106/332 f.184
59. Arthur Bryant, *Samuel Pepys, The Years of Peril*, Cambridge, 1933, p.209
60. Catalogue Pepysian MSS, NRS, Vol IV 612
61. TNA ADM106/330 f.468
62. British Library, BL534 k5
63. BL534 k5
64. *Dimensions of Old Ships* MSS, Author's Collection
65. Boymans-Van Beuningen Museum, Rotterdam, MB1866/T327
66. TNA ADM106/36
67. TNA ADM106/342 f.281
68. TNA ADM106/330 f.336
69. TNA ADM106/342 f.201
70. *Dimensions of Old Ships* p.21, Author's collection
71. TNA ADM106/322 f.260
72. *Dimensions of Old Ships* p.22, Author's collection
73. TNA ADM1/3549 f.715
74. Cat Pepysian MSS, Vol. IV, p.630
75. TNA ADM106/41
76. TNA ADM2/1749
77. TNA ADM106/42 and ADM2/1749
78. Peter LeFevre, Naval Dockyard Society Newsletter, 2003
79. TNA ADM106/342 f.192
80. BL Add MS60386 f.93
81. BL Add MS60386 f.107
82. *The Mariner's Mirror*, Vol. 12, 1926, p.435
83. TNA ADM3/278, March 1681, pp.10, 24, 29
84. TNA ADM106/342 f.192
85. National Maritime Museum SPB50
86. Pepys Naval Minutes p.128
87. *Journal of Edward Gregory*, MSS, Author's collection
88. TNA ADM106/395 Part1 f.304

Belander

Chapter 3

1. TNA ADM106/3119 f.94, TNA ADM106/341 f.365
2. TNA ADM106/380 Part 2 f.128
3. TNA ADM106/3119 f.92, f.94
4. TNA ADM106/341 f.354
5. TNA ADM106/342 f.421
6. TNA ADM106/350 f.198
7. TNA WO49/111
8. TNA ADM106/3119 f.231
9. Bodleian Library, Oxford, Rawlinson A177 f.112

10. Photographs and tracing of lines are courtesy of Michael Wenzel and Willibald Mieschel.
11. TNA ADM106/336 f.289
12. J.D. Davies, *Pepys's Navy*, p.27
13. TNA ADM 106/431 f.241, f.248
14. TNA ADM1/3552 25
15. TNA ADM106/3541, Part 1
16. TNA ADM106/3539, Part 2
17. TNA ADM3/278 f.67
18. TNA ADM106/3553 f.661
19. TNA ADM106/356 f.222
20. TNA ADM106/356 f.271
21. TNA ADM106/356 f.293, f.295
22. TNA ADM106/361 f.173
23. TNA ADM106/361 f.175
24. TNA ADM106/361 f.183
25. Pepys Naval Minutes, Naval Records Society, p.160
26. TNA ADM106/3538, Part 1
27. TNA ADM1/3553 f.361
28. J. D. Davies, *Pepys's Navy*, Barnsley, 2008, p.28
29. TNA ADM106/371 f.28
30. TNA ADM106/372 f.113
31. TNA ADM106/370 f.51
32. TNA ADM106/3556 f.11
33. TNA ADM106/375 f.25
34. TNA ADM106/58, Bodleian Library, Oxford, Rawlinson A464 f.11
35. Bodleian Library Oxford, Rawlinson A464 f.59, TNA ADM106/378 f.11
36. Bodleian Library Oxford, Rawlinson A464 f.61, TNA ADM106/378 f.424
37. Bodleian Library Oxford, Rawlinson A464 f.58
38. Bodleian Library Oxford, Rawlinson A464 f.29
39. Bodleian Library Oxford, Rawlinson A464 f.110
40. Bodleian Library Oxford Rawlinson A464
41. Pepys, *State of the Navy*, p.33, TNA T38/657 28
42. Pepys, *State of the Navy*, p.27
43. Pepys, *State of the Navy*, p.38
44. BM Harley MS7476 f.66v
45. Pepys *State of the Navy*, p.107, TNA T38/657 f.28
46. TNA T38/657 f.28

Chapter 4

1. TNA ADM8/1
2. TNA ADM106/68
3. John Charnock, *Biographica Navalis*, Vol. II, p.98
4. *Journal of Edward Gregory* MSS, p.15
5. TNA ADM2/1741 f.415
6. Bodleian Library, Oxford, Rawlinson A189 140
7. TNA ADM2/1741, f.392
8. *Journal of Edward Gregory*, p.15
9. John Charnock, *Biographica Navalis* Vol. II, p.15
10. National Maritime Museum ROM/4
11. John Charnock, *Biographica Navalis*, Vol. I, p.385
12. John Charnock, *Biographica Navalis*, Vol. II, p.214
13. NMM L/A/134
14. TNA ADM51/4115 f.3
15. Pepys Library, Magdalene College, Cambridge, PL1339
16. *Dimensions of Old Ships*, pp.21–22, Author's collection
17. Pepys Library, PL1339
18. *Dimensions of Old Ships*, pp.21–22, Author's collection
19. TNA ADM106/389 f.451
20. Richard Endsor, *The Restoration Warship*, London, 2009, p.184
21. TNA ADM2/1741 f.249
22. TNA ADM1/3555 f.855
23. TNA ADM1/3556 f.137
24. TNA ADM106/3542

25. TNA ADM1/3556 f.429
26. TNA ADM1/3557 f.105
27. TNA ADM1/3556 f.423–4
28. TNA ADM106/698
29. TNA ADM2/1741 f.420
30. NMM SGN/A/2
31. TNA ADM2/1741 f.245
32. TNA LS9/99
33. *Barlow's Journal*, transcribed by Basil Lubbock, London, 1934, Vol. II, p.384
34. *London Gazette*, 15 September, 1687
35. TNA ADM106/382 f.255
36. TNA ADM1/3556 f.673
37. TNA ADM1/3556 f.674–5
38. TNA ADM1/3556 f.825
39. TNA ADM106/380, Part II, f.128
40. TNA ADM1/3556 f.825
41. TNA ADM1/3556 f.823
42. TNA ADM1/5253 f.47–48v
43. TNA ADM1/5253 f.51
44. TNA SP71/3 f.165
45. TNA ADM33/132
46. Bodleian Library, Oxford Rawlinson A186 f.321
47. TNA ADM33/132
48. Additional details from *The London Gazette,* 14 November, 1687
49. TNA SP71/3 f.184
50. *The London Gazette,* 22 December 1687
51. J. D. Davies, *Transactions of the Naval Dockyards Society*, Vol. 5, p.82
52. TNA ADM106/397 f.434
53. *London Gazette,* 8 March, 1687
54. TNA ADM33/132
55. Bodleian Library, Oxford, Rawlinson, A179 26

Chapter 5

1. TNA ADM106/3541 Part 1
2. Bodleian Library, Oxford, Rawlinson MS A171 145
3. TNA ADM1/3556 f.783
4. *Journal of Edward Gregory*, MSS, Author's collection, p.15
5. British Library, Harley 7466 f.14v
6. Bodleian Library, Oxford, Rawlinson C429
7. TNA ADM106/384 f.195
8. TNA ADM106/389 f.373v
9. TNA ADM8/1
10. TNA ADM/389 f.391
11. TNA ADM/389 f.414
12. TNA ADM/389 f.420
13. TNA ADM/389 f.441
14. TNA ADM/389 f.449
15. TNA ADM/389 f.460, ADM1/3558 f.505
16. TNA ADM/389 f.469
17. TNA ADM106/2908
18. TNA ADM106/388 f.80
19. TNA ADM1/3558 f.783
20. *Dimensions of Old Ships*
21. National Maritime Museum, CHA/L/1
22. TNA ADM2/170 p.29–33
23. NMM CHA/L/1, TNA ADM1/3560
24. ADM10/15, John Charnock, *Biographica Navalis*, Vol. II, p.32

25. TNA ADM2/170 f.104
26. TNA ADM106/401 f.371
27. TNA ADM106/397 f.231
28. TNA ADM1/3560 f.807
29. TNA ADM2/170 f.118, 119
30. TNA ADM1/3560 f.805, ADM49/29
31. TNA ADM106/401 f.291
32. TNA ADM49/29 f.45
33. NMM CHA/L/2
34. TNA ADM106/400 f.359
35. NMM CHA/L/2
36. TNA ADM106/401 f.293
37. TNA ADM106/398 Part1 f.157
38. TNA ADM51/3881 1 and ADM52/58 f.1
39. TNA ADM106/402 Part II, f.184
40. TNA ADM51/3881 1 and ADM52/58 f.1
41. TNA WO55/1762
42. Many thanks to Frank Fox and Dr Peter LeFevre for sharing their research
43. The Earl of Torrington's speech to the Commons, 1710, p.50
44. TNA ADM 52/30/4
45. The Earl of Torrington's speech to the Commons, 1710, p.29
46. The Earl of Torrington's speech to the Commons, 1710, TNA ADM52/30/4, TNA ADM51/3881/1, Josiah Burchett, *Transactions at Sea*, 1720, p.425
47. TNA ADM106/401 f.295
48. TNA SP8/7 ADM52/30/4
49. Richard Endsor, *The Restoration Warship*, London, 2009, p.152
50. Account by Ashby and Rooke 1691, p.7
51. TNA ADM51/4127
52. TNA ADM 52/30/4

A view of Deptford and Greenwich showing the site where it is proposed to build a replica of the *Lenox*, a ship built to the same specification and at the same time as the *Anne*. Author

53. TNA ADM106/401 f.295
54. TNA SP8/7
55. Account by Ashby and Rooke, 1691, p.21
56. Account by Ashby and Rooke, 1691, p.20
57. TNA ADM51/3984
58. TNA ADM106/3023
59. TNA ADM82/13
60. TNA ADM106/401 f.295
61. TNA ADM51/3984
62. The Earl of Torrington's speech to the Commons, 1710, p.35
63. TNA ADM52/123
64. TNA ADM106/401 f.297
65. TNA ADM106/401 f.295
66. TNA ADM52/123
67. TNA ADM51/3984
68. TNA ADM106/401 f.297
69. Josiah Burchett, *Transactions at Sea*, 1703, p.49
70. TNA ADM1/3562
71. TNA ADM3/3
72. TNA ADM106/401 f.295
73. TNA ADM106/397 f.247
74. TNA ADM106/401 f.299
75. TNA ADM106/401 f.301, f.303

Chapter 6

1. Recent archaeology carried out by Steve and Carol Ellis, licensees of the *London*
2. TNA ADM7/677
3. TNA ADM49/123
4. Pepys MSS, Vol. IV, p.407
5. TNA WO49/111
6. Bodleian Library, Oxford, Rawlinson A185 f161 and BL ADD MSS 9316 f.226
7. TNA WO49/111
8. *Dimensions of Old Ships*
9. Pepys MSS, Vol. IV, p.425
10. TNA ADM49/123 TNA ADM7/827 f.76–f.80
11. TNA ADM2/1748 f.132, f.139
12. TNA WO50/13
13. TNA ADM49/123 and ADM2/1748
14. *Dimensions of Old Ships*, pp.16–17
15. TNA WO55/1762 and records in the Staffordshire Record Office D(W)1778/V/44
16. TNA ADM7/827
17. Richard Endsor, *The Restoration Warship*, London, 2009, p.155
18. TNA WO49/112
19. TNA ADM106/406 f9
20. *Dimensions of Old Ships*, pp.21–22
21. TNA WO50/13
22. ADM7/827 f.81
23. NMM ROM/4
24. TNA ADM8/3
25. TNA WO51/34 f.48v
26. TNA WO51/34 f.100
27. TNA ADM51/4115 f.3
28. NMM ROM/4
29. TNA WO51/34 f.202v
30. TNA WO51/34 f.100
31. TNA WO34 f.118
32. NMM ADM/L/A/134
33. TNA WO51/36 f.135
34. WO 55/1762
35. WO 55/1763 and Staffordshire Record Office D (W)1778/V/44
36. Archaeological evidence, Seadive Organisation
37. TNA WO51/40 f.170
38. TNA WO51/41 f.81v
39. TNA WO51/43 f.137
40. TNA WO51/40 f.167v
41. TNA WO51/41 f.77 and WO51/42 f.38
42. *Ibid* WO51/42 f.38v
43. TNA ADM95/13 f.139

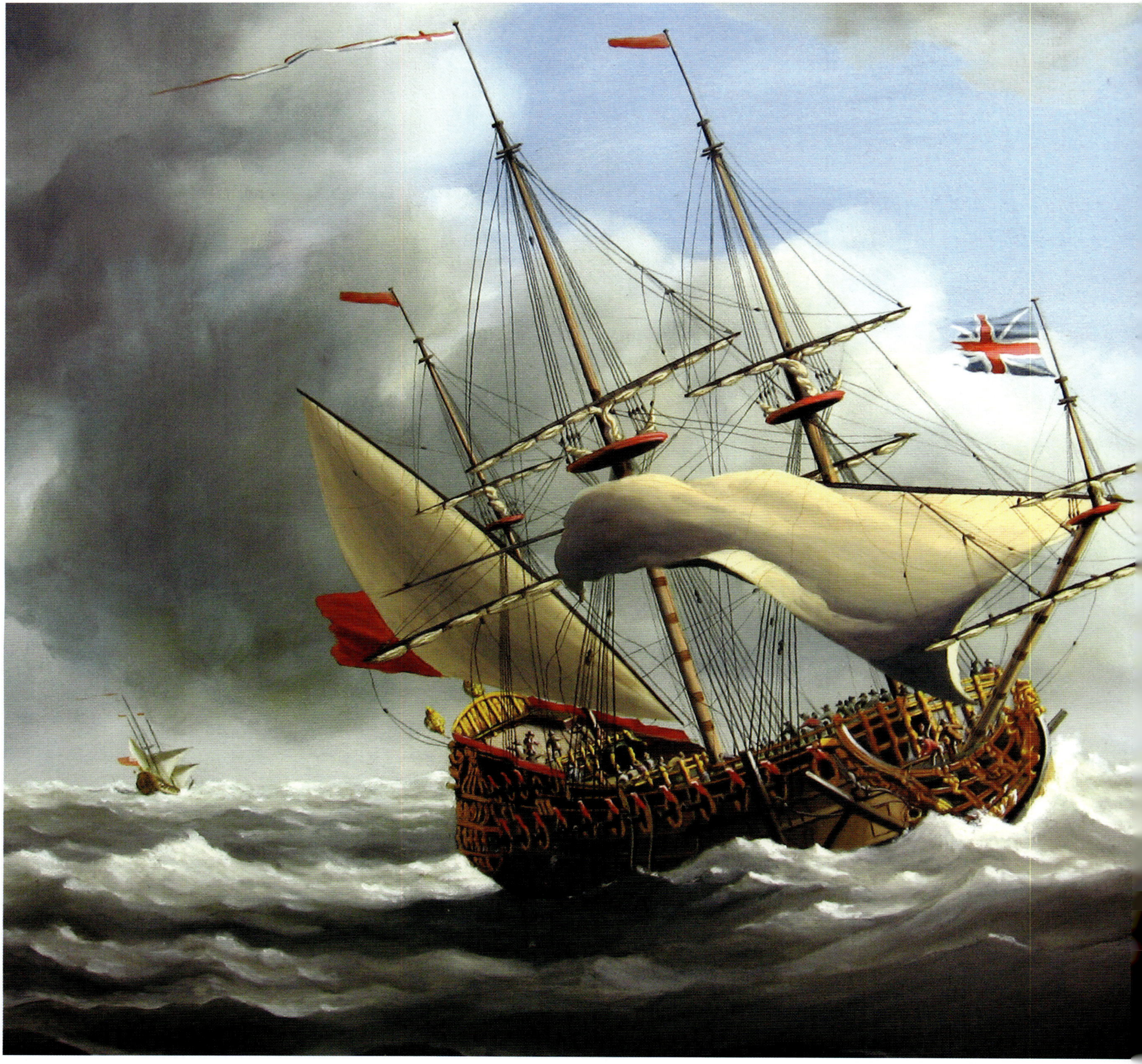

44. TNA WO51/41
45. TNA WO51/42 f.75v
46. TNA ADM1/3563 f.181–182
47. TNA WO51/43 f.142
48. TNA Prob11/514/33
49. TNA ADM106/494 f.398
50. TNA Prob11/514/33
51. TNA ADM7/827 and Cumbria Record Office, D/Lons/L
52. TNA WO51/43 f.142
53. TNA WO51/44 f.57
54. WO51/44 46v
55. TNA WO51/44 f.111v
56. TNA WO51/44 f.46v
57. TNA WO51/44 f.93
58. TNA WO51/44 f.111v

Chapter 7

1. Correspondence with Historic England, 29 May, 2008
2. D. Robinson & R. Williams, *The Sussex Coast Past and Present*, 1983, p.53, quoted by Peter Marsden
3. P. Marsden and D. Lyon, *International Journal of Nautical Archaeology*, 1977 6.1, p.12
4. Marsden and Lyon, IJNA, 1977, 6.1, p.12a
5. Marsden and Lyon, IJNA, 1977, 6.1, pp.9–20
6. Louise Martin, 'The Wreck of the Anne, Pett Level, East Sussex: Report on Geophysical Survey', for Historic England, May 2008: http://research.historicengland.org.uk/Results.aspx?p=1&n=10&t=the%20anne&ns=1
7. Frank Fox, *Great Ships: the Battlefleet of Charles II*, London, 1980, p.158
8. The National Archives ADM106/3071

The *Lenox*, a ship built as part of the 1677 programme and very similar to the *Anne*. Author

Index

Page numbers in *italics* refer to captions and illustrations

Adams, Thomas 86, 115
Admiralty 16, 17, 35, 38, 48, 49, 104
   Admiralty Commission 6, *11*, *14*, 46, 48, 49
   see also Navy Board
Advice 89
Albemarle 87
Algiers 70–1, *71*
anchors 56, 58
Anglo-Dutch fleet *see* Battle of Beachy Head
Anne 25, *62–3*, 72
   Barbary States mission 7, 53, 60, 70–81, 109, 145–7
   Battle of Beachy Head (1690) 7, 87–99, *90*, *91*, *93*, *100–1*, *113*
   construction of *see* building the *Anne*
   dimensions *18*
   fitting out 56–9
   guns *see* guns
   Historic England policy 131
   laid up in ordinary 42–9
   launch 35, 36
   Portuguese mission 52–60, *57*, *61*, 109, 145
   reconstruction (drawing) *36–7*
   run aground and burned 98, 114–16
   Van de Velde drawing *34*, *37*
   Warship Anne Trust 126, 127
   wreck of and wreck site 120–31, *120*, *121*, *122*, *123*, *124*, *125*, *128*, *129*, *130*
Arlington, Henry Bennet, Earl of *11*, 104
Assurance 87

Bachelors Hoy 116
ballast 35, 49, 79
Barbary pirates 52, *72*
Barbary States mission 7, 53, 60, 70–81, 109
Barlow, Edward 64
Barnaby, Walter 53
battles
   Bantry Bay (1689) 85
   Barfleur-La Hogue (1692) 98
   Beachy Head (1690) 7, 87–99, *92–3*, *96–7*, *100–1*, *113*, 114
   Dutch raid on the Medway (1667) 7, 11, 14, 16
   Four Days' Battle (1666) 10, *12–13*
   Lowestoft (1665) 10
   Sedgemoor (1685) 84
   Solebay (1672) 19
Beach, Sir Richard 19, 22, 23, 27, 30, 32–3, 34, 35, 36, 38, 39, 46

beer 56
Bennett, Robert 114
Berkeley, Lord 68, 69, 78
Berry, Sir John 49
Berry, Captain Thomas 53
Berwick 32, 36, *37*, 87, 129
Bingham, Joseph 116
Bloody Assize 84
Board of Ordnance 104, 108, 114, 116
Boatswain's stores 57
bolts 23, 25, 36, *128*
Bonaventure 91, *92*, 94
Breda 85, 87, *91*
Bristol 60, 66
Browne, Mary 104
building the *Anne* 20–35
   build costs 22, 34, 38
   finishing works 34–5
   frame timbers 23–7, *128*
   gun decks 30–1
   keel 22–3, *26*, 127
   planking 27, 130
   timber *see* timber

wages cost 36, 38
bulkheads *37*, *44*, *45*
Burford 85, 86

Cadiz 81
cannon balls 124
capstans *45*, 57–8, 141
Captain 16, 17, 85, 86, 87
carlings 31
Carpenter's stores 57
carvings 34, 144
Castle, William *43*
caulking 43, 47
Charity Hoy 116
Charles II *10*, *17*, 30, 38, 39, 47
　Anglo-Dutch Wars 10–14
　　death of 48
　　and the Popish plot 35–6, 46
　　shipbuilding programme 7, 15–17, 19, 46
Charles Galley 60, 68, 69, 70, *72*, 81
Chatham Dockyard *19*, 22, 45, 49, 85
chocks *26*
clamps 30, 128, *129*, 140
Colbert, Jean-Baptiste *11*, 14, 85
Concord 31
Cornwall 108
Coronation 87
courts martial 69
Cox, Captain John 19
cross pillars 129–30, 140
Crown 79, 80

Danby, Thomas Osborne, Earl of 14, *14*, 84, 104
Deane, Sir Anthony 19, 39, 48, 49, 69
Defiance 87
discipline, enforcing 46–7, 60, 69–70

Dolphin 87
Dorothy 87
Dragon 68, 80
Duchess 84, 87
Duke 86, 88
Dummer, Edward 36, *37*
Dutch Golden Age 7, 14
dysentery 81

Eagle 105
Eason, Robert 23
Edgar 87, *91*, 95
Elizabeth *43*, 87
Elswout 95
Endeavour of Weymouth 70
Essex 85, 89
Exeter 91, *94*, 95
Expedition 87

Fagge, Thomas *24*, *28*
fighting instructions 60
fill-in frames 27
fireships 87, 89, 98
Fitzjames, Henry 56, 74, 78
food and drink 56–7, 64, 79
footwaling 128–9
Foresight 87
fourth-rate ships 89

frame bends *24*, *25*, *128*
frame timbers 23–7, *24*, *25*, *26*, *27*, *28–9*, *31*, 128, *128*
French fleet 85, 86
　see also Battle of Beachy Head
Friesland 95
Fubbs yacht 39, 60, 64, 87
Furzer, Daniel 48
futtocks 23, *24*, 25, *25*, 27, *28*, 31, *128*, 139

Galloper Sands 60
Garland 68, 87
Gekroonde Burg 98
Gibraltar 67–8, *67*, 80
girdling 104
Glorious Revolution (1688) 80, 84–5, 105
Goodwin, Sir John 47
Gourden, Sir Robert 58
Grafton 52, 86, 87
Grafton, Henry, Duke of 52, *53*, 56, 58, 60, 64, 67, 68, 69, 70, 74, 78, 79, 81, 87
graving 43, 47
great cabins 59

Gregory, Edward 38, 39, 58, 85, 98, 105
gun decks 26, 30–1, *30*, 139, 140
gun ports *31*, *37*, *42*, 47, 104.140
guns 56, 102–17
   3-pounders 104, *108*, 116
   6-pounders *111*, 114
   12-pounders 104, 105, *105*, *107*, 112, 115, 124
   24-pounders 104
   brass guns 104, *111*, 112, 113, *113*, 114
   cartridges 105
   chase guns 104, *105*, *106*, 113
   costs 104
   culverins *106*, 113, *113*, 124
   demi-cannon 104, *106*, *110*, 112, 114, *114*, 115, 124
   demi-culverins 104, 105
   gun carriages 108, 109, *110*, *111*
   gunpowder 105, 112
   re-proved guns 116
   'Rupertino' guns 114
   sakers 104, *105*, *107*, *108*, *111*, *113*, 116, 117, *117*
   shot 105, 112

Haddock, Sir Richard 46
Hampshire 52, 60, 64, 66, 68, 70, *73*
Hampton Court 87
Harwich 89
hawsers 58
Henrietta 52, 60, 64

Hewer, Will 49, *49*, 69
Historic England (formerly, English Heritage) 131
Holmes's Bonfire (1666) 10, 14, 16
Hope 42–3, 86, 87
Hopewell Hoy 114
hoys 115

impressment 19, 31, 32–3, 87
Isabella yacht 39, *59*, 60, 66, 70, *72*, 81

James II (earlier, James, Duke of York) 7, *14*, 48, 49, 52, *52*, 58, 78, 80, 84, 85
James Galley 56
James and Mary 58
Jeffreys, Judge 84
John and James 114

keels 16, 17, 22–3, 127, 138
keelson 25, *26*, 139
Kent 89
Killigrew, Vice Admiral Henry 86, 88
knees 30–1, *30*, 35
Knights of Malta 78

Lancaster 106
Lark 52
launching *32*, 35, *35*, 36
Lawrence, Joseph 26
Le Fleuron 91
Le Grande 92
Le Modéré 91
Le Terrible 91, 92
Lee, Robert 19, 30, 47, 48, 52, 67, 69, 85, 86
Lemontree 69
Lenox 17, 58, 86, *96*, 105, 127, 130

Leopard 67, 81
Lewis & Cliff 87
lifting gear *25*
L'Illustre 95
L'Intrépide 95
Lisbon 64, *65*
Livorno 79–80
Lloyd, Captain David 84
Lodgingham, Robert 58
logbooks 53
London 34, 35, 104, 105
London Merchant 76
Louis XIV, King of France 14, 15, 85
Lyon 87

Maagd van Enkhuizen 98
maintenance and repairs 47, 48–9, 67–8, 79, 80, 84, 85, 86
   costs 49
Malta 77–9, *78*
Maria Sofia, Queen of Portugal 52, 60, 64, 87, 109
Marsden, Dr Peter 6, 124, 125, 126, 129

Martin, Louise 120, *125*, 126
Mary 86
Mary II, Queen of England 84, *89*, 90, 98
masts 56, 57, *59*, 66–7, *68*, *68*, 69, 79
Mees, Captain 93
men overboard 76, 81
Mermaid 60, 67, 70, *73*, 81
messengers 58
midshipmen 56
Monck 89
Monmouth 85, 89
Monmouth, James, Duke of 84
moorings 42–3, *42*, 44–5, 84
Mordaunt 87
Moreland, Sir Samuel 58

Narborough, Sir John 46
Nautical Museums Trust 126
Navy Board 16, 23, 26, 35, 36, 38, 46, 48, 49, 52, 85, 98, 104, 116, 127
Neptune 89, 98
Neville, Captain 79
Nonsuch 52, 87
Noord Holland 98
Northumberland 89

Oates, Titus 35–6
Onslow, Sir Richard 126
Orange Tree 64
Ossory 89, 98

Peace of Breda *10*, 11, 14
Pearl 52, 60, 66, 68, 69, 70, *73*, 76, 78
Pedro II, Don 52, 64
Pembroke 87
Pendennis 32

pensions 95
Pepys, Samuel 6, 7, 11, 15, *15*, 16, 19, 27, 39, 46, 47, 48, 49, 68–9, 80, 81
Pett, Sir Phineas 17–19, 22, 23, 26, 27, 30, 31, 32–3, 34–5, 36, 38–9, *38*, 48–9, 67, 69, 127, 128
Pett Level 7, 98, 114, 120
Phoenix 64
planking 27, 130
Plymouth 87
Popish plot 35–6, 46, 48
Portsmouth yacht 58
Portugal Merchant 70, *73*, 74, 76, 79, 80
powder rooms 105
Prince Royal 17
Princess 44, 46
pumps 58

Resolution 87
Restoration 86, 92, 93
Richard & Samuel 87
Richmond 52, 60, 66
riders 129, 130, 139
rigging 56, *59*, 69, 80
rigging plans *54–5*
River Medway

Dutch raid on 7, 11, 14, 16
silting up 43–4
Rooke, Rear Admiral 87
Royal Charles 10, 11, 14
Royal Katherine 81, 85, 87
Royal Oak 84
Royal Sovereign 46, 87
Rupert, Prince 10, 16, 114
Ruyter, Michiel de 14

sailing instructions 60
St Andrew 87
St Michael 85, 89
St Michel, Balthasar 49
Sandwich 87
Sapphire 68, 69
scantling list *18*, 128, 135–7
Schomberg, Duke of 87
scuppers 34–5
Second Anglo-Dutch War 10–14
Sedgemoor 52, 58, 60, 64, 66, 70, *72*, 76, 78, 81, 84
Shaw, John 69–70
Shipwreck Museum, Hastings 6, 116, 126

Yachts

shipwrights 32–4
   apprenticeships 17–18
   Master Shipwrights 16, 17–18, 23, 30, 48
   pay and arrears 18, 32, 38, 84
Shovel, Captain Cloudesley 53, *53*, 56, 57, 58, 64, 67, 69, 70, 71, 74, 76, 79, 80, 89
shrouds 57, 68, 79
signals 60
Silvester, Edward 108, 112, 114
slaves 70–1, 80
smacks *115*
Southampton 107
Sovereign 87, 90, *96*
Sovereign of the Seas 17
staterooms 58–9
stems 16, 19, *131*, 138
Stephen & Anne 114
stern post 130, *130*, 138
Stirling Castle 86, *96*, *110*, *111*, 114, 127
stores, ships' 56–7, 79
Success 53
Suffolk 58, 87
Sutherland, William 23, 39, *59*, 72, 130
Swallow 95
Swan 67, 68
Swiftsure 89

Third Anglo-Dutch War *11*, 14, *14*, 19
third-rate ships 17, *28–9*, *32–3*, *42–3*, 89
   approved dimensions *18*, 134
   building contracts 138–43
Tholen 95
timber
   decay 47, 67
   elm 22, 23, 27, 127
   oak 22, *22*, 23, 27, 30, 31, 48, 49
   supplies of 22, 23, 27
Tippetts, Sir John 19, 35, 39, 46
Torrington, Arthur Herbert, Lord 87, 90, 91, *93*, 98
Tourville, Comte de 88
Treaty of Dover (1670) 14
Triple Alliance 14
Tripoli 76, *77*
Tunis 74–6, *75*
turned over men 87
Tyrrell, Captain John *86*, 87, 92, 95, 98, *99*

Velde, Willem van de, the Elder 14, *15*, *34*
Velde, Willem van de, the Younger 14, *15*
Victory 106
volunteers 56

Wherry

wales 31, *31*, *37*, *48*
Wapen van Utrecht 95
warrant officers 46–7, 86
water casks 76, 81
William III (William of Orange) *14*, 80, 84–5, *84*, 87
Windsor Castle 87
Witt, Johan de 11
Wivell, Lieutenant Francis 53, 80

Yarmouth 138–9
York 95
York, James, Duke of 36, 46

Yawl